Process Mapping and Management

Process Mapping and Management

Sue Conger

Process Mapping and Management
Copyright © Sue Conger, 2011.

First published in 2011 by
Business Expert Press, LLC
222 East 46th Street, New York, NY 10017
www.businessexpertpress.com

ISBN-13: 978-1-60649-129-4 (paperback)
ISBN-10: 1-60649-129-6 (paperback)

ISBN-13: 978-1-60649-130-0 (e-book)
ISBN-10: 1-60649-130-X (e-book)

DOI 10.4128/9781606491300

A publication in the Business Expert Press Information Systems collection

Collection ISSN (print): 2156-6577
Collection ISSN (electronic): 2156-6593

Cover design by Jonathan Pennell
Interior design by Scribe Inc.

First edition: May 2011

10 9 8 7 6 5 4 3 2 1

Printed in the United States of America.

To my daughter, Katie, and my students and colleagues Diane de La Fon and Brett J. L. Landry, who worked with me during the development of this book

Abstract

As the economy moves toward a services orientation, companies are struggling with how to improve their offerings. Process management is a key component of the services that companies provide. This book has three main parts: mapping, improvement, and error-proofing and metrics. In the first part—mapping—the reader will learn how to map a process so that the map is immediately understandable for identifying the roles, work steps, and automation support used in process delivery. The second part—improvement—provides a series of techniques for defining, prioritizing, and analyzing problems from several perspectives. The first perspective is called "leaning," and its purpose is to remove waste from an existing process. The second perspective is "cleaning," during which the remaining steps following leaning are analyzed for possible improvement. The third perspective is "greening," which explores opportunities and trade-offs for outsourcing, coproduction, and environmental improvements related to the process. The final third of the book—error-proofing and metrics—presents several techniques for ensuring risk mitigation for the new process and for measuring changes that define their impacts, and illustrates a method for proposing changes to executives in a "case for change." Overall, the book provides a blueprint of how to develop a discipline for process management that applies to any type of work.

Keywords

Process, improvement, statement of work, value-added analysis, root-cause analysis, Six Sigma, quality function deployment, statistical process control, failure-proofing, metrics, case for change

Contents

Figures

Chapter 1

Chapter 2

Chapter 3

Chapter 4

Chapter 5

Chapter 6

Chapter 7

Chapter 8

Chapter 9

Chapter 10

Appendix A

PART I

Opening Gambit

The opening gambit includes activities and skills that are assumed for any project. If you embark on a process improvement without these, then you jeopardize its success from the beginning. Much like a chess game that has risky first moves, these activities are crucial to success but hidden from most client organization staff, and therefore the risks of not having these activities and skills is assumed by the project team.

The first chapter in this part describes activities that should be conducted for all projects in order to situate the project in the context of its organizational environment. The discussion focuses on the duties, roles, and responsibilities of the project team and how to articulate them so that contingencies can be planned as needed.

The next two chapters discuss the mechanics of process mapping. Process maps are icon-based shorthand ways of describing the steps for performing some process. They identify all of the key roles and, to the extent possible, all steps in a process. Chapter 3 describes the icons and how to use them to develop a process map. Chapter 4 discusses common novice errors in process mapping and shows proper techniques for each type of error.

CHAPTER 1

Introduction

The early years of the 21st century brought astounding changes to industry: the dot-com crash, the globalization and widespread outsourcing of business functions, increased regulatory and standards pressures, and a peek at a future full of nanotechnology, artificial intelligence, and bio-engineered products that will far surpass human capabilities. All of these changes have forced organizations to become "leaner and meaner" to survive, but being lean and mean alone does not guarantee survival.

A 2004 study by the London School of Economics and the McKinsey Company[1] shows that companies that managed both processes and their technology deployments to support their business processes experienced significant gains over those who did not. Companies that neither had much technology support for work nor managed their business processes experienced no gains from business investments relative to other companies. Companies that minimally managed their business processes but had a high level of technology support experienced a 2% return on their investments. Companies that actively managed their business processes but had a low intensity of technology for work support experienced an 8% gain. This shows that simply making no other changes than managing business processes can lead to higher returns. And companies that both actively managed business processes and had a high intensity of technology support for work experienced, on average, 20% gains in returns on the investment. These results highlight the importance of both intelligent process management and strategic, intelligent technology deployment in supporting business processes.

Thus in the search for survival capabilities, organizations have come to understand that excess of any sort is costly and should be removed. The first step in removing excess is to understand business processes, the work those processes accomplish, and how that work relates to the organization's mission. Any process, process step, or process product (e.g., document, e-mail, data, or other product of a process step) that does not contribute to the organization's mission, or its ability to meet its mission, is waste.

But just removing excess does not guarantee survival. Processes need to be not only efficient but also effective. Where *efficiency* is driving out waste and minimizing costs (or doing things right), *effectiveness* is doing the right things to generate revenue. Both efficiency and effectiveness are required for survival. In striving for effectiveness, companies need to plan and deploy technologies and other aids in order to accomplish the work that will not only speed the process but also enhance the company's image, provide new ways to do work, and otherwise improve internal operations. Further, companies annually spend an increasing amount on planning, developing, monitoring, improving, and automating their processes.

Automated business processes model some organizational work to a very detailed level. Such a business process definition is important for the success of many activities, including the following:

- Management is difficult, if not impossible, if the processes being managed are not completely and explicitly known.
- Organizational structuring or restructuring (e.g., changes accomplished during reengineering efforts) requires knowledge of the importance and contribution of business processes.
- Installation of cross-functional software, such as enterprise resource planning software (ERP; e.g., SAP), requires intimate knowledge of business functions and their processes.
- Application scoping, definition, and development are unlikely to be successful if not based on fully defined processes and all supporting detailed information.
- Servitizing of the information technology (IT) function is the application of process management to IT; therefore, it requires knowledge not only of IT processes but also of how to manage those processes across organizational silos.

Business process analysis uses business process maps to determine the appropriateness of changes relating to restructuring or the introduction of new business technologies, such as computer applications or new manufacturing technology. Sets of process maps are developed to define the current business and proposed changes, which may result in one set of maps per proposed alternative. While other techniques for graphically depicting an organization have been used, business process maps are generic and not specifically technology driven—they are therefore more easily accepted by business executives.

This book is about removing waste from organizations by business process mapping, analysis, change, measurement, and continuous improvement. The book is also about optimizing and measuring the efficiency and effectiveness of processes in order to improve the overall revenue of an organization, thereby improving its chances of survival. While this is not specifically a technology book, we will discuss how to analyze and select technologies that can optimally support work once the processes have been streamlined. Keep in mind that without a good process foundation, technology is unlikely to obtain the expected gains. An understanding of process must come first.

Other ingredients of survival include being innovative, being future oriented in trying new techniques and technologies, being capable of continuous change, being able to time changes to optimize the probability of success, and luck. While luck cannot be guaranteed, the book does address the future orientation, innovation, and continuous change aspects of organizational management and timing.

Why Do We Care About Processes?

We cannot say why we care about processes without first defining what a process is. A *process* is the set of activities (repeated steps or tasks) that accomplishes some business function. In a perfect world, a process consists of the following components (as illustrated in Figure 1.1):

- *input*—that is, data, information, or materials that are used in the process
- the *process steps* to transform or otherwise manipulate the input
- some *output*—that is, a good or service that results from the process
- *feedback* in the form of monitoring and metrics on output quality that are used to regulate and improve the process

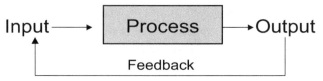

Figure 1.1. Process = IPO + feedback.

So why do we care about processes? Business processes involve how work gets done. Process understanding is important because you cannot manage what you do not know or understand. Further, processes are the basis of organizational functioning. Therefore, any business improvement involves process analysis and process improvement.

Managing process understanding and conduct ensures process repeatability. As whole organizations follow standardized processes, the resulting organizational maturity should improve all aspects of business conduct, including customer satisfaction. Thus managing processes—or not—affects organizational outcomes, including profitability.

Every project of any type that spans organizational boundaries has some characteristic phases in common. These phases relate to process improvement projects, which are explained in the next section.

Overview of Project Conduct

Any project follows similar phases of work. These phases are mentioned here because they are assumed in any process improvement endeavor. However, the details of these phases are not covered here because they divert attention from process understanding and improvement, which is the primary focus of this book.

A generic project ideally includes stages for organization strategy development, which spawns development of tactical initiatives, which then spawns development of individual projects. While mature organizations may develop strategy, tactics, and projects in this way, many companies are less sophisticated and more ad hoc in their approaches to management. Such less sophisticated companies may only realize a problem when it results in lost sales or customer complaints.

Process architecture is an abstraction depicting an overview of an organization as a set of critical processes, often in the form of a matrix. The architecture documents all critical processes for the organization and includes items such as the date of last improvement, process success, business functions that participate in the process, and organizational process interrelationships and dependencies. As processes are monitored, problems in work conduct can be identified and process improvement projects recommended. Thus process architecture is a tool to identify continuous improvement needs of the organization.

All projects require project management. Project management includes activities for planning, coordinating, scoping, costing, time estimating, quality assuring, staffing, communicating, procuring, and risk managing. Project management issues relevant to process improvement projects are addressed in the next chapter. However, project management is a significant topic in its own right and is therefore not covered in detail in this book.

Similarly, all process improvements are essentially change projects. Change management has its own requirements, and it is a complex activity that relates to organizational culture and the radicalness and type of change. Many fine books are available on this subject, so it is only briefly discussed here in the context of key issues.

Thus the phases of strategizing, architecting, managing, and changing relate to any project and, as a result, are considered beyond the scope of this book. This book concentrates on the actual process improvement activities needed to architect and engineer a well-designed, appropriate process. The next section describes the key aspects of process improvement activities and identifies the chapters in which these topics are discussed.

Process Improvement Project Conduct

Process improvement projects proceed through their own process in the steps depicted in Figure 1.2. Process improvement projects begin with an initiation activity, which results in mapping and documenting the target process (or processes). Once documented, the target process proceeds through three types of problem analyses for improvement: leaning the process of unneeded tasks, cleaning the process to further improve the remaining process steps, and greening to minimize the environmental impact of the process. Following analysis, the process is redesigned, a case for change is developed, and changes are recommended. Once the changes are approved,

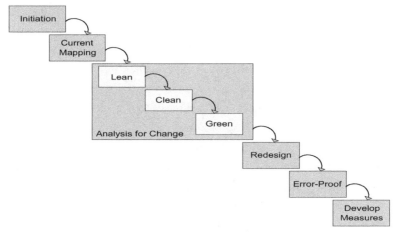

Figure 1.2. The process of process improvement.

implementation planning begins, with error-proofing used to remove the potential for problems and to guarantee identification of problems should they occur. Measures or metrics are developed to monitor the success of the changes and to take the process into the future.

Initiating a process improvement project begins with a series of interviews, the goal of which is to develop sufficient understanding for staff and to plan the improvement project. In chapter 2, we introduce these concepts and a call-center case that is used throughout the book to illustrate many concepts.

After identifying processes through interviews and determining one or a small number of processes for further analysis, the processes are mapped. Process mapping is discussed in both chapters 3 and 4. Process maps depict roles, tasks, process steps, and all initiating and terminating events and conditions. Many processes cross organizational boundaries, and to ensure optimal improvement, all stakeholders should be part of any improvement project. Chapter 3 develops the technique of process mapping, defining each icon and its usage and a method for mapping processes. The chapter also describes alternative techniques sometimes used for process mapping and the knowledge behind each step required for optimal improvement.

Chapter 4 expands on mapping techniques and develops techniques for dealing with time, geography, and other variations that can alter the ways in which maps are drawn. In addition, common errors are depicted with an example of the error and an example of the correct mapping technique. Process improvement requires knowledge behind process (or process step) history, purpose, problems, method of conduct, current metrics, reliance on information from external sources, and so on. Process understanding includes all of these and is required for map validation and documentation, which are also discussed.

When process steps are identified as having problems, techniques for determining the extent, severity, and impact of the problems are used to determine the focus of improvement. These techniques include matrices, checklists, and various graphical forms, which are addressed in chapter 5.

Problem-finding techniques may surface all of the critical needs for change, but these techniques can sometimes miss historically accepted process steps or wasted movements that are also unneeded. The next chapters deal with identifying and removing any unnecessary steps. Chapter 6 discusses lean manufacturing methods as applied to process improvement. Lean tenets allow us to find and remove waste from processes. Then, in chapter 7, other techniques that lead to process "cleaning" assist in improving remaining process steps. Both of these chapters also rely on Six Sigma concepts to improve process activities and outcomes.

Alternatives for spreading or shifting responsibility for process steps are evaluated in chapter 8. A key motivation for these alternatives is environmental friendliness that reduces paper input, paper use, or production through a particular process. Thus this step is referred to as an analysis for "greening" the process. One alternative is automation. Process automation not only reduces paper but also increases throughput of a process while allowing automated tracking of workflows through service jobs. Alternatives for automation range from adaptations of off-the-shelf software capabilities, to use of process automation tools, to customized applications that track workflows. Each alternative requires careful analysis and deployment in order to ensure a positive outcome.

Another alternative for spreading or shifting responsibility is the shifting of activities to customers (or others) as a coproduction initiative. Coproduction off-loads work to others who add unpaid, value-adding capabilities to a product. Coproducers can be the public, customers, or other companies with some stake in the outcome. Since coproduction, as discussed here, takes place mostly on the Internet, it, too, can reduce paper that would otherwise be created to deal with user concerns.

Once a process has been leaned, cleaned, and greened, it is ready to be reconstructed for optimal performance. Chapter 9 addresses the redesign of the process map, which shows all proposed changes. Redesign includes the application of ideas from all analyses as well as the evaluation of innovative approaches for performing the work that might be beyond those considered in the greening section. The seemingly simple task of developing a proposed process can spawn many other tasks, for instance, for outsourcing. Therefore, making a case for change that encompasses all expected forms of change and spawned projects is important. Chapter 9 describes the types of financial analysis required for the case for change.

Once changes are approved, process error-proofing is performed. Process error-proofing seeks to identify all possible points of failure (including human) and to design the resulting solution to reduce the likelihood, provide detection, and otherwise manage potential points of failure. The more complex and automated the process, the greater the possibility that points of failure will occur and the more critical this step becomes.

Final activities relate to proving that recommendations for change were successful and developing the case for change in a final report. Chapter 10 describes the development of metrics for both daily management and customer reporting. Once the redesign and engineering is complete, the process is ready to be implemented. The remainder of chapter 10 defines how to document the process improvement project and its recommended outcomes—organization and technology changes. Building on the case for change, the accompanying financial analysis, which highlights the cost-benefit analysis for the recommended change, is presented. As an example, a sample final project report is presented in appendix A following chapter 10. The sample report is presented as evidence that all aspects of work require evaluation, as the presenting problem is often merely a symptom of other problems.

Finally, many changes in process orientation are actually performed as precursor activities to the development of a service orientation for the company. In this book, I often distinguish between immature and mature "servitized" organizations. This distinction is important, as the companies in both camps have clear, relevant differences that constrain or facilitate different solutions for process improvement.

Mature organizations are managed through "formal, repeatable, and secure operational processes."[2] Many of these organizations—for example, Proctor & Gamble and Johnson Controls—are the best in their industries. Through discipline, these companies have mastered cross-functional management through a service orientation to deliver a quality customer experience.

Change management for continuous improvement is embedded in the processes of mature organizations as a normal consequence of any breakdowns in quality experience delivery. Therefore, process change initiation, while having more "ceremony," is one facet of risk management that pays off, leading to nearly 100% successful change efforts in mature organizations as compared with about 40% success for immature organizations.[3]

Contrast this well-oiled machine of an organization with an immature organization. Immature organizations buy in to Nicholas Carr's notion that "IT doesn't matter,"[4] treating IT as a necessary evil that drains assets. Such organizations frequently believe the controlled management of IT is not possible. Immature organizations frequently throw technology at a problem because it is cheaper than changing people. These firms are lucky to get any returns from their IT investments.[5]

Immature organizations frequently have cultural clashes between IT and the rest of the company, which works based on adversarial relationships that rely on last-minute heroics to achieve IT changes. As IT changes are implemented, little attention, if any, is paid to the people doing the work that IT supports. Training, if present, is incomplete, and support is inconsistent.

Most organizations fall somewhere between these two extremes. The important distinction is that in mature organizations, the ideas in this book are already embedded in daily work life, while in immature organizations, this book's ideas seem radical, overkill, or even impossible to accomplish.

Ironically, every organization *can* become a mature, servitized organization, but doing so requires great and unwavering management, a commitment to excellence, and an understanding of what servitizing means. The last chapter both summarizes this book and discusses the path to servitizing through a discussion of IT service management. The book's body of knowledge is summarized with expectations for the future of process management and its role in the servitizing of business.

Summary

Businesses have come to understand that to be efficient and effective, they need to manage their work processes and support good processes with IT. Process management is important because you cannot manage what you do not know. Since processes are the basis for all organizational operations, development of lean, clean, and green processes support organizational cost savings and quality management goals.

CHAPTER 2

Process Improvement Project Initiation

Introduction

This chapter describes project initiation and the development of a contract for a process improvement project, sometimes called a "statement of work" (SOW). Organizational entry to initiate a project differs among different organizational maturity levels and among consulting organizations.

In developing an SOW, the organization and target process need to be understood well enough to ensure that the scope of the process improvement project is appropriate. Developing an understanding of an organization requires information elicitation skills, usually through interviews, although other methods can be useful, depending on the context. Different elicitation techniques are discussed, along with the pros and cons of each, while interviewing, the most commonly used skill, is discussed in detail.

Upon completion of the initial interviews, a contract or SOW is created. An SOW documents the project, its sponsor, contacts, current status, team members and their roles, client responsibilities, work breakdown with staffing and work plan, deliverables, change management conduct, and other topics relevant to accomplishing the process improvement project.

This chapter's appendix introduces Support Center Inc., a call center, and provides a sample SOW for a process improvement project.

Organization Entry

During project initiation, entry into an organization is either as an employee or as a consultant. If you are an employee in an immature organization, entry usually consists of introductions with a meeting or interview to ensure that the scope of the project is appropriately defined and that the project team is acceptable. After the initiation meeting, the initial client interview should take place, and the project begins.

In a mature organization, a steering committee of information technology (IT) and non-IT executives collectively determines projects for the year based on direction from the executive committee and the organization strategy. Project initiation tends to be formal and follows the consulting model, with a contract for the project and documented expectations of goals and outcomes. Outcome descriptions may include service-level expectations for the number of users and locations, the number of transactions with peak periods, help-desk needs, and recovery in case of outages.

If you are a consultant, there may be a series of "marketing" meetings to scope the project, develop a cost, and conduct the initial client interviews. From that exercise, the SOW, which is a contract describing the work to be accomplished, is developed and, if accepted, becomes the basis for subsequent work. Contracts can include some sort of feasibility report, project approach, budget, work plans, staffing plans, technology requirements, constraints, information on expected user participation, needed documents, and assumptions used in developing the project. Consulting firms refer to an SOW as a proposal, which contains relatively fixed work schedules.

If you thought these descriptions of entry involving employees versus consultants sound similar, it is because they are. The differences are mostly in the length of time from first meeting to start of work and the formality of acceptance of project initiation. Therefore, a more detailed understanding of the initial situation, work conditions, and project constraints is desired to ensure project success and profitability. Consulting firms frequently suggest two or three people as project leads and allow the client to make the selection. Project risks are identified and mitigated, removed, or accepted. The proposal, however good, might be rejected or might be the subject of further negotiation. Therefore, at the start of an engagement, the time and depth of understanding tend to be greater for consultants than employees.

Understanding the Organization

The basic model of an organization shown in Figure 2.1 defines an organization as the composite of its functions, processes, and supporting

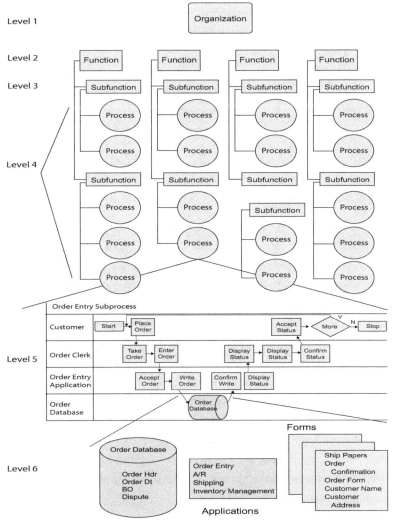

Figure 2.1. Model of the organization.

detail. Development of this model of the organization provides a basis for business process mapping. The first three levels provide an overview of the organization, while levels 4 and 5 are the focus of business process mapping and analysis.

Level 1: Organization

Level 1 defines a business entity that exists to accomplish some mission. Mission definition is the responsibility of organization executives. If there is no existing mission, then one should be defined as a prelude to any improvement project to ensure alignment of the process with the business mission.

An organization may be an actual company or a component of a company (e.g., a division or a business unit). The organization's mission usually documents the type of business and its competitive environment in addition to defining orientation toward quality, price, customers, and employees.

Level 2: Function

The accomplishment of the organization's mission requires the coordinated efforts of too many people who perform too many different functions to be organized, with everyone reporting to a chief executive. Therefore, an organization typically structures functions to mirror its supply chain, plus needed support organizations. Functional needs depend on both the size and type of organization. For instance, a large manufacturing firm might have functions defined for purchasing, manufacturing, distribution, sales, accounting, information technology, marketing, finance, and human resources. A service organization might have functions for sales and marketing, service management, service delivery, accounting, and legal management.

Keep in mind that organizations vary in their design from functional to matrixed to projectized. Matrixed organization diagrams should include the functions, their project counterparts, and dotted-line responsibilities. Project-oriented organizations should identify both permanent projects and temporary projects that exist at the time of diagram creation, each within its respective reporting structure. Temporary project teams should be shown in dotted-line, rounded rectangles to indicate their temporary nature.

As companies move toward a service orientation, they are sensitive to the notion that functional silos need to be transcended in managing processes that are the joint responsibility of many functional areas. An example of such a process is order fulfillment, sometimes called names like "quote-to-cash" to identify the scope of silo involvement. A quote-to-cash process would likely include sales quotes, sales, inventory management, manufacturing, order fulfillment, shipping, invoicing, and accounts receivable. For process improvement projects, companies assign cross-functional management teams. Such teams require management of new or potential issues arising from organizational silo priority differences.

Level 3: Subfunctions

The larger the organization, the more likely each function consists of several subfunctions. For instance, marketing might have subfunctions for market development, advertising, and product development. To the extent that they exist, subfunctions should be documented in the organizational model.

Level 4: Business Processes

The people in each functional area accomplish their work goals by completing a set of processes. A *process* is a series of repeated tasks or steps that may or may not be interrelated with other processes. Clearly identify each process with the subfunctions that perform it. Typically, only part of a process is shown within a single subfunction. For instance, a shipping organization would show the pick, pack, and ship steps of the overall quote-to-cash process.

Level 5: Business Process Detail

Process details describe the individual work steps that compose the conduct of single processes. While the first step of business process analysis is to develop an organizational map that describes the areas of interest, business process details compose the focal point of business process mapping.

Each process is composed of starting and ending events or conditions with decisions and work steps in between. An *event* is some occurrence or demand that triggers actions in a process (e.g., a date). A *condition* is a state of some process, product, or work item in an organization that requires action. For instance, "out of stock" is a condition. The work steps might themselves be processes that may or may not require further elaboration depending on the purpose of the analysis.

A business process may have steps performed by individuals, organizations, application systems, or organizational roles. Each of these is explicitly identified in the diagrams that document the process, with the interdependencies illustrated.

Level 6: Supporting Detail

The details of accomplishing work are specific to the entity performing the work step. Most white-collar job descriptions specify outcomes required of the job incumbent without describing how to obtain the outcome, that is, without specifying a process. White-collar jobs allow a fair amount of discretion in actual job conduct that, while encouraging creativity, allows people to introduce their own bad habits to their work processes. Therefore, a good practice when collecting supporting information is to identify not only the information source but also its purpose and whether it is required (e.g., for auditability).

If an individual, role, or organization performs the work, then the details might include documents, e-mails, forms, policies and procedures manuals, or other reference and work materials used in the conduct of the step. If the work is performed by an application, then the supporting detail would include the input and output formats of messages and screens, input and output media, programs, database tables, database attributes, and so on that are used as work is performed. Further information might include file and database storage locations, frequency of usage, backup schedule, recoverability plan, audit requirements, compliance requirements, and other aspects of the work relevant to the task.

The process improvement team should create either an intranet repository or a set of files, binders, and data sets to form the official copy of project documentation. Mature organizations usually have intranet repositories for documents needed for a process improvement project. As a result, access to the repository by the improvement team is critical and, ideally, documents collected or created by the improvement team use an intranet for documentation, storage, and accessibility.

Process Mapping

Function-Level Mapping

Developing a business process map starts with an organization chart that identifies the major functions, with focus on the functions that are the target of activity for business process analysis. While the diagram in Figure 2.1 is only three levels deep, the larger the organization, the more likely the diagram will require several levels of detail and management structure. For simple organizations, one or two levels of detail may be sufficient for a process map, while for a complex organization, there may be as many as 10 levels to fully articulate the functions of interest.

Most organizations can provide an organization chart for their specific structure. However, if the organization does not have an organization chart, then the team should develop one as a work product. The task of the analyst is to understand and diagram individual functions, map them on the organization chart, locate the process owner for all processes and subprocesses, and identify the areas that are the targets of analysis.

Therefore, analysts start their work by interviewing the client contact in order to obtain an organizational overview and to determine their next interview chart, then the team should understanding of the context and expectations for the project. These tasks are required background for creating the SOW.

In general, the client directs the work in terms of identifying the key areas of interest and related areas that may also need analysis. The interview subjects are considered *stakeholders*, that is, the people whose jobs or management areas are likely to be affected by the process improvement project and, hence, should participate in the project.

The analyst interviews the stakeholders, including the client, functional managers, IT representatives, and several people who actually do the work to ensure that both automated and nonautomated tasks are fully understood. Other interviews might be conducted with, for instance, auditors or compliance officers in order to gain understanding of job monitoring requirements that may not be fully understood by the incumbents.

One responsibility of the process analyst is to ensure that organizational interrelationships are not overlooked. Usually this assurance is accomplished by verifying the findings and interrelationships during all interviews. In addition, the IT representatives might not only confirm organizational interrelationships but also identify other hidden relationships that are embedded in the software or operational environment.

Functions are documented by identifying the overall organizational purpose or roles performed within the organization. Organizational roles vary for manufacturing, distribution, retail, and service organizations, and many companies have elements of each of these organization types. Therefore, the interviews can be used to confirm, from a global list of functions, those that apply to the subject organization and how they are placed in the organization's structure. Global functions can include the following:

- human resources
- benefits administration
- executive compensation administration
- marketing
- sales
- advertising
- research and development
- product development
- product engineering
- manufacturing planning
- manufacturing
- purchasing
- raw materials management
- returns management
- rework management
- inventory management
- accounts receivable
- accounts payable
- accounting
- financial planning
- financial management
- buildings and grounds maintenance

- machine maintenance
- shipping and receiving
- audit
- compliance
- information systems management
- IT operations
- systems development
- systems quality assurance
- customer support or service

Once the list of applicable functions is developed, functions are mapped onto the organization chart to develop Level 2 of the diagram. When validation of the function mapping has been completed by the client, the analysts turn to the focal process and its conduct.

Process-Level Mapping

Recall that a process is a set of steps that accomplish some business function. One functional manager is designated as having primary responsibility for each business process even though each process might be carried out by tasks conducted in many different functions. This cross-functional management of business processes is one reason why process improvement is not simple. Each function has its own priorities and tasks. Yet improvement within a functional area, while relatively easy, is likely to suboptimize the overall process. Gaining support and cooperation from multiple functions requires careful planning and stakeholder participation. A process improvement project that provides sufficient inclusiveness across the organization is more likely to be successful than one that is not very inclusive.

As processes are identified, the process owner should be identified as well. The *process owner* is the person responsible for the process as the overall decision maker in the event of a process-related dispute. Ideally, as processes are identified for improvement, the process owner then becomes the "client" for the improvement project.

Initial Project Understanding

The first step in the process project is initiating the project. This may entail gaining entry to an organization as a consultant or simply being assigned as an employee project manager for an improvement project. In either case, once assigned a project, one must quickly gain an understanding of the work to a level of detail that allows the project work to be planned. Such understanding is documented in an SOW that becomes a contract between the process project team and the client.

In eliciting information, the consultant or project manager should *triangulate*, obtaining three sources of information about every aspect and topic area to be covered. Triangulation provides more confidence that the information is correct. Politics, faulty recall, and simple sabotage can occur in the best of projects, but triangulation with public review of diagrams and data-gathering results can minimize problems stemming from poor information.

Developing a quick understanding requires at least one project sponsor interview. Sponsor interview topics include the following:

- project motivation, client expectations, and project goal
- project team authority
- dealing with inconsistencies
- project communications
- project status reporting
- interview scheduling and interviewees
- project deliverables
- client involvement
- deadlines
- constraints and risk
- target process

Project Motivation, Client Expectations, and Project Goal

The project motivation defines the situation to be analyzed, while expectations and goals relate to the desired executive outcomes. The goal is the overall outcome expected from the project. The project purpose, expectations, and goal may not be consistent, and frequently, the stated goal is not the real goal. If the team has a goal that differs from the organization's goal, then the project is unlikely to succeed. Through recognizing the purpose, expectations, motivations, and stated goals, the project manager's role is to help the client articulate the "real" goals.

As interviews proceed, the project goal should be reviewed with each interviewee. Each person develops his or her own filtered version of the goal, which may not necessarily be consistent with reality. Therefore, to help the organization develop a harmonized understanding of the goal, it should be repeated often and consistently.

Project Team Authority

While the process project team has responsibility for project conduct, it frequently lacks authority to resolve conflicts. Discussions regarding project authority should resolve issues about eventual problem management and define the extent to which the client expects the project leader to deal with issues. The purpose of this discussion is to surface authority limitations. It is best to define authority and responsibility boundaries before problems arise to ensure clear lines of communication and to ensure notification of the proper authority when issues occur.

Dealing With Inconsistencies

A plan for dealing with inconsistent information should be approved before any inconsistencies arise. The team can then take action without arousing the politics of the organization. This topic relates to authority issues and is best understood before the event. One method for identifying inconsistencies—*triangulation*—requires compiling three sources for all facts in order to increase the probability that they are accurate. Another method for dealing with inconsistencies is to gather information from a single source and then attempt to verify the information with peers or managers of the source. This is a form of triangulation, but rather than the interviewees providing the information, they only confirm its accuracy.

Project Communications

Process improvement projects, by definition, alter power structures and change the nature of jobs. As a result, everyone involved should be made aware of the project and its status as a way to minimize erroneous gossip and undercutting of the team. Communications initiation, audiences, and timing should be carefully mapped out and modified, as needed, for the entire project.

The communications strategy should be summarized and published in a table that matches stakeholder groups and roles to the types of communications to be used (e.g., status reports). The cells of the table should contain the timing and media type (e.g., e-mail) for each type of communication.

As stated before, organizations vary in their design from functional to matrixed to projectized. Organization structure is important to communication decisions because, typically, the more projectized the organization, the more communication is a project team responsibility, while the more functional the organization, the less communication is a project team responsibility.

Thus depending on the organization structure, the client, the project manager, or someone else in the organization may be designated as having overall communications responsibility. In any case, it is important to define who is responsible and to develop a communications plan that informs all stakeholders of project actions and outcomes at appropriate times.

Project Status Reporting

Similar to project communications, but usually with a smaller group receiving regular reports, the content and list of recipients for status reports should be defined as early in the project as possible. If the client has no preference, status reporting should be weekly and should include, at a minimum, tasks accomplished (by staff member, as appropriate); outstanding issues or problems, who is responsible for their resolution, and by what date; and plans for the next week that require client participation. If defining the recipient list is left to the process improvement team, every major stakeholder in the outcome should receive status reports.

Interview Scheduling and Interviewees

The team should identify the list of interviewees as part of their definition of the target business areas. Initially, however, the client may set several interviews with affected managers to gain their buy-in and increase their cooperation for the project. The who, what, when, where, and how of interviewing should be discussed, planned, and modified, as needed, to ensure that project needs are met. The initial interviewee list is almost never adequate enough to ensure full team understanding. Therefore, the list of interviewees needs to be supplemented, as needed, within project time constraints.

A good plan is to suggest client (or higher level executive) participation in the initial set of interviews to ensure staff understanding of the level of support for the project and to instill a sense of urgency about the importance of the work. The client opens the meeting, introducing the team and describing the goals, and then the meeting is turned over to the project team to complete.

Project Deliverables

Once the initial scope of the project is understood (by defining the goals and purpose), an initial set of deliverable products can be defined with the client. The deliverables can be modified as needed, but the definition should be about 90% complete after the initial meeting. The minimum documents produced are an SOW (or project contract), status reports, and final report.

Client Involvement

Ongoing client involvement is needed for project-related information, functional information, and details of process steps. Often, the project sponsor delegates daily coordination responsibility; the team then works with this delegate as the client rather than the sponsor. Keep in mind that when this book refers to client, it may be the sponsor or the delegate.

In addition, the project must be viewed as "the client's" rather than as "the project team's" to convey ownership for the final products. If the project is not viewed as owned by someone in the target organization, the change effort is less likely to be successful and is more likely to be difficult. The difficulty derives from the team's having to sell the ideas to the people whose jobs will change first and then make the change. If the project is perceived as being owned by the client in the first place, then the sales job is either unneeded or reduced.

Further, different levels of staff will be involved at different times during the project. The process improvement team should be relatively free to determine the managers who should be interviewed and the skill levels of the subordinates to be chosen by respective managers. However, client involvement should always be discussed and roles should be clarified in advance of project planning. If a company insists on conducting a process improvement project without user involvement, then the team needs to strive for project communications to serve that role.

Deadlines

The discussion of deadlines focuses on time as a constraint in the project plan. Many companies tend to want deliverable products at least quarterly to demonstrate momentum and interim success. The project plan needs to incorporate client deadlines to be useful for the life of the project.

Any expected end dates for the entire project should be surfaced. A project team can manage two of three aspects of a project: time, budget, and scope or functionality (see Figure 2.2). If time and budget are both constrained, the level of detail for functionality is automatically constrained. Therefore, in situations when the client defines both time and budget, the project manager needs to discuss with the client the limitations to obtaining a full understanding. A time-boxing technique may be applied so that, for instance, 30% of time is devoted to obtaining information and developing understanding, 40% of project time is allocated to process analysis, and 30% of project time is spent documenting findings and recommendations. This allocation of percentages can work with any duration—1 week, 1 month, or 1 year. The variance in the level of understanding gained by the project team is a risk that the client must be willing to bear.

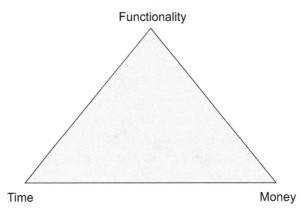

Figure 2.2. Three controllable project attributes.

Constraints and Risk

As stated previously, constraints relate to project scope in terms of functionality, time, budget, and human resource availability. Once the team has defined the scope and project plan (which includes time, budget, and resources), any change to any of the constraints means that one or more of the other constraints must be compromised to ensure the others. Project plans are accurate to the extent that they include consideration of all aspects of the project, including all constraints.

In addition to constraints, understanding risks involved in the project is important. Risk can relate to personnel, management support, budget, technology, machines, or methods. The most common risks relate to personnel changing jobs, insufficient budget, or technology that does not work as advertised or is not available when needed. In any case, project risks should be assessed for ways to mitigate or manage the risk.

Target Process

Once the parameters of project conduct are agreed upon, the target process becomes the focus of the client interview. Problems with the current process are surfaced and should be compared to the project motivation to ensure consistency. To the extent possible, detailed process conduct should be documented, as it provides the scope and basis for time and staff estimates. The target process is the focus of every first interview with every stakeholder and is further elaborated in the next topic on interviewing.

As you can see from these topics, quick understanding relates not only to the project but also its management, conduct, and constraints. The knowledge gained from the first interview is then evaluated to determine that sufficient information to create the SOW has been obtained. But before we discuss that, now that we have the interview topics defined, conducting the interview is next.

Interviewing

An *interview* is a structured meeting during which one person questions one or several person(s) to obtain information. Interviews are the basic form of information transfer from the client organization to the process improvement team. The team's professionalism, credibility, perceived expertise, and basic trustworthiness are initially judged by the manner in which they set up and conduct their interviews. If the interview processes run smoothly, then the team gains the trust and cooperation of the client stakeholders more quickly. If the interview processes run poorly, then the team may likely be fired. Take a minute and write down what you think the steps of the *interview process* are, from setup to follow-up. Compare what you wrote to the recommended process discussed next.

The initial interview sets the stage for the project and may actually take place before a consulting firm is engaged or before the project is officially begun by the organization. The next level of interviews serves to determine the structure, functions and subfunctions, and processes of the organization. Usually, one or more interviews per subject are required.

At least two interviewers should attend each session. While an interview is proceeding, one person does most of the actual interrogation, while the other takes notes and asks probing questions as needed. The notetaker may try to sketch a preliminary process map but has the main task of taking text notes. If the interviewee agrees, recording the session provides a completely accurate record. The other reason to have two interview attendees is that *two* people hear what is said. Moreover, each person may hear it differently. Having both interviewer and notetaker ensures at least two versions about what was said and results in a more complete record of the interview.

Interview topics proceed from function definition and mission to the processes that compose the function, the work steps of the processes, and the details of the process steps. If all information can be obtained in a single interview, then the next step is development of diagrams and accompanying details for verification. Most often, multiple interviews will be required, and initial diagrams provide a basis for subsequent interviews. Interview topic hierarchy should follow the following:

- organization
- mission
- functions and subfunctions
- process
- process work steps
- details of work steps or contacts for further interviewing

Interviewees can be asked if they mind being recorded so that key information is not lost. If the interviewee agrees, then the session should be recorded, and a rough process map then becomes the notetaker's main goal. If a process map is sketched during the interview summary, then any diagrams created are immediately reviewed for accuracy and completeness.

Every interview, regardless of topic, should include the following steps (compare this against your list of interview process steps):

1. Make an appointment for the interview with location, topic, and start and stop times identified. Make appointments 2 to 5 business days before the meeting (or even earlier if the person requests more lead time). Never *show up* without an appointment and expect to get someone's time.

   First interview appointments should be made via phone call or in person to introduce the analyst and the project to the interviewee. After the first interview, other appointments can be made via e-mail. If an appointment is made via an e-mail system, such as Lotus Notes, then make the list of attendees visible to all. Interviews should be no more than 2 hours in duration with 1 hour being ideal.

2. At least 2 days before the interview, provide the following:

 a. Meeting agenda

 b. Any review materials for the interviewee

 c. A list of any items to be gathered as documentation for the interviewers

3. Be on time and dress appropriately. If you are unsure of the dress code, ask about it when setting the interview time. Never wear blue jeans, T-shirts with decorations, or sneakers, regardless of the company's dress code. Never show belly or back skin. Remove any visible piercing jewelry not in the ear. If the company dress code is business casual, wear a shirt with a collar, dressy slacks (or a skirt, for women), and dressy shoes. If the dress code is business attire, a suit of some kind is required. If you are concerned about overdressing, it is far better to be overdressed than underdressed.

4. Conduct the interview, making sure you include all beginning, middle, and ending activities:

 a. To begin the interview, do the following:

   i. *Greet* the interviewee.

   ii. *Introduce* all interview attendees and their roles. Interviews should be cordial but formal. During the introductions, it is nice to talk of sports, family, and so on *if* you know the person well. If not, be friendly without being personal. Humor and opinion should be omitted from an interview until you know the interviewee well.

   iii. *Give a brief summary* of the project status, *purpose* for this interview, and the overall *outcome expected* for the session. For instance, "At our last interview, we covered the initial setup for a new client. For this meeting, we would like to review and correct the diagrams we developed from that process discussion and continue with procedures for new client processing."

 b. During the middle of the interview, do the following:

   i. *Ask questions*, beginning with open-ended and moving to closed-ended questions for each topic. Questions vary from open-ended (or nonspecific) to specific on each topic, with probing questions about the meaning of terms or manner in which an activity is accomplished or for more detail about a subject.

ii. *At the end of each topic, summarize* what you have heard. For instance, "I'd like to do a quick summary so we're all sure we understand what you have said." This summary builds client trust by demonstrating your understanding and provides feedback and correction on any misunderstandings before you leave the session.

iii. *Actively listen. Active listening* means paying close attention to what is said, letting the client say what they want, and not cutting the speaker off or finishing sentences or thoughts for him or her. The person asking questions actively listens to ask, evaluate an answer, develop follow-up questions, and develop probing questions to get more information on subjects of interest. The interviewer also keeps the interview moving, stays on the topic, and ensures getting the right level of detail. The notetaker attends to getting complete and accurate notes of the interactions.

iv. *Mind the time* and cover all topics as best you can. If the time is clearly insufficient, plan the interview with only the number of topics that can be completed in the time allowed. The notetaker also is the timekeeper, prompting for the summary when there are 10 minutes left to the session. Then, as needed, ask to extend the session if you are within a 15 to 30 minutes of completing the data gathering for this person, or begin the summary for the session.

c. At the end of the interview, either when the interview is complete or the time is almost expired, do the following:

i. *Summarize* the current session. If a diagram has been sketched during the session, walk through the diagram. Otherwise, paraphrase the interviewee's answers to questions to ensure correct understanding.

ii. *If there are follow-up activities, confirm* them and *get commitment*, if the activity is for the interviewee, in the form of a completion date. For instance, if you will send a copy of notes and diagrams for review and correction, say when that will happen (which should be within 48 hours), then state what you expect from the interviewee's review. For instance, "We will send you a copy of the diagrams by e-mail tomorrow. We would like you to review and mark them up with corrections, if any. E-mail corrections to us or tell us that the information is correct by [2 days to 1 week]. We would like to schedule another interview to discuss changes and continue discussion on [topic and date]."

   iii. *Thank the person* for his or her time and leave.

Immediately after the meeting, the team members should compare and complete the meeting notes to ensure that if there are conflicts or topics for which notes were not complete then they can be resolved while the information is fresh.

After interview follow-up is complete, develop the accompanying diagrams. When developing the diagrams, ask yourself if you have enough detail to make decisions about your next steps (e.g., if you are interviewing for functions, then can you now start talking about processes?). If your answer is "no," then write down questions you need answered to complete your information for the next interview, or e-mail the questions if only short answers are needed.

Continue a cycle of "interview, document, review, and correct" until you have a sufficiently detailed understanding of the environment to develop the next steps of your change process. This concept, *"enough to continue,"* becomes the rule of thumb[1] by which you determine completeness of a step.

A formal review of results, called a walk-through, is conducted after all interviews are complete. A *walk-through* is a formal presentation of a work product to all stakeholders (e.g., affected managers not interviewed), interested parties (e.g., auditors), interviewees, and the project team. The purpose is to find errors or misunderstandings in the work product and to ensure that all stakeholders have the same understanding about the product content and project direction. Material to be walked through is given to all participants when the meeting is set up. One person, not the author, presents the material while the reviewers ask questions and try to find errors. One person is the scribe, taking notes on errors found and the reasoning for any corrections. After the meeting, not during, corrective action is taken to perfect the work product and the item or document is sent for final review. After the deadline for final review, the document is officially approved via client signature and finalized. Walk-throughs should not be optional, as errors found early in a project cost 10% of the cost to fix compared to when they are found late in the project.

As work documents and diagrams are collected and completed, the "official" version should be added to the documentation intranet site or binders to ensure that the official version remains accurate, complete, and current.

Creating an SOW

After project initiation, the first task is to develop a quick understanding. Using the knowledge gained from the initial interview(s), an SOW[2] is created in order to define the work to be conducted, the deliverables, a schedule, and expectations of both parties in the project. This document becomes a contract between both the team and the organization as to project scope, project schedule, budget, deliverables, client involvement, and other issues. In this discussion, we define the SOW sections and the type of information provided in each.

The contents of the SOW are summarized in the next sections, with further discussion following the document summary. The SOW should contain all of the sections and contents described here.

Title Page

The title page contains the title of the project—for example, "Statement of Work for [Project Name]"—centered about halfway down the cover page in 16-point type, a list of team members—[Prepared by:]—right justified, 10- or 12-point type, and report date right justified and under the "prepared by" list. The next section begins a new page.

Executive Summary

An executive summary should identify the project, sponsor, goal, and deliverables in fewer than 100 words and in 2 to 3 sentences. Text should be set at 1.5 spacing and formatted for readability. The next section begins a new page.

Introduction

The introduction explains the purpose of the project. Most often, this section summarizes a *brief* history of the company, department (as appropriate), reason for the project, and a clear statement of the purpose of the project.

Project Description

The project description summarizes the functional area of project in enough detail to permit the reader to evaluate work plan adequacy. The scope should be clearly delineated, identifying the event or condition that initiates the process and the event or condition that signifies an end to the process. All process stakeholder organizations should be identified. Details should be added, as needed, to discuss assumptions, risk, budget, technology, or other areas that might be controversial.

Deliverables

The "deliverables" section contains a bulleted list of the deliverable documents and work products to be developed as part of project work. Required documents for a process improvement project include the following:

- SOW
- current "as is" process map
- process description
- analysis of current process
- recommended changes
- recommended "to be" process map
- metrics and benchmarks
- project documentation
- project report

Client Responsibilities

This section contains a bulleted list of client responsibilities, including but not limited to the following:

- signed acceptance of the SOW
- review and approval of all work products
- signed acceptance of the final project and all deliverable items

Additional items may include time and budget commitments expected, interview scheduling, documents or electronic resources to be provided, special workspace or equipment, and so on, as the project requires.

Work Plan

The work plan is a work breakdown, providing a list of tasks, the assigned responsible person (can be team member or client), start and end dates, and required time (see Figure 2.3). Required client time commitments, such as interviews and reviews, should be included in the work plan.

Change Control

Once the SOW is signed, if either team members or a client require a change of scope or requirements beyond what was outlined previously, a request for change should be prepared as an addendum to this document, and, once approved, signed by all parties. The change should be reviewed by all parties and may or may not be accepted, depending on the change of the scope and time left for project work. The date after which changes are not accepted should be identified. A blank change control form should be attached to the SOW as an appendix.

Start Date	End Date	Work Hours	Task	Person(s) Assigned

Figure 2.3. Template for work plan.

Signatories to the document include the client and project manager, and it should be formatted something like the following:

[Client Company Name]:
For example, SCI Corporation

_____   _____

Client Name,   Date
For example, Richard Madison, CFO   October 1, 2010
Project Team: (This section should contain one line for sign-off by each team member)

_____   _____

Member Name,   Date
For example, Mary Jones   September 30, 2010

Appendices

Appendices are optional and should be omitted if not relevant to the project. If used, then each appendix begins on a new page. Appendices include supplementary material that is not appropriate in the body of the report. Optional documents might include supporting organizational reports, organization charts, or other information used in the conduct of the work. If you use jargon (e.g., military units, medical terms) or unfamiliar terms, then include a dictionary of terms. If change management is anticipated, then a blank form should be provided in this section. If the project team is responsible for the communication plan, then it should be added to the SOW as an appendix.

References

The references section is optional and should be removed if not relevant to the project. If used, then references should begin on a new page.

All research documentation (e.g., the analysis of the current process) should provide a reference citation to the previous research or ideas used in the development of a solution or argument. The entries have the following elements: author(s), year of publication, title, and source (i.e., publisher and place of publication in the case of books and reports only). Book and journal titles are italicized. A journal title is followed by the volume number, issue number within the volume (or the month or season, depending upon the journal's style), and the page numbers.

Use the American Psychological Association (APA) format for references, with a second-line indent and single spacing. Within the document, refer to a source by author surname, comma, and year: for example (Foster, 2005).

The following are examples of appropriate layout:

Anderson C. (2004, October). The long tail. *Wired, 12*(10). Retrieved from http://www.wired.com/wired/archive/12.10/tail.html

Foster, I. (2005, May 6). Service-oriented science. *Science, 308*(5723), 814–817.

Garrett, J. J. (2005). *Ajax: A new approach to web applications.* Retrieved from http://www.adaptivepath.com/publications/essays/archives/000385 .php

Summary

Process improvement projects consist of several main tasks: understanding and mapping the current process, analyzing the current process for possible improvements, recommending a revised process, creating benchmarks and metrics, and documenting the project and all process information. Before attaining a complete understanding of the current process, which might take weeks, a quick understanding is gained through one or several interviews to allow development of an SOW. The SOW constitutes a contract between the team and the client organization, describing the project schedule, project outcomes, and client responsibilities.

A process improvement team must first understand the environment and organization within which it is working. To do that, interviewing skills are required. An interview is a structured discussion with one party asking questions and probing for details on answers, with the other party or parties answering the questions and providing backup documentation as requested or required. The interview is important in setting the tone of cooperation with the interviewees. Interviews should be set formally and have specified start and stop times. The interview should have a beginning, middle, and end. The beginning of the interview introduces everyone and sets session goals. During the middle of the interview, the interviewer asks a series of questions that vary from open-ended to closed-ended, obtaining both general and specific information. The end of the interview confirms what was heard, identifies follow-up actions, timing, and responsibilities, and thanks interviewees for their time. Interview results should be compiled as soon as practical after the session in order to minimize forgetting of unwritten details. Any taping of interviews must be agreed to in advance of starting the session.

From interviews, the process improvement team develops organization charts, as needed, and maps functions to organizations, identifying the processes conducted within each function. From this understanding, processes for evaluation are identified and verified for scope with the client or project sponsor.

Once a quick understanding of the project is acquired, the team develops an SOW, which constitutes a contract between the team and the client. The SOW is a comprehensive document, lacking many details, but defining the who, what, and when of a project. The document contents are customized for process improvement but can be modified for almost any type of project.

The project plan's work breakdown structure may be incorporated in the document or may be a separate document created from software such as Microsoft Project. Hourly work assignments allow better project control and give a clearer picture of project progress, but planning software that states durations in days can be used.

Appendix 1: Support Center Inc. Call Center

Support Center Inc. (SCI)[3]—a $300 million, 200-person call center—is used as a case study throughout this book. SCI was the product of a merger between three call-center companies to create one entity that provides first- and third-party collections and sales. First-party collections are situations in which the call-center customer service representatives (CSRs) act as if they are the client organization. These positions use scripts for all customer interactions. Third-party collections are situations in which the CSRs identify themselves as SCI employees (e.g., a collection agency) and use no scripts in their collections activities. Sales employees do no collections, conduct scripted transactions, and are legally required to record all transactions for proof of voluntary customer assent.

The project team was charged to evaluate the technology used in the call-center processes. As a first step in understanding technology needs, the team interviewed the chief operating officer (COO, sponsor), the call center manager (client to whom the COO delegated daily project responsibility), several call center supervisors, the "dialer administrator," and several CSRs. In addition, the team observed 10 CSRs and the dialer administrator in order to gain a deeper understanding of their issues in using the technology.

The team began with an organization chart to facilitate organizational understanding (see Figure 2.4). The team developed the chart based on interviews, as SCI did not already have one on hand.

The team also developed two diagrams of the collections and sales processes that are shown in Figures 2.5 and 2.6. The diagram in Figure 2.5 shows how the organization works to bring in a client, perform collections activities, and bill for their services.

Figure 2.6 depicts the call center's processes by identifying start-up and shut-down activities with iterative collections and sales activities

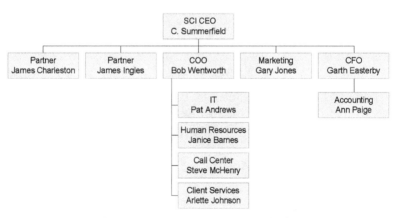

Figure 2.4. Initial functional SCI organization chart.

Figure 2.5. SCI client process overview.

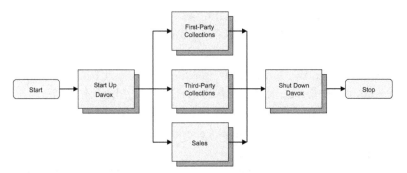

Figure 2.6. SCI collections process overview.

between those events. A complete process analysis of the call center, then, requires looking at the details of all of the boxes illustrated in Figure 2.6.

SOW

The next pages reproduce the SOW for the SCI case.

Statement of Work for
Support Center Inc.
January 20, 2010

Developed by:
David Birch
Enrique Estevez
Anil Henry
Brad Powell
Sheri Jones
Cindy Allison

Executive Summary

This project is an analysis of the technology used for SCI's call center operation. The goal of the project is to determine more effective use for technology in collections and sales processes. Recommendations on technology and, possibly, process improvements will be the major deliverables.

Introduction

SCI is a call center performing both collections and sales activities. SCI was formed from the merger of three call center organizations owned by Charles Summerfield, President of SCI, Jim Charleston and Jim Ingles, both SCI partners. Bob Wentworth was hired to help determine the causes of technology problems and to improve organizational functioning. This project was initiated to detail technology issues and problems in the call center and to develop recommendations to improve call center operations.

Project Description

The project includes interviewing and observing call center employees and representatives of other SCI organizations relating to call center work. In addition, documents, such as measures of call center efficiency and effectiveness both of people and of the applications will be evaluated.

The call center consists of first-party, third-party, and sales operations (see Figure 2.6). A Davox predictive dialer for which start-up and shutdown processes are required on a daily basis supports these. Calls are made, evaluated, and forwarded by the Davox for processing after the formatting screen displays the proper script, if required, and customer information.

Agents performing first-party collections act as agents of the client organization, announcing themselves as employees of that organization. Agents performing third-party collections are agents of SCI in the transaction. Both collections groups seek to collect past-due debts, updating databases at both SCI and the customer site (as required) with monies collected. Sales agents follow scripts to sell products via telemarketing. As a sale is made, an audio recording of the payment terms and sale confirmation is made as proof of the transaction.

At the end of a workday, CSRs all log off of their machines, and the Davox proceeds to end-of-day processing to generate reports and close down database and client processing.

Deliverables

Documents to be developed include the following:

- SOW
- organization chart
- current process maps for the following:
    - dialer administration start-up and shutdown
    - first-party collections
    - third-party collections
    - sales
- process descriptions, as needed
- analysis of current processes and use of technology for those processes
- recommended changes, including both technology and process
- recommended "to be" process map
- metrics and benchmarks
- project documentation
- project report
- weekly status reports

In addition to the documents, an interim report on progress will be presented at least once during week 5 of the project. Further presentations, such as a walk-through of work products with all participants, will also be scheduled.

Client Responsibilities

This section contains a bulleted list of client responsibilities including but not limited to the following:

- signed acceptance of this SOW
- review and approval of all work products
- approximately 4 hours over the first 2 weeks with Steve McHenry; approximately half an hour weekly after that.

- approximately 40 hours of observation acceptance of this SOW of CSRs, dialer administration start-up and shutdown, quality assurance, and supervisors.
- approximately 20 hours of interviews with added time for document review with IT representatives.
- approximately 15 hours of Bob Wentworth's time over the 10 weeks.
- in addition to time needed with various people, reports, policies, procedures, applications reports, operational reports, and other documents will be evaluated as part of this work. Items will be requested during interviews and originals will be returned upon completion of our analysis.
- signed acceptance of the final project and all deliverable items.

Additional items may include time and budget commitments expected, interview scheduling, documents or electronic resources to be provided, special workspace or equipment, and so on, as the project requires.

Work Plan

The work plan details all tasks and responsible persons, with estimated start and end dates and work hours. Changes will be reflected in the work plan as needed.

The work plan assumes that Figure 2.7 accurately depicts the scope of the engagement. If the work is substantially different from that in Figure 2.7, new dates will need to be developed.

Change Control

Once the SOW is signed, should either team members or client require a change of scope or requirements beyond what was outlined previously, a request for change should be prepared as an addendum to this document, and once approved, signed by all parties. The change should be reviewed by all parties and may or may not be accepted, depending on the change of the scope and time left for project work. *Neither party will accept changes after the 4th week of the project.* A change control document is attached to this document (Figure 2.8).

Start date, weekday	End date, weekday	Work hours	Task	Person(s) assigned
Jan 25	Jan 26		Statement of work	Team
Jan 25	Jan 25	3	Organization chart	Team
Jan 25	Jan 25	2	Meet with Steve McHenry	Team
Jan 26	Jan 26	2	Meet with Pat Andrews	Rick, Anil
Jan 26	Jan 26	2	Dialer administration start-up and shutdown	Anil, Brad
Jan 25	Jan 26	2	Meet IT staff	
Jan 26	Jan 29	15	Observe and interview call center CSRs, supervisors, and managers	Rick, Anil, Brad, Sheri, Cindy
Jan 29	Jan 29	2	Create process map: dialer	Rick, Brad
Feb 1	Feb 1	5	Create process map: first-party collection	Anil, Sheri
Feb 2	Feb 2	5	Create process map: third-party collection	Anil, Sheri
Feb 3	Feb 3	5	Create process map: sales	Rick, Brad
Feb 3	Feb 3	2	Review maps	SM, David
Feb 1	Feb 1	5	Create process descriptions as needed	Brad, Cindy
Feb 3	Feb 3	2	Revise and finalize maps	Anil, Rick
Feb 4	Feb 4	5	Walk through all maps	Team, BW, SM, PA, JH, KL, AP, AC, CO, BY, SP, CY, JO, AC, others?
Feb 4	Feb 4	2	Revise and finalize current maps	Rick, Anil, Brad, Sheri, Cindy
Feb 5	Feb 5	5	Analyze current processes: dialer	Rick, Brad
Feb 5	Feb 5	5	Analyze current processes: first party	Anil, Sheri
Feb 5	Feb 8	5	Analyze current processes: third party	Anil, Sheri
Feb 5	Feb 8	5	Analyze current processes: dales	Rick, Brad

Figure 2.7. Work plan.

Start date, weekday	End date, weekday	Work hours	Task	Person(s) assigned
Feb 8	Feb 9	5	Develop recommendations: dialer	Rick, Brad
Feb 8	Feb 9	5	Develop recommendations: first party	Anil, Sheri
Feb 9	Feb 9	5	Develop recommendations: third party	Anil, Sheri
Feb 9	Feb 9	5	Develop recommendations: sales	Rick, Brad
Feb 10	Feb 10	2	Discuss and present recommendations	BW, SM, Team
Feb 10	Feb 10	5	Develop "to be" process maps: dialer	Rick, Brad
Feb 10	Feb 10	5	Develop "to be" process maps: first party	Anil, Sheri
Feb 10	Feb 11	5	Develop "to be" process maps: third party	Anil, Sheri
Feb 10	Feb 11	5	Develop "to be" process maps: sales	Rick, Brad
Feb 12	Feb 12	5	Walk through all recommendations and "to be" maps	Team, BW, SM, PA, JH, KL, AP, AC, CO, BY, SP, CY, JO, AC, others?
Feb 12	Feb 15	5	Revise and finalize recommendations and maps as required	Rick, Anil, Brad, Sheri, Cindy
Feb 15	Feb 16	5	Develop metrics and internal benchmarks: dialer	Rick, Brad
Feb 15	Feb 16	5	Develop metrics and internal benchmarks: first party	Anil, Sheri
Feb 16	Feb 16	5	Develop metrics and internal benchmarks: third party	Anil, Sheri
Feb 16	Feb 16	5	Develop metrics and internal benchmarks: sales	Rick, Brad

Figure 2.7. Work plan (continued).

Start date, weekday	End date, weekday	Work hours	Task	Person(s) assigned
Feb 17	Feb 17	2	Discuss and present metrics and benchmarks	BW, SM, Team
Feb 18	Feb 19	18	Complete project documentation	Team
Feb 18	Feb 19	5	Final presentation and project turnover	Team, BW, SM, PA, JH, KL, AP, AC, CO, BY, SP, CY, JO, AC, Others?

Figure 2.7. Work plan (continued).

Approved By:

SCI Corporation:

_____   _____

Bob Wentworth, COO   Date

Project Team:

_____   _____

David Barth, Project Manager   Date

Change Request Form	
Requested date:	
Requested by:	
E-mail address:	
Phone:	
Priority:	High ___ Medium ___ Low ___
Change type:	Enhancement _____ Error correction _____
Change description	
Justification for making the change and impact if the change is not made	
Change request resolution	
Client decision:	Approved _____ Denied _____
Decision date:	
Project team decision:	Approved _____ Denied _____
Decision date:	
Reason for decision	

Figure 2.8. Change control document.

CHAPTER 3

Process Mapping I

Introduction

As preparation for process mapping, interviews are conducted with all parties who perform steps in, or are customers or suppliers to, the process being reviewed. In the previous chapters, we discussed the interview process and the information to be obtained during the interviews. Some of that information should include samples of all documents and data, regardless of medium, generated for or by the process. In this chapter, we discuss what to do with all of that documentation, starting with its review and ending with its addition to a documentation archive.

Once all of the documents and interview results are digested thoroughly, the process description and process maps are developed. We define the icons used throughout this book for developing a process map, which is also called a swimlane diagram. Then, with several examples, we discuss how to map a process.

Process Documentation

In chapter 2, we described the call center and provided the results of interviews that included process documentation and customer service representative (CSR) observation notes. In this section, we discuss (a) how to analyze the documents and interview data and (b) methods for storing the document and data samples as part of the process documentation.

Document and Data Analysis

Documents relating to the target process should be obtained from interviewees or observation subjects. The documents should then be analyzed to determine how the information in the documents fits (or does not fit) with what you know already about the situation. Sometimes the documents will not garner any new information, but other times the documents will confirm, disagree with, or otherwise relate to the interview information. If the documents confirm information, then they can be used as part of the triangulation requirement. If the documents disagree or shed light on new areas not covered in the interviews, then they should be used as the basis for formulating new questions to be raised with the person from whom they were obtained at the next interview session.

For instance, in a factory, one might have setup instructions for a specific machine. A process description for running the machine may have omitted discussions about machine setup. Therefore, the next interview would include questions on setup and how it relates to day-to-day operation of the machine.

Once documents are collected and reviewed, they become part of the project documentation.

Storage of Document and Data Artifacts

Documentation is required to provide teams that may follow the current process improvement team with background and understanding so that they may circumvent some of the start-up costs of beginning a related process improvement exercise. Therefore, any documents that add to understanding a "whole" process should be kept. Documents, whether electronic or paper, should be created, as required, and stored in a specific "official" process library. This typically starts out in the process improvement project manager's office for manual libraries but should be in some other designated "library" by the time the project is completed.

Document storage can be formal, with a librarian and formal check-in and check-out procedures, or can be less formal, with entries made in a binder that is known as the "official" documentation. Most companies opt for the less official version, as it is significantly cheaper. The disadvantage of the cheap alternative is that by not controlling access, the "official" version of documents can easily become corrupted. Further, using "small" databases as repositories can be dangerous unless they are both printed and backed up often. Small databases (e.g., Microsoft Access) are unpredictable with any volume of data (i.e., more than 1 million records) and become increasingly unreliable as the volume increases. With these disadvantages for hard copies and databases, digital storage via an intranet website is preferred. A website is easily maintained, can be set up to track who made the last update, and can be backed up as part of an information technology (IT) operations center's normal daily backup.

Project Document Organization

Regardless of the storage technique selected, the process of storing and accounting for documents is essentially the same. A binder, or series of binders, is created for each process. The front and side of the binder should identify the process and, as needed, the binder number. The front page of each binder should be a table of contents with dates of entry for each item. Within the binder, tab separator pages should be labeled for each section's contents. The item should then be stored in that section. Digital files should be on a semipermanent medium, such as a CD, DVD, or memory stick, which can be stored in a binder's tab section(s). For voluminous paper or books, the sheet in the binder's tab area should contain the title, location, date, size (in pages), and summary of contents for the item. One copy of the all documents, whether original or copied, should be set aside as part of project documentation. As process maps and other deliverables are created, and as other documents are collected, a copy of each is collated and stored in the documentation binder(s).

The web analogue to the binder is a directory structure that approximates the binder tabs. The table of contents provides menu entries for the project or process home page with simple JavaScript updating the date of last update for each. Within each menu item, another menu can expand the contents for that item. Information such as file name, hyperlink to the document, date, size, and summary of contents can all be used to identify contents.

An example of an electronic documentation structure is shown in Figure 3.1. This figure hierarchically relates corporate policy to all documentation levels, ending at detailed documents that support and are used in process steps. This type of structuring simplifies information finding. Plus, by allowing universal read-only access to all documents, everyone can be made responsible for knowing the process and no one has an excuse for not knowing.

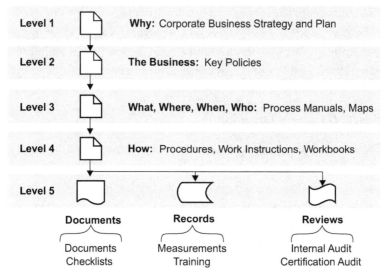

Figure 3.1. Document structure.

Automated Process Maps

Organizations that have process maps should eventually automate them so they are readily accessible to all employees. Each icon or role on the map should be clickable and have hyperlinks to its related details. If you were to click on the role "Sales Manager," for instance, you might go to a job description and list of all sales managers, which would then be clickable to get location and contact information. If you were to click on a summary diagram process box—for instance, 1.4—you would link to the more detailed diagram as a "drill-down" to a more detailed version of the process. If you then were to click on box 1.4.4, you would link to the next level diagram showing even more detail about the topic. At the final level of detail, clicking on any process box should link to related documentation, such as the task documents or application software, databases, tables used, and so on.

Thus by automating a set of process maps (Level 3 in Figure 3.1), eventually all significant information about the roles, processes, decisions, and applications underlying the maps are documented. Process maps, after all, are a summary of real-world items that have significantly more information relating to them than can be conveyed in a diagram.

Once finalized, process maps are then automated, and they can be used for training of new employees, for reference material for existing employees, and for auditors as evidence of process documentation.

Individual Documents

Each document should contain a cover page with title, authors, and date of completion. The next page should be the "change page," containing a list of all changes, in a sequential order from oldest to most recent, and the specific pages that are replaced, with the reason and contents update summary. Next, the original table of contents and their starting pages are presented. As documents change, the changes should be redlined down the left margin to clearly identify them. Occasionally, a new baseline document should be created to refresh the document so it starts anew with no redlined areas.

If using a website, some topic areas may simply contain a page that consists of a list of downloadable documents, with summary information to identify each. The information entry with the hyperlink is similar to the cover page for paper documents, including title, authors, and date. Each document should follow a format similar to that for individual documents in order to facilitate content understanding.

Document Use

Documents provide a history of organizational priority differences, decisions, coordination, and process conduct that sometimes surface details that were unstated during interviews. For example, information about data, allowable contents of data fields, problems with data accuracy or origin, and so on may be found. Similarly, process discussions with any client tend to surface key common factors that cover about 80% of normal functioning and the most common 20% of errors or problems experienced by the person being interviewed. This is not uncommon. In fact, recency, the effect that describes our tendency to remember what we have done most recently, is a well-known phenomenon that must be factored into interviews and document review plans. Document reviews help identify topics that have not yet surfaced but that may be integral to a process.

The type of documents or other artifacts that might be collected include memos, e-mails, help-desk trouble reports, problem analysis reports, program code listings, operations run books, work instructions, project reports, and so on. From memos, e-mails, and trouble and problem reports, one might better understand the types of problems with the current process and its application support. From program code listings, a complete understanding of current data structures, automated data definitions (do not confuse this with understanding the semantic data definition), and allowable data may be gained, if validation is performed.

If the work domain of the target process is completely new to the work team, then the members can circumvent irritation with their ignorance by collecting as many documents, databases, and so on as possible and reviewing them before any interviews.

In summary, all collected documents may be used to add to the team's developing process understanding and to determine what is known and unknown about a process. Copies of all documents should be used to create "official" project documentation. After interviews and document collection, process maps are developed.

Process Map Icons

Before developing a process map, it is necessary to understand the icons and how they are used. Process mapping icons are graphics that represent types of activities or data. Later in this chapter, we use these icons to draw several examples of initial process maps. In the next chapter, we look at several anomalies and conventions for dealing with more complex situations as well as common errors and their corrections.

Swimlane and Swimlane Orientation

In this section, each icon is shown with an explanation of its use in a process map (Figure 3.2). The actual process map, also called a swimlane diagram, has one row (or column, if vertical) for each person, role, application, or organization that interacts with the process in some way. The following are types of interactions:

Figure 3.2. Process map swimlanes. Process maps may be organized horizontally, as the left graphic, or vertically, as the right graphic. Although either method is accepted, most people seem to prefer the horizontal type of map.

- providing or creating information or materials
- changing, manipulating, retrieving, or otherwise using information or materials
- receiving information or materials
- storing information

Regardless of its column orientation, *the diagram should be drawn so it can be read top to bottom and, generally, left to right.* In a horizontal diagram, each "row" is a swimlane and should be named with the person, role, organization, application, or other entity that is involved in the process. In the vertical diagram, the columns are the swimlanes, and each column should be named. Only named swimlanes should be in a diagram; that is, there should be no blank swimlanes. Each named swimlane must participate in at least one process step; that is, there should be no empty swimlanes.

Starting and Ending a Process

Each diagram should have one start icon and at least one stop icon. Starts and stops both use the same icon, as shown in Figure 3.3. Rarely, a process may have more than one start if it truly is initiated from different roles in the process. If you have more than two start icons, then you probably have more than one process.

Icon	Definition and use
Start	The start icon signifies the event or condition that begins a process.
Stop	The stop icon signifies the event or condition that ends a process.

Figure 3.3. Start and stop icon. Both are drawn as rounded rectangles.

A process can have any number of stop points, but most people find that a single stop with many connectors from multiple stop points is easier to comprehend. Connectors are defined and discussed more fully in a later section of this chapter. Events and conditions initiate and end a process. A process consists of all tasks required for an enterprise to respond to a business event or condition.

An *event* is an occurrence or demand that triggers actions in a process. Examples of an event are the arrival of an order, a work request, a problem report for a service or product, a date, or an information request.

A *condition* is a state of some process, product, or work item in an organization that requires action, such as an out-of-stock condition or a need for office supplies.

Flows

Arrows connect all of the icons in a process map. The arrows signify process flow, showing the sequence of steps.[1] There is *one* flow (arrow) *out* of a start icon, with no flow *into* the start icon. Similarly, there is *one* flow *into* a stop icon, with no arrows *out* of the stop icon. Processes (described in the next section) have *one* flow *in* and *one* flow *out* of the process box. *If there are converging or diverging process steps, they converge or diverge into a flow arrow, not the process.* Decision diamonds (described in a later section) have *one* flow *in* and *two* flows *out*—one for each yes or no decision.

Different types of arrows show the sequence of a process, sequence with a delay, telecom transmissions, and document movement. Each of these items is defined in Figure 3.4. Each arrow shows a flow of some type. In all cases, the sequencing of process steps is understood by the use

Icon	Definition and use
⟶	A plain, directed arrow depicts process flow, showing the sequence of steps in a process. It has no relationship to data, documents, applications, and so on unless they are on one end of the flow.
(zigzag arrow)	A zigzag arrow depicts an electronic transmission, such as an e-mail or a fax, or a document transmission. It would be used to show request and delivery of service application components that occur outside the company. It is not necessary for flow sequencing of internal applications because digital data transmission is understood as required.
(fat black arrow)	A "fat," black arrow depicts physical flow. For example, a document delivery through interoffice mail or a document arrival from some external source, such as as the government. The document name can be identified above the arrow.
(fat dotted arrow)	A "fat," dotted arrow depicts temporary delays due to human action or inaction, such as waiting until 3:00 p.m. to process new hires for the day, or waiting for five trucks to be present before starting any weigh-in process. Duration rules of the wait should be written inside the arrow.

Figure 3.4. Flows.

of arrows. There are four types of arrows: simple process flow, electronic transmission flow, physical item flow, and flow with delay or inactivity.

In general, the most descriptive icon for an item or flow should be used in a process map. However, there is leeway in flow description arrows. For instance, if there is a single electronic transmission in a process map, and it is not an object of concern, then a process flow arrow might be used to simplify diagram readability for users. However, if there are concerns over time, accuracy, or something else relating to a particular type of flow, the transmission flow arrow is used regardless of the number of times the type of flow occurs.

Processes

A process box is a square-cornered (or round-cornered in some software) rectangle that is used to depict a step, or set of steps, in a process. Three types of process boxes are described in Figure 3.5.

Regardless of type, all processes must be named. A process must have a verb to identify the action being taken and a noun to identify the object of the action. Occasionally, some type of participial phrase identifies details of the action-object relationship. The strongest process name constructs are verb-noun and verb-noun-object.

Figure 3.6, read left to right, shows how to properly draw a simple diagram with, in this case, three nonatomic processes, all with names of the verb-noun form. There are several things to point out in this diagram. First, notice what is missing—swimlanes. If a single person does all of the work, or if the diagram is simply to summarize a complex process that would have many swimlanes involved in each subprocess, the swimlanes could hamper understanding. Therefore, one rule of diagrams is *"don't be a slave to the process."* Draw a diagram in a way that makes the most

Icon	Definition and use
Atomic Process	An atomic process or process step is one that cannot be subdivided any further and retains its process characteristics (i.e., having input, process, output, and feedback).
Nonatomic Process / **Nonatomic Process**	A nonatomic process summarizes several atomic processes to add to the understandability of a summary diagram. Nonatomic processes are also called subprocesses. An example might occur in an accounting process, which could have subprocesses for receivables, payables, and payroll.
Automated Process	An automated process is one conducted by a computer application.

Figure 3.5. Process types.

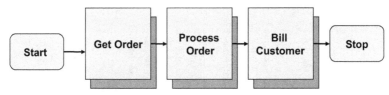

Figure 3.6. Summary process diagram.

sense for its users. High-level summary diagrams are often most readable without showing swimlanes.

The simple diagram in Figure 3.6 shows how to put process boxes, arrows, and start and stop icons together. Most of the process flows you see will also have swimlanes. Notice, too, that the start and stop icons, process boxes, and arrows are all the same size. This consistency lends continuity to the diagram and enhances its readability. In addition, short arrows are desirable in order to enhance readability and to minimize the number of pages used.

In general, "do" and other nonspecific process verbs are not used as process names because they do not convey enough information. Rather, the verb should describe a specific action. "Give," "send," and other words that imply movement of some data or form are always accompanied on the receiving end by a parallel verb such as "get" or "receive."

Sample good and bad names for processes are provided in Figure 3.7. When defining process names, the most direct name is usually the strongest.

Handoffs

There is a special type of process relationship when process steps move between swimlanes. These are called *handoffs*. Handoffs come in pairs with a "send" process from the source and a "receive" process at the destination. Therefore, if an e-mail is sent to someone, then the sender process might be "generate e-mail" and the receiver process might be "receive e-mail." Notice there is no indication of what is in the e-mail or of the actions taken by the receiver. These would be different process steps. Another example is a hand-off between a person and computer application. The sender process might be "enter help request," and the application receiver process might be "get

Good process name	Poor process name	Explanation
Get new hires listing	Give list of new hires to department manager	"Department manager" should be a swimlane that will "get new hires listing," so does not need to be identified as the recipient
Display acknowledgement	Display "ack"	Ack is an abbreviation that might not be universally understood. If used, abbreviations should be in a dictionary.
Create marketing query	Create marketing query of all people in zip 75222	The poor process name is too detailed and implies that only people in zip 75222 will ever be someone the sender queried. Qualifications, such as 75222, may indicate a need for a condition (see next section) and are removed once the condition is reflected in the diagram.
Assign staff	First available staff	There are two problems with "first available staff": no verb and insufficient information since it is not clear how "first available" is defined. It is better to be deliberately ambiguous and explain the details in the process description or a subprocess diagram.
Schedule visit	Schedule visit with client	This should probably be shown as a multiswimlane process with "schedule visit" shown in both the enactor's swimlane and the client swimlane. Swimlane name is omitted from process names.
Receive customer request	Client receives request from the customer	Poor process name is wordy and need not contain the swimlane name "client." The best names are verb-noun or verb-noun-object constructions.

Figure 3.7. Samples of good and poor process names.

help request." Any interaction between humans and computer applications requires two handoffs—one to initiate the computer steps and one to show the computer's response. All handoffs should be explicitly shown because they are frequently the source of errors or they may identify extraneous data movements in a process. An example of a handoff is depicted in Figure 3.8 for the requirement "Mary sent John an e-mail asking him to help her move and he agreed."

Human-computer interaction that results in digital data storage of some type requires a handoff with processing by the computer. Figure 3.9 shows a salesperson entering data into an application, which accepts the information, processes it in some way, stores the information, and displays the saved information to the salesperson. Processing then continues. The handoffs in this scenario are the "enter-get" and "display-get" process pairs.

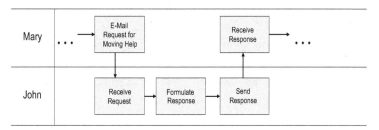

Figure 3.8. Handoff example.

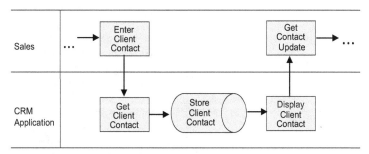

Figure 3.9. Data storage with handoff.

Decisions and Conditions

Processes never flow in a single direction, especially before they are improved. There are decisions, flows from one swimlane to another, and other shifts that can take place. The condition icon shown in Figure 3.10 is used to depict a decision point and the alternate flows of a process depending on whether the condition is met or not.

Frequently, decisions are more complex than a simple yes or no choice; instead, they have many possible choices for actions. In that case, each choice is placed in its own decision diamond with the yes and no actions for only that one choice. Figures 3.11 and 3.12 show alternative ways to handle multiple possible choices. In Figure 3.11, there is a definite yes and no action for each of three choices. In Figure 3.12, there are only two choices, and if choices A and B do not exist, then choice C is the default. Both of these constructions are legal. Please note that the three dots, or ellipses, signify that this is part of a larger diagram and that only the part of interest is being displayed.

The syntax of a condition is object-verb (or verb-object, or verb, or object, e.g., "Pass?"), with the verb indicating the condition being tested and the object indicating the item on which the test is applied. Examples of decisions might be "design accepted?" or "processing correct?" For checks to determine correct processing, examples are "transaction on time?" or "service complete?" As you can see from these examples, the

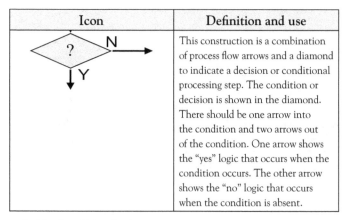

Icon	Definition and use
? N ↓Y	This construction is a combination of process flow arrows and a diamond to indicate a decision or conditional processing step. The condition or decision is shown in the diamond. There should be one arrow into the condition and two arrows out of the condition. One arrow shows the "yes" logic that occurs when the condition occurs. The other arrow shows the "no" logic that occurs when the condition is absent.

Figure 3.10. Condition logic.

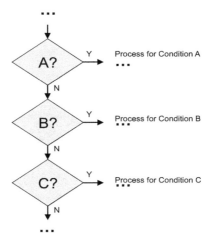

Figure 3.11. Three conditions; error if no condition is met.

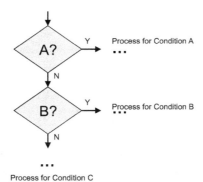

Figure 3.12. Three conditions; last condition occurs if the other two are not met.

decision should be described succinctly, with yes and no alternatives and without any details of the alternatives. If there is complex reasoning logic that is not apparent from the diagram, then document it separately in the process description.

Good and bad examples of condition names are presented in Figure 3.13. In general, the decision is being taken by the swimlane role where

Good condition	Poor condition	Explanation
Staff available?	Check staff availability	Condition or decision should be in the form of a question.
Alternate staff OK?	Client OKs alternate staff?	The good condition is less wordy and the condition would be in a "client" swimlane, thus indicating that the client is making the judgment. The swimlane name should not be repeated in every question or process.
Questions?	Are there any questions to be answered?	The good condition is less wordy.
"Inspection passed" or "pass inspection"?	Truck inspected?	The poor condition has a yes or no answer but you would also need to ask the "Pass" question. It is better to ask one clear question than two. If inspection includes three items, then there should be three questions. Unless there is some doubt about what is inspected, the truck need not be mentioned.
Specific staff available?	Check specific staff	The poor condition is not a decision or, if it is, it should be in the form of a question.

Figure 3.13. Samples of good and poor condition descriptions.

the icon is located. Good condition names should be direct, not wordy, and indicate the question being answered.

Storage

Process maps contain swimlanes for digitally stored information as well as manually stored information, and all information can be permanent or temporary. The icons for types of storage are illustrated in Figure 3.14.

For complete analysis of an application area, the name of a data store or queue should be as specific as possible. E-mail provides a good example of how to use different types of storage icons. E-mail would be identified as being in a temporary queue until read. Then it might stay in the queue or be moved to a data store. Alternatively, e-mail might be printed and placed in a physical store, in which case it would be depicted in an upside-down triangle.

Another example might occur in a situation in which three databases and applications are used in performing a single task. Applications should

Icon	Definition and use
Data Store **Data Store**	A data-store icon symbolizes *digital files or databases*. Both icons are legal, but the horizontal one can be stretched sideways to make room for a long name without making a swimlane wider and without making the vertical sizes of icons larger.
Physical Store	The upside-down triangle depicts *physical storage*, such as a filing cabinet, off-site file, or permanent storage in someone's desk.
Queue or Temporary Storage	The "bullet" is used for temporary *data queues* or for *temporary digital storage*, and temporary storage of *unknown type*. The data or item in the queue or temporary store should be identified in the name along with the range of time spent in the queue.

Figure 3.14. Different types of storage.

each have an individual swimlane, and the databases should have their own identities in the form of database icons. The analysis may show that there is significant movement between applications or databases in conducting a single transaction and, therefore, that they should be combined or integrated in some way. Without individual swimlanes for each application and database, this problem would not be identified. This type of problem frequently occurs in older applications that were developed at different times for different reasons and, over time, have evolved into use for a single process.

Frequently, for instance, for interoffice mail, there may be a handoff without an accompanying required receipt. Figure 3.15 illustrates such an occurrence. Ordinarily, interoffice mail may show up on a process diagram as a "human delay" dotted arrow. In the case of document losses, every role, person, organization, or application that touches a document, including "interoffice mail" would be depicted in order to allow the source of any errors to be found. In one process analysis engagement, lost interoffice mail was part of the problem: telecommunications bills amounting to millions of dollars were lost. The solution for this problem was the creation of a tracking system for telecom bills that started with their receipt, ended upon their payment, and included their paths through the interoffice mail system.

Figure 3.15 shows two types of delays. Delays in both interoffice mail departments are shown in dotted arrows in order to depict human delay. The second delay—in this case, the U.S. mail—cannot be fully controlled by the company but can be tracked for its contribution to delays in bill processing. If the U.S. mail was a source of delay, either a different method of handoff or a different class of service might be warranted.

In another example (see Figure 3.16), placing a physical item (e.g., paper) in a temporary queue is shown by a downward-facing triangle.

Documents

Paper documents are used in most processes and are identified with an icon symbolizing torn paper (see Figure 3.17).

For manual storage, such as a physical, personal file (i.e., on paper), the process relationship is the only exception to the one-arrow-in and one-arrow-out rule for processes. For documents, arrows can bidirectional,

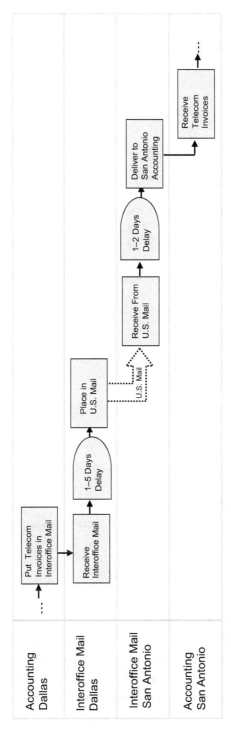

Figure 3.15. Delay with handoff example.

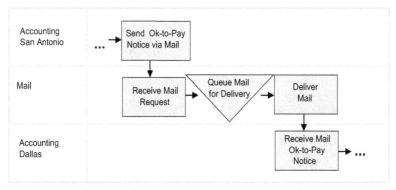

Figure 3.16. Queue delay.

Icon	Definition and use
Document	The document icon is used to identify paper documents, such as memos or computer-generated reports that are used or generated in a process.

Figure 3.17. Paper documents.

signifying retrieval and updating; however, since a physical file cannot, by itself, perform actions, no related handoff is shown (see Figure 3.18). The physical form then has a bidirectional arrow showing that process flow control does not leave the originator of the action. If paper is generated and moved to another process step, an out-arrow to its next process step is also legal.

Delays

In a previous section, the use of bullet icons to depict temporary data storage delays was discussed. For completeness, this is depicted again in Figure 3.19. The fat arrow depicting "human delay" is also shown in Figure 3.19, since it can be used to represent a "real world" delay of unknown type.

Human delays, such as those related to an in-box or a wait for a time or condition, do not necessarily qualify as problems. They are, however,

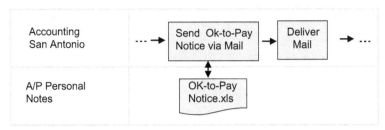

Figure 3.18. Manual data store.

Icon	Definition and use
Data Queue or Temporary Storage	The bullet icon shows a temporary delay due to electronic queuing (as for an e-mail) or temporary storage, such as an in-box.
Human Delay	A "fat," dotted arrow depicts temporary delays due to human action or inaction, such as waiting until 3:00 p.m. to process new hires for that day or waiting for 5 trucks to begin safety inspections.

Figure 3.19. Physical delays.

extremely important in determining actual cycle time for a process, and if omitted, then the process cycle time will be incorrectly computed.

Connections

The final icon is for connectors (see Figure 3.20), which are used to add to diagram readability. Connectors are used in several situations:

- to link multipage diagrams
- to link to a single "stop" icon from multiple locations
- to add readability to a diagram that would otherwise have many crossed lines or confusing links across many swimlanes
- to simplify a multipage diagram

Icon	Definition and use
# #	A circle depicts a connection to or from some other location within a single diagram.

Figure 3.20. Connectors.

Connector numbers should be consecutive. If it is unclear how many connectors will be required, it is conventional to use "9" or "99" for multiple connectors to a "stop" icon. Directions to map reviewers can identify "99" as a cue that the connectors go to an "end process."

The same number is used to show a connection linkage in both the "to" connector circle and the "from" connector circle. If the connection is entering a process that already has an incoming arrow from another process, the connector process arrow enters the other incoming process arrow (see Figure 3.21).

Creating a Process Map

Recall that a *process* consists of all tasks required for the enterprise to respond to a condition or event. The *scope* of a process ranges from the condition or event that initiates it to the satisfaction of the condition or event.

Creating a swimlane map, then, is the documenting of process steps that encompass all activities performed in the conduct of a single business

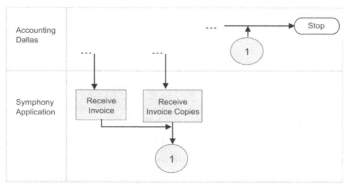

Figure 3.21. Connector example.

process and to a level of detail that allows analysis of the process for its improvement. The level of detail *does* differ from one analysis to another. For instance, if a call center that collects money as a service is the focus of analysis, then the details of the actual collection process and all interactions with the call management, script, and collections software applications are needed to the extent that they (a) are required for completeness and accuracy, (b) vary between personnel, (c) are the subject of study, or (d) have some other purpose in the documentation, such as training new hires in the business process.

For beginners, a good approach is to develop an outline of steps used in conducting the process and then evaluate the list to consider what steps might be similar and candidates for consolidation. Consolidation often occurs with computerized steps. For instance, you may have a step for opening Microsoft (MS) Word (see Figure 3.22a). Then, other steps might identify the documents worked on. By including the opening of the MS Word program as well as the documents worked on in the same level of the outline, it appears that they are independent when in fact they are not. That is, starting a computer process (application) such as MS Word for each occurrence of its use is inefficient and unlikely.

Usually, a computer process is started, all subprocesses are conducted, and then the process is closed (Figure 3.22b). For instance, MS Word might be opened, multiple documents worked on and saved, and then the application is closed. This set of events, along with added detail for the "Daily Report" is shown in Figure 3.22b. This list shows more detail but also has an implied loop: for every document to be worked on, there is a set of steps that include open-update-save process steps. On a process map, this sequence requires analysis of the documents being worked on. If the documents are always the same, then the sequence in the middle column of Figure 3.22 would be transcribed to the diagram as it is. If the documents can vary, then use of document names is incorrect, and a loop is required to perform a condition check to determine if there are more documents to be updated. If this case, Figure 3.22c would be a correct rendition of the consolidated steps for a generic process.

Once the list appears complete and correct, sticky notes on a whiteboard or flip chart can be used to develop an initial map so that steps can be easily moved to increase readability. To use this technique, write each process (or other icon, if not a plain arrow) on a sticky note, then place the sticky notes in the desired configuration. Review the configuration for accuracy, then move the notes into swimlanes. If you do this on a whiteboard, then you can draw the lanes, identify them, and place the sticky notes in the appropriate lane. Start each diagram with "start" and "stop" icons so they are not forgotten. Then, fill in the steps to the process. If you developed a process description or list of steps, then use them to guide the process-mapping exercise. If not, then use your notes, memory, or other devices to develop the map.

Now, try to draw the process map outlined in Figure 3.22c. It should look like Figure 3.23—not something like it or close to it, but *exactly* like Figure 3.23. When you have a clear understanding of the process and have the steps properly detailed, anyone who draws a process map will develop the same process map. For maps with more than two pages of detail or over 80 or so icons, there will be variation, but the basic process should be the same. This makes process mapping a repeatable process and shows that, when everyone in an organization uses it, your organization has reached a high level of maturity.

Once a process map is created, it should be completely reviewed by the process team for completeness, accuracy, and correct level of detail, and to make sure everyone shares the same understanding of the process. Upon agreement, a draft digital process map is created using MS Excel, MS Visio, or any number of other software programs. The draft map is then ready for review (verification) and approval (validation) by the interviewees and the client, respectively.

Other Methods of Process Mapping

This book teaches a generic method of process mapping, using icons that are generally accepted for the task. However, there are many methods of process mapping,[2] and each has its own custom icons for some tasks. In this section, we discuss two other methods of process mapping. The purposes of this discussion are, first, to illustrate several methods and, second, to recognize that there are other methods of process mapping, so that everyone is aware that when starting a new job or switching jobs, a new method may need to be learned. The two methods discussed are Information Definition for Function Modeling (IDEF), which is used by

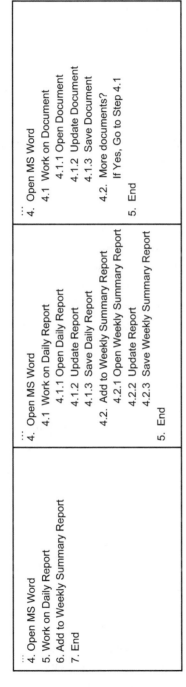

4. Open MS Word	... 4. Open MS Word	... 4. Open MS Word
5. Work on Daily Report	4.1 Work on Daily Report	4.1 Work on Document
6. Add to Weekly Summary Report	4.1.1 Open Daily Report	4.1.1 Open Document
7. End	4.1.2 Update Report	4.1.2 Update Document
	4.1.3 Save Daily Report	4.1.3 Save Document
	4.2. Add to Weekly Summary Report	4.2. More documents?
	4.2.1 Open Weekly Summary Report	If Yes, Go to Step 4.1
	4.2.2 Update Report	5. End
	4.2.3 Save Weekly Summary Report	
	5. End	

Figure 3.22. Example of initial steps: (a) initial process steps, (b) consolidated process steps, and (c) generic process steps.

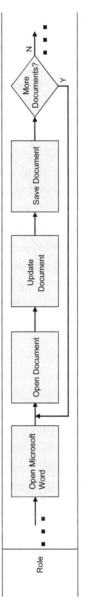

Figure 3.23. Process map of generic process steps.

the U.S. government, and Business Process Execution Language (BPEL), which is an automated language for performing process mapping.

Information Definition for Function Modeling (IDEF)

IDEF is a U.S. government method for diagramming processes that has widespread use in the defense industry. IDEF numbers diagrams according to a hierarchic level of detail, starting at level 0 to define the functional model, IDEF 1 to define an information model, and IDEF 2 through n to develop a dynamic model. The models each start at level 0 and progress sequentially through level n, where n is the highest, most detailed level.

IDEF diagrams are not process maps per se. Instead, they are meant to show both the scope of the process and all inputs, outputs, internal organizations, and external organizations related to the process. External organizations, recall, are usually not of importance to a process improvement project unless they are under the control of the client organization. However, it is still important to identify them, especially when they are contractors performing some service, as the external organization may be integral to the process.

IDEF diagrams use boxes (to identify a function) and arrows (to depict data or objects related to a function). In general, at the highest level, a function, has a series of in or out arrows depicting inputs, outputs, controls, calls (as in a procedure call), or mechanisms involved (for embedded software functions).

A level 0 diagram is shown in Figure 3.24 for the call center case's first-party collection process. This diagram is relatively simple to understand and provides a context for an entire area. Over the course of analysis, formulating the requirements definition, and diagram development, the function box is progressively decomposed into its constituent parts (see Figure 3.25). Since much of the work of the U.S. Department of Defense (DOD) includes embedded software, such as missile guidance systems that are only a part of a missile's functioning, the diagrams involve some necessary complexity. However, even simple diagrams can be complex to understand because of complex semantics in the meaning of every item on a diagram as well as multiple meanings to arrows.

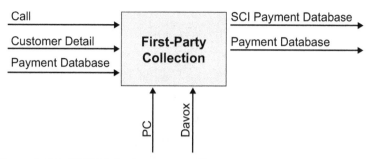

Figure 3.24. IDEF 0 for first party collections.

IDEF embeds such complexity because it uses multiple purposes for some icons.[3] IDEF diagrams are "talking" points for requirements, are the basis for communication between requirements analysts at DOD and implementing-development engineers at a defense contractor, and are used as the basis for implementation of automated process workflows.

Business Process Execution Language (BPEL)

Automation of process management requires an underlying specification language that can be translated into digital concepts. The drive for automated process management has led to the development of several computer "languages." The Business Process Execution Language (BPEL, pronounced "bee-pell") was developed in 2003 by IBM, BEA Systems, Microsoft, SAP, and Siebel Systems in an attempt to develop an automated process language. They then applied to the *Organization for the Advancement of Structured Information Standards* (OASIS), a global consortium that drives the development, convergence, and adoption of e-business and web service standards for standardization of the standard, which eventually became WS-BPEL 2.0.[4] (WS stands for "web services.") The major goals of BPEL are the following:

1. Define business processes such that they can interact in a computer environment via a service architecture called *Web Service Definition Language* (WSDL). This means that messages between processes are in the form of messages that use WSDL.

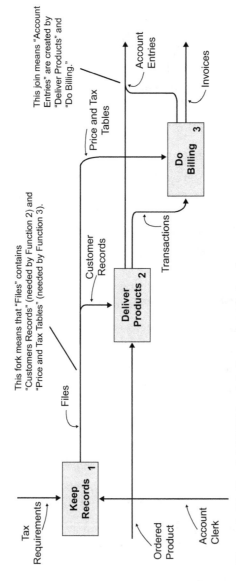

Figure 3.25. Partial IDEF level 1 diagram with details.

Source: U.S. Department of Defense (1993), p. 24.

2. Define business processes using a generic language, in this case the *Extensible Markup Language* (XML), absent of any particular design method for business processes. This means that the processes are defined as abstract templates for which an *instance* identifies the data details of a particular process.

3. Provide data manipulation capabilities to allow process and data flows. This capability is also implemented via WSDL.

There are many other goals for BPEL, but they relate to technical aspects of supporting transaction processing through a business process using an object orientation.

BPEL, then, is a language that supports service-oriented, automated transaction management. As such, there is no standard notation or modeling method; however, Business Process Modeling Notation (BPMN) from the Business Process Management Institute (BPMI) is often used. The simple process map specified in IDEF in Figure 3.25 is rendered as a BPMN business process diagram (BPD) here.

BPDs use different notations and slightly different icons from the method in this book and from IDEF (see Figure 3.26).[5] There are no swimlanes in this sample, but a complete BPD would have swimlanes, called *pools* or *lanes*. A pool is a swimlane as discussed in this book. A lane is a subpartition within a pool, that is, a swimlane with multiple sublanes. The processes are in rounded rectangles and can be either subprocesses or tasks. Decisions are still in a diamond, though the decision, called a gateway in BPD terminology, may be specified outside of the diamond. The decision legs ("yes" and "no") need to be specified. Arrows can be straight or curved. When multiple arrows enter a process, they need not be joined first.

There are three types of events in BPEL notation—start, intermediate, and end—each with a trigger and a result. There are also three types of arrows: sequence, message, and association. Sequence arrows are similar to the use of arrows in our notation; this BPD only uses sequence arrows. Message arrows identify a communication between two process participants. Association arrows identify text or data that relate to the diagram in some way. The open-ended rectangles are *annotations*, which allow the modeler to provide notes to future diagram users.

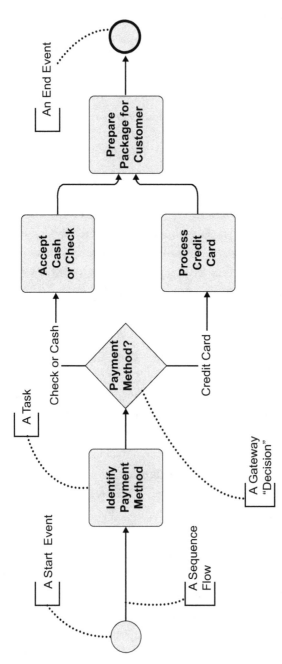

Figure 3.26. BPEL-BPD example.

While not fully mature, the appeal of executable processes is cheaper, more customizable, interoperable processes that provide interorganizational flexibility. BPEL and its descendent methods have led to the development of automated workflow software that is discussed in a later chapter.

Summary

Process documentation consists of the set of documents, applications, reports, faxes, e-mails, and so on that are used in the conduct of a process under review. Icons used in process mapping include start and stop; atomic, nonatomic, and automated processes; arrows showing process flows, transmissions, and physical flows; digital data stores and databases; temporary data stores; temporary physical storage; delays; and connectors. In drawing a process map, a good practice is to start with some method, such as using a whiteboard and sticky notes, that allows movement of swimlanes and icons for reading ease. After team review, a process map is drafted and is ready for review with the client for accuracy and completeness. Two alternative methods for process mapping are IDEF, used by the U.S. government, and BPEL, used in industry for automated transaction processing.

CHAPTER 4

Process Mapping II

Introduction

This chapter continues the discussion of process map variations and different methods of depicting aspects of processes. In addition, many maps are so complex that they are difficult to understand unless they are summarized in logical "chunks." This chapter explains the reasoning for creating summary maps. Once the variations have been discussed, we move to validating and verifying a process map.

Novices make errors in process maps that slow their learning of the techniques. Therefore, several common errors are discussed along with correct mapping techniques.

Process Map Variations

Process maps may contain many variations, including the following:

- multiple inputs or outputs to a single process
- multiple conditions
- use of connectors
- multiple swimlanes participating in a process step
- handoffs
- loosely coupled processes
- multiple methods of accomplishing a process step
- manual data processing
- time-driven processes

Each of these variations is discussed in this section. Please keep in mind that all examples in this section show partial process maps and hence may have no "start" or "stop" icons or swimlanes.

Multiple Inputs or Outputs to a Process

Frequently, a process will be preceded by more than one parallel activity. For instance, an approval on a document may have parallel client reviews that converge to a joint "approve project" process. Figure 4.1 shows the form of such a figure.

Similarly, a map may have multiple following-process steps, as in Figure 4.2. An example of such an outcome might be "approve project," which spawns both a printing activity and an activity to put the project documents on an intranet.

Multiple Conditions

Another situation that frequently arises is one in which there are multiple outcomes from a single decision. This discussion recaps an example from chapter 3. The constructions are determined by the selection of a default.

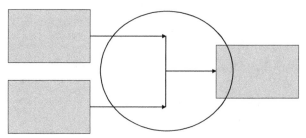

Figure 4.1. Simultaneous predecessor processes.

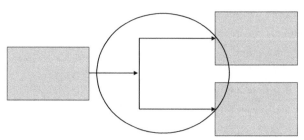

Figure 4.2. Simultaneous outcomes.

A *default* is a process step that is executed when none of the options explicitly checked is chosen.

Multiple decision constructions have two alternative forms depending on whether or not there is default processing. The construction shown in Figure 4.3 has a default error process if none of the four alternatives specifically tested is selected.

Figure 4.4 shows the fourth subprocess as the default. In this construction, there is no error processing, and, if options one, two, or three are not selected, then the fourth is automatically selected.

Another example might be months of the year. There would be 11 decision diamonds, with the 12th month as default if there is no error processing. Conversely, if there was error processing or some "other" process where none of the options is selected, then there would be 12 decision diamonds with the "other" option as the default.

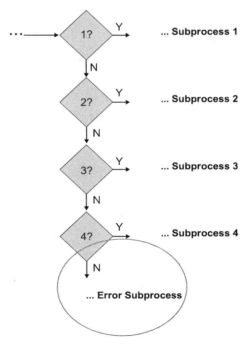

Figure 4.3. One subprocess with four alternative actions, each with a "no" process.

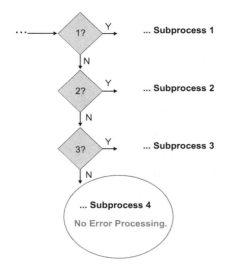

Figure 4.4. One subprocess—four alternative actions.

Use of Connectors

Recall that connectors are small circles that are used to improve the readability of a diagram. Figure 4.5 repeats the definition of a connector.

Connectors are the source of many diagram errors because they are frequently misused. As Figures 4.6 and 4.7 demonstrate, a connector is created as an output of a process and reused to show input to the next sequential process step. Figure 4.6 shows connector "1" as created to change the flow of the process.

Figure 4.7 shows connector "1" as indicating that the process flow continues at the process step to which it points. Each number set is used once except, as discussed, in the case of using single connectors from multiple locations that stop a process.

Connectors are used in a number of situations to improve diagram readability. Connectors can be used to indicate a single process stop point, manage flow of process details, or manage complex diagrams so lines do not cross. In general, connector numbers should be sequentially assigned. In the case of having a single "stop" icon, many process steps may have a connector that goes to a single stop. All of the process steps going to a single stop should have the same number.

Figure 4.5. A connector, shaped like a small circle, is used to show a change of process flow and to connect to the point where the flow continues.

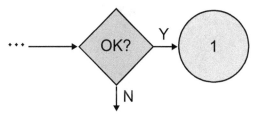

Figure 4.6. Connector change of process flow.

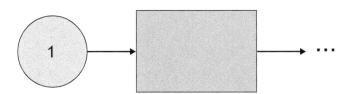

Figure 4.7. Connector connects where flow continues.

Another reason for using connectors is to simplify complex diagrams. Connector use increases readability, especially in situations where a set of decisions has many possible outcomes. Figure 4.8 shows such a situation. The important item here is the set of decisions and their criteria. The lesser important items are the connected-to logic, showing what happens in each situation.

Figure 4.9 shows a diagram for which connectors could be used to avoid overlapping lines and complex logic. When lines cross, go backward rather than forward, or span many swimlanes, readers tend to get lost, and diagrams become unreadable. By using connectors to untangle

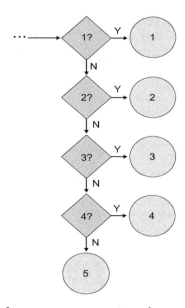

Figure 4.8. Multiple connectors—a variety of reasons.

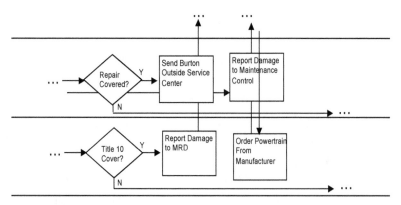

Figure 4.9. Connectors could enhance readability.

the lines, and by keeping the arrows short and of consistent length, readability is enhanced.

Finally, Figure 4.10 shows a simple example of connectors used to identify multiple stop points in a process. Imagine a more complex diagram with 10 possible stop points. Using ten connectors all number "99" to connect to a single stop point clarifies the diagram.

Another convention is to use a number that would otherwise not occur to signal a "stop" connector, such as 99. As more process maps are created, use of a single "stop number" provides a visual cue that facilitates user understanding of the maps.

Multiple Swimlanes in a Process

For meetings, interviews, group decisions, or other types of multiperson activities, multiple swimlanes may participate in a single process. Figure 4.11 shows a larger box enclosing multiple swimlanes that participate in a single process.

When the swimlanes are adjacent, the process box is drawn once, with one set of words in the box, centered to identify that both parties take place in the process. If more than two swimlanes participate in the process, and the swimlanes are adjacent, one process box would span all required lanes.

Process-step actions taken may differ by participant, in which case multiple process boxes can be placed within the multilane box to show the details. Actions requiring multiple swimlane participation include

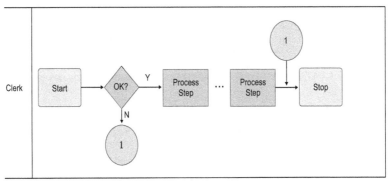

Figure 4.10. Connectors manage stop points.

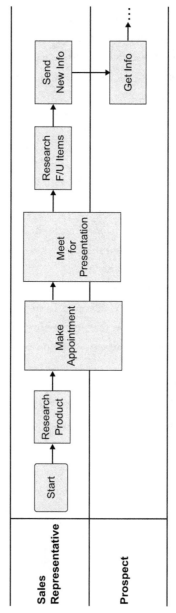

Figure 4.11. Adjacent swimlanes—preferred arrangement.

phone conversations and meetings. Both of these may have participants discussing a situation, with one of the participants making a decision. In such a situation, multiple process boxes would be in the multilane process box.

An example is the "present product" and "examine product" process step in Figure 4.12, where the sales representative is making a sales call. Both swimlanes participate in the process, so a large, shaded box is drawn, but each swimlane has a different step, each in its own process box.

Since swimlane diagrams should be read from top to bottom and from left to right, swimlanes may participate in a single process step but may not be adjacent. Figure 4.12 also depicts this situation by the drawing of one large box—which can be a different shadow color or have a dotted line when no colors are used—to show that multiple swimlanes are involved in the process step. Then, for the participating swimlanes, a process box is drawn, with the same words in each of the process boxes, or different words if the actions taken during the joint activity differ.

Handoffs

Using a diagram similar to a previous one, appointments might be stored in some type of software. The processing for software handoffs is shown in Figure 4.13.

Each side of a handoff has a process step for each handoff that matches the real-life interaction. A sales representative, for instance, enters contact information into an application and presses "enter." The application takes the screen information, processes it, and confirms the process by displaying some type of acknowledgement. The sales rep views the display that confirms the outcome of the data entry.

Handoffs occur between people, between people and applications, or between people and roles (i.e., a person with a nonspecific title, such as "customer"). Handoffs are a frequent source of error both in process maps and in the actual process because they tend to be taken for granted, which allows the information transferred to be lost. As a result, when mapping a process for which the sources of errors are unknown, it is important to include all handoff details in order to ensure complete analysis.

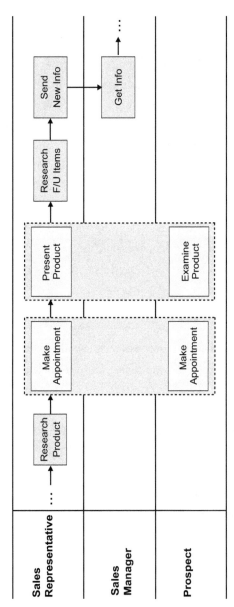

Figure 4.12. Nonadjacent swimlanes.

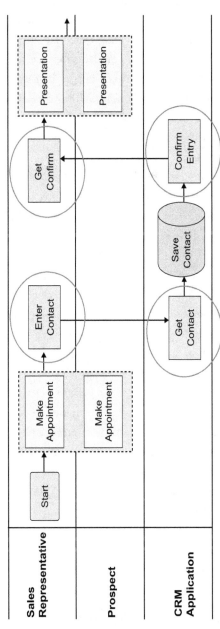

Figure 4.13. Application handoffs.

Loosely Coupled Processes

A *loosely coupled process* is one that contains discontinuous processes with long or planned delays, no direct interaction, and no necessary impact on one part of the discontinuity when changes are made to the other part of the discontinuity. Therefore, loosely coupled subprocesses, when embedded in complex processes, can be broken out as their own processes. An example of this situation frequently occurs in business when a request is entered on a website or intranet site and, at some specified time, someone checks for requests and handles them. Examples are customer-order entry and help-desk requests.

Loosely coupled processes could be handled as a single process, with a dotted arrow showing the discontinuous wait time, or as two processes. If the process is simple, then there may be nothing served by separating it into two processes. If the process is complex, however, then separating the subprocesses can enhance understandability. Examples of split subprocesses are shown in Figures 4.14 and 4.15. Figure 4.14 shows an employee entering a request via an intranet, receiving a confirmation of request completion, and ending the activity. Figure 4.15 depicts a human resources (HR) employee getting requests, verifying request completeness, and either rejecting or accepting the request and then updating the request status and continuing with other processing. This is a complex process that does not involve direct interaction between HR and the employee; therefore, there is no real need for the employee subprocess to be shown with the HR subprocess. The intranet links the employee to HR. Since interaction is through an intranet, the subprocesses can be split, and each subprocess becomes its own process.

The risk of splitting a large process into two subprocess diagrams is that a delay between the two parts (in this case, request entry and request processing by HR) could be overlooked. Therefore, when decoupling subprocesses, care must be taken so that the linkage delay is not forgotten during process analysis.

Multiple Methods of Accomplishing the Same Work

Another variation occurs when a swimlane is defined as an organization or a department, such as HR, where different people execute the

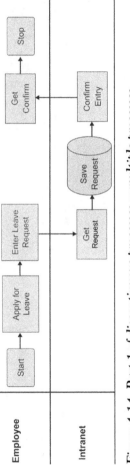

Figure 4.14. Part 1 of discontinuous processes = multiple processes.

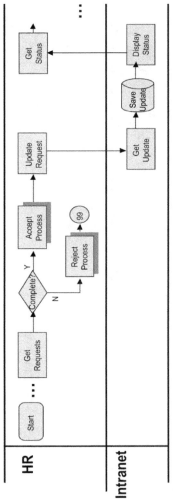

Figure 4.15. Part 2 of discontinuous processes = multiple processes.

process differently. There are four ways of depicting this situation, and the reasoning behind which one is appropriate depends on the context. The four methods include the following:

- separate swimlanes
- condition within a swimlane to show differences
- subswimlanes
- different processes

Separate Swimlanes

These techniques show several ways to depict the same work. The first method, separate swimlanes, has two variations that both identify the organization in some way but draw wholly separate swimlanes. This variation is shown in Figure 4.16. This method would be selected if there were many points of divergence or the processing of one or both of the sublanes is complex.

Condition Within a Swimlane

Trivial divergences can use a condition within a swimlane via a condition diamond, as shown in Figure 4.17. The conditional treatment shows one of the possible people (clerk) performing the subprocess. The disadvantage of this method is that the reader is left guessing who the other person is. The manager could be mentioned rather than using "no" as a leg of the process, but that naming convention is not the best.

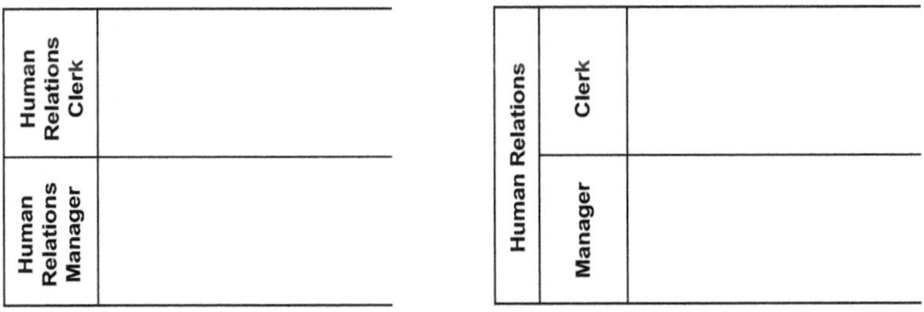

Figure 4.16. Multiple subprocesses shown as swimlane alternatives.

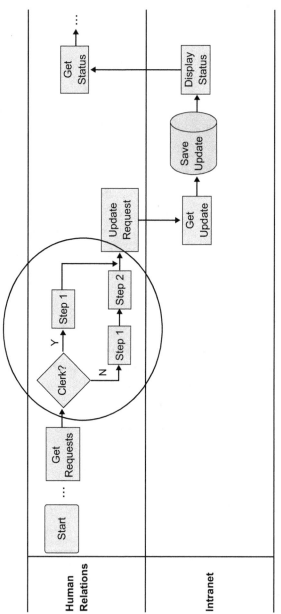

Figure 4.17. Multiple subprocesses shown as alternative.

A variation that would remove this disadvantage would be to include a condition to check for "whom"—one leg would identify "clerk," while the other leg would identify "manager" rather than showing "yes" or "no" alternatives. The advantages of this method are brevity and improved clarity of action.

Subswimlanes

The preferred method for minor divergences is to embed subswimlanes at the point at which they diverge. Figure 4.18 shows the condition leading to either a manager or clerk sublane.

Different Processes

A mapping exercise to make processes consistent might find a merged or acquired organization with its own process. Trivial differences should be mapped using one of the previously mentioned techniques. If there are significant differences, each organization's process should be mapped completely and separately, and then each process should be compared to the acquiring (or desired) organization's process to identify and reconcile the differences.

Manual Data in Processes

Manual data offer another complication to be dealt with in diagrams. One method is to use a bidirectional arrow between the paper document and the person using it. The other method is to show the flow of the process continuing from the document to the next process. A bidirectional arrow is preferred, since a paper document cannot, by itself, further a process.

A document's movement or content might alter what a person or application does, but the interactions with the document take place before the subprocess step.

When a document's content can alter or move a process forward, it is acceptable to use an arrow from the document to show its significance (see Figure 4.19). However, this subtlety is missed by most readers, and therefore, the bidirectional arrow is more commonly used. Companies develop their own local standards for process mapping, and this is one of the areas needing a decision on how it will be handled.

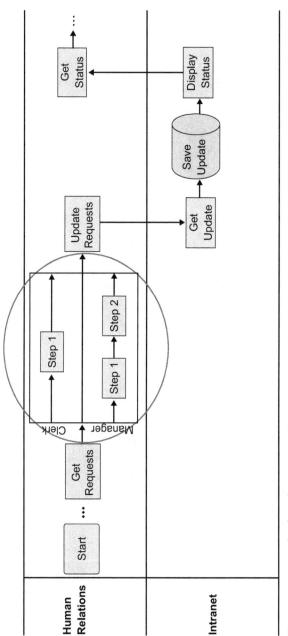

Figure 4.18. Multiple subprocesses shown as subswimlanes.

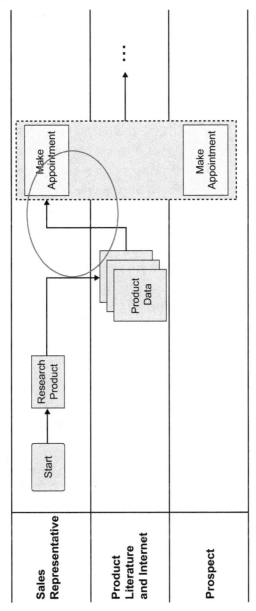

Figure 4.19. Document content directs process flow.

An alternative to this process depiction is to show the entire Internet interaction from which product data are retrieved. Depending on the goal of the mapping exercise, showing the interactions may be crucial to defining improvements and would therefore be the desired mapping approach.

Time-Driven Processes

Another variation in process maps is the depiction of time-, geography-, or event-driven process steps. Figure 4.20 shows a time-driven process example for a church service during which visitor cards may be available on the seats. If a card is present, and the swimlane is for a new attendee, then the person must decide whether or not to put the card in an offering basket. The time-driven aspects of the process are the start and end of the service. There might also be process steps for collection of money or other aspects of the service. Another example might be a time-driven process that has no specific end date, such as university graduation, obtaining a patent, consolidating organizations, and so on. In these examples, the end date is time zero or t_0. All other dates are some number of days, such as 10, which would be t_{10} from the event date. The times then act as a count down to the t_0 event date.

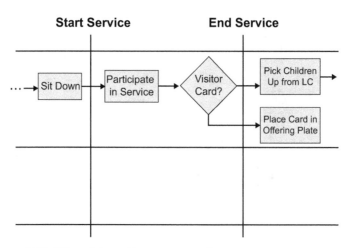

Figure 4.20. Time-driven diagram example.

Summary Process Maps

Frequently, process maps will be complex, span multiple pages, and require their own "map." When a team is developing process maps, it becomes clear that summaries are needed. Usually, a junior or part-time team member will say something like, "I wish I had a map to the maps!" or "I've lost my train of thought on this process." Comments such as these are clues that summaries are needed. Summary maps are created as an aid to understanding. In this section, we develop a process for creating summary maps and discuss how best to automate them.

Creating a Summary Map

There are two basic methods for developing map sets: bottom-up and top-down. Neither is preferred, but each person will probably have a preference—relating to how he or she tends to think—since most people are more comfortable with one or the other method. It is important that whichever method is chosen, the maps are numbered so that connectors are consistent within the set and so that when a number is used, its meaning is consistent within the set of maps. Bottom-up mapping is discussed first.

Bottom-Up Process Analysis

A bottom-up process for creating summary maps is as follows:

1. Create the process map(s).
2. Identify subprocesses on the original map.
3. Convert the subprocesses to summary icons.
4. As needed, repeat steps 1–3 until you have a one-page overview map.
5. Create "drill-down" maps for each subprocess.

The advantage of bottom-up development is that complexities and details that might alter a complete view of the process are known early on. The disadvantages of bottom-up development are that the details may obscure the recognition of the subprocesses and the analysis may result in an incomplete or skewed view of the overall process. Summary maps help overcome the risks possible with bottom-up process map development.

Top-Down Process Analysis

Conversely, some people think of the major process steps first and then follow to get the details. This is a frequent strategy in the initial interview in defining the scope of a process. In this case, the process of creating diagrams is top-down, and the steps are as follows:

1. Identify the major subprocesses.
2. Create and validate a summary process map.
3. For each subprocess on the summary map, do the following:
   a. Research, interview, or observe to obtain the process details.
   b. Create a process map for each subprocess.

The advantage of top-down process analysis is that all major steps are identified first so that completeness is verified and details can be deferred until the major steps are known. Two disadvantages of top-down process analysis are that the complexities affecting the time to complete analysis may not be known until late in the data-gathering activity and that details altering the outcome of the analysis may be skipped altogether.

Analyze your own thinking processes as you progress through the book to determine which type of thinking you are most comfortable with, and then follow that method on any projects you develop. Some may find that a combination of top-down and bottom-up will work best. Obtain as many details as possible to develop a summary diagram, and then switch to bottom-up thinking to develop the individual detailed maps.

Compiling a Diagram Set

Complex processes may have multiple levels of diagrams developed to allow discussions with executives (least detailed), people managing the work (more detailed), and people who actually do the work and systems developers (most detailed). Regardless of the number of levels in a diagram set, all stakeholders should review a set of the maps, each one with an appropriate level of detail. A final set of process maps should include the summary map and all related detail or "drill-down" maps (see Figure 4.21).

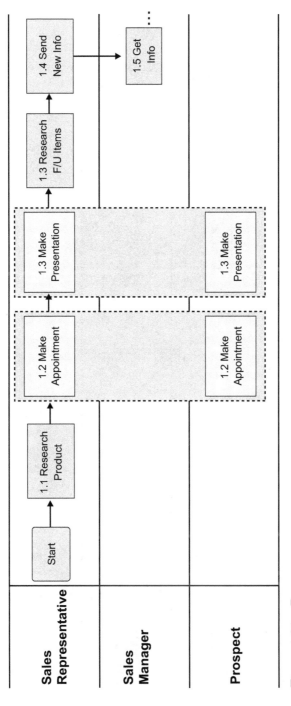

Figure 4.21a. Process map sets.

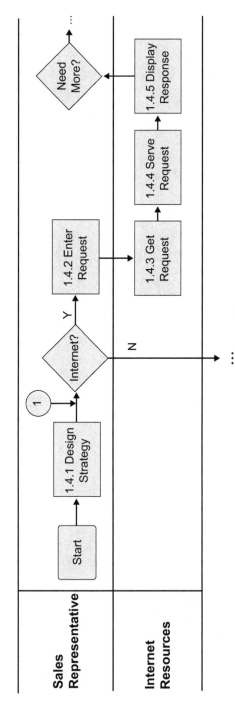

Figure 4.21b. Process map sets.

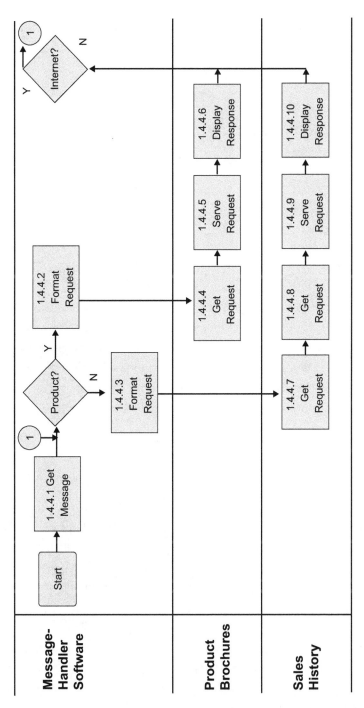

Figure 4.21c. Process map sets.

Each level of map should be numbered starting at either zero or one for the highest level and moving down through the hierarchy in a logical system, such as what follows:

1. Level 1—Summary map
   1.1. Level 1, Process box 1
      1.1.1. Level 1, Process 1 detail diagram process box 1
      1.1.2. Level 1, Process 1 detail diagram process box 2
   1.2. Level 1, Process box 2
      1.2.1. Level 1, Process 2 detail diagram process box 1
      1.2.2. Level 1, Process 2 detail diagram process box 2
   1.3. Level 1, Process box 3

Verifying and Validating Process Maps

Verification is the act of confirming accuracy or truth of some item. *Validation* is the act gaining confirmation or official sanction.[1] In terms of process improvement projects, verification is done with individual stakeholders, usually those who were interviewed to provide the information that formed the basis for the process diagrams. Validation is done via a *walk-through*, which is a structured meeting to review the verified process maps and officially sanction them.

Process Map Verification

The purpose of process map verification is to ensure that the interviewees and people who perform tasks in a process agree about the details and substance of the process. Apply the principal of triangulation to the review of processes (i.e., three people should verify every process step, conclusions about summary processes, and the placement of process steps in swimlanes).

Interviewees should have an opportunity to review the process maps developed as an outcome of their consultation. Within 2 days of an interview, the interviewee should be given a copy of the interview notes and any diagrams developed from the discussion. Not all discussions lead directly to process maps, but when enough information has been collected to develop process maps, the reviews should be completed by each interviewee as soon as possible.

In addition, several—usually 3 to 7—people who actually perform the work should review process maps to ensure that correct and complete information was given. This can be via e-mail and remote review as with interviewees or in person in a single group meeting or in individual meetings. Each of these modes of review is useful, but they are likely to result in different results unless everyone involved is highly motivated to participate in the project. Without having had interviews, e-mail and remote review are unlikely to result in more than superficial comments and are less likely to result in problem finding. Similarly, individual one-on-one reviews are likely to result in the deepest level of comments, but only one person's verification is acquired. Group meetings can result in the best outcome but may not be warranted as they may also take more time for users than individual meetings. For all types of sessions, project background, goals, and discussion of results to date (that are not confidential) should be a prelude to any feedback requests. These sessions serve to find errors and correct them before the validation meeting. The other alternative is to both verify and validate at the same time.

Process Map Validation Using Walk-Throughs

After process maps are complete and verified, a walk-through should be held to validate the maps. The steps involved in a walk-through are as follows:

1. Premeeting
   a. Gather the process maps and any process descriptions developed to explain the diagrams.
   b. Develop an agenda for the meeting.
   c. Invite all participants, sending them the agenda, process map(s), and other material to be reviewed.
2. Walk-through meeting
   a. A senior analyst conducts the walk-through by reviewing each diagram in detail.
   b. A project team member acts as scribe, noting any errors found. No attempt is made to fix errors.

c. A third person acts as timekeeper to ensure that the meeting meets its goals and stops at a designated time, usually about 1 hour.

d. Other participants include the process experts, managers interviewed, workers used to verify the process maps, or other stakeholders in process accuracy (e.g., internal auditors).

e. Meeting participants find errors of logic, syntax, or semantics in the diagram(s) being reviewed.

f. At the end of the meeting, the group decides if another group meeting is needed (i.e., the errors are severe or numerous) or if the corrections can be reviewed via e-mail.

3. Postmeeting

a. The scribe types notes and circulates them to all participants.

b. The project team members work through the errors found, addressing and rectifying each.

c. As errors are corrected, a notation is made on the error list as to where the correction is placed within the diagram set.

d. When all errors have been addressed, the outcomes are documented and circulated with corrected process maps to all participants to ensure correct and complete updating.

The walk-through can serve two purposes: one, to verify the process maps in a group setting, and two, to validate the maps, thus defining the "official" version of the processes.

Common Errors and Corrections

This section presents correct techniques to help avoid common novice errors. The most common errors include the following:

- incorrect role identification
- incorrect arrow placement
- incomplete handoffs
- incorrect handoffs to applications or databases
- dangling processes, connectors, or decision outcomes
- misnumbered connectors
- sloppy diagram style

Incorrect Role Identification

Misnamed or incorrectly named roles are a common problem. When a role is wrong, all icons in the swimlane are also likely to be wrong. Therefore, good practice is to ensure that roles are properly named before beginning the process map. Roles can be individual names, a job role, an organization, or an application—some entity that can perform independent actions. A database does not follow that definition but is a special case of a role when application support for a process is being analyzed.

Disk drives that contain shared documents are not swimlanes because a disk drive cannot, without direction from an application, perform independent actions. The shared repository could be a role, but care would be needed to ensure that the commands for actions were clearly differentiated as human or application process steps.

Another error concerning the definition of roles is use of an individual's name (e.g., "Sharon"). Sharon may be the person who currently holds responsibility for some tasks, but she would be representative of a title or role in that regard. The role name is preferred over a person's name. The same reasoning holds if Sharon is a supervisor who has added duties beyond those normally performed. The title "supervisor" would be used to distinguish the role.

Incorrect Arrow Placement

There are two ways that arrows are used incorrectly—the first is to have them crossing each other; the second is to violate the rules for numbers of arrows in and out of each icon type.

The "before" side of Figure 4.22 depicts crossing arrows and, because of the arrows crossing, the author was unaware that the process was dangling (i.e., it did not have any out arrow). The "after" side of Figure 4.22 shows the fixed diagram with no crossing arrows and the dangling process now connecting to the "stop" icon.

The second type of arrow problem violates the rules of arrows in or out for the icon type. Several wrong examples are shown in Figure 4.23. In the "before" side of the map, the two arrows out of the "save schedule" process and the two arrows out of the next process violate the rule of one arrow out of a process box. To fix the problem, diverging arrows emanate

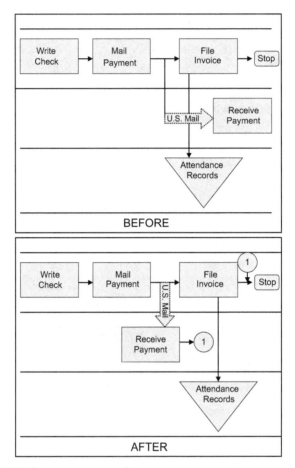

Figure 4.22. Incorrect arrow placement.

from one of the "out" arrows. The "after" side of the figure shows how to fix these problems. There is another unrelated problem with this diagram. Can you find it? The answer is at the end of the chapter.[2]

Incomplete Handoffs

Handoffs seem to cause significant problems for novice process mappers. If the sending side of a handoff shows the preparation of an item, then the receiving side must show receipt of the item. Handoffs are important because they are frequently the source of problems such as lost material

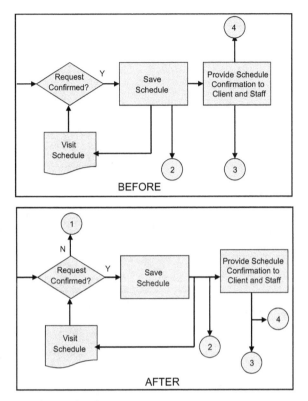

Figure 4.23. Example of wrong arrow use.

or documents, delivery delays, or technology bugs. Handoffs, especially those across organizational boundaries, represent the "white space" on an organization chart (or process map) and are error sources because no one has responsibility for monitoring them.

One handoff problem is deciding whether or not the handoff is a joint activity, requiring the outer multilane process box. Think of the top swimlane in Figure 4.24 as referring to a "client" and the bottom swimlane referring to a "vendor." The "before" diagram shows a handoff of payroll checks as being a joint activity. This would be correct if the delivery is in person and both sides of the handoff in fact participate in the delivery and receipt. If not (e.g., if the checks were delivered electronically or via mail), then the "after" diagram would be correct. Thus for this example, both before and after diagrams *could* be correct, depending on the context.

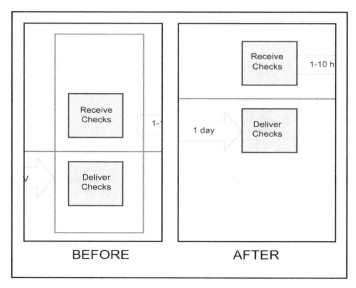

Figure 4.24. Example of handoff issue.

A different type of problem is shown in Figure 4.25. In the "before" map, the author assumed that passing inspection was acceptable as the start of a handoff. This is wrong. When inspection is passed, the inspector gives approval to the person receiving it, as shown in the "after" side of the figure. The left side is wrong because giving specific approval implies that some verbal approval, e-mail, piece of paper, or other evidence of approval is provided. The left side does not provide for the passing of anything to the receiver. Therefore, nothing can be received. To correct this situation, the passing of inspection occurs, and then the "give inspection approval" task occurs in order to start the handoff. The receiving side of the handoff is correct in both diagrams.

Incorrect Handoffs to Applications or Databases

Handoffs to applications and databases are a bit trickier because not only one send-receive interaction takes place but also a second send-receive is required to display results and the next steps of a process. In the middle of the two handoffs, the processing takes place. The processing, if simple,

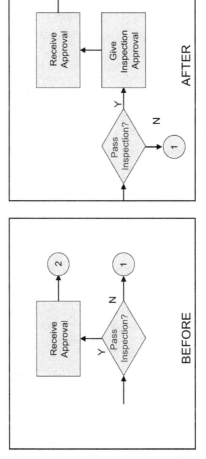

Figure 4.25. Example of incomplete handoff.

can be depicted within a database icon. If more complex or application work is completed before the database is involved (e.g., computations on data are performed), then more process steps are shown. Figure 4.26 shows both application and database handoff errors.

The first error in Figure 4.26 relates to "retrieves entry ticket." The actual handoff, "get-retrieve," is acceptable, although the wording could be improved by changing the warehouse manager's entry to "request entry ticket" and the database system entry to "retrieve (or get) ET request." This revised wording more clearly identifies a handoff. The problem is that the "retrieves" process output should be the step in which the data are obtained, followed by a process step to display the response, which is then followed by a process step to get the response, leading to the creation of a new pickup note entry.

The second error, "saves new pickup notes entry," occurs at the database end of the process. This entry should be a receipt of the pickup note request, followed by the process of creating a new entry with a database icon, followed by a display of the new pickup note status. An improvement from "database" as a swimlane name would be to identify the application as the "pickup note application." The corrected diagram is shown in Figure 4.27

While this diagram is quite a bit more complicated, it is also much clearer. Every process box in the "entry ticket" and "pickup note" application swimlanes requires some programming to accomplish those tasks. If the handoff processing is omitted or abbreviated on the process map, then it is likely that programming errors would occur. In addition, omitting these handoffs on the current process map would result in incomplete analysis and potentially missed opportunities for improvement.

Dangling Processes, Connectors, or Decision Outcomes

Often, it is easy to forget to complete temporarily incomplete areas of a diagram as the main logic is being developed. Figure 4.28 shows two common errors. This summary diagram has a connector that is unused in the rest of the diagram, and the "daily process" is unconnected to anything else. Another common error not in this example would be to omit "yes" and "no" outcomes for a decision. After drawing a diagram, as part of its team review, one person should be tasked with ensuring that all connections and lines are correct and that the diagram is syntactically

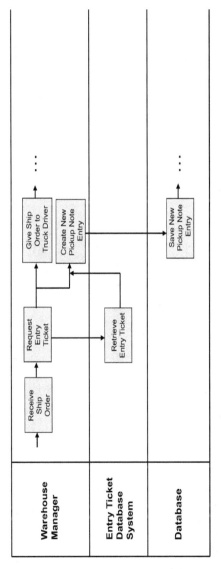

Figure 4.26. Incorrect application and DB handoffs.

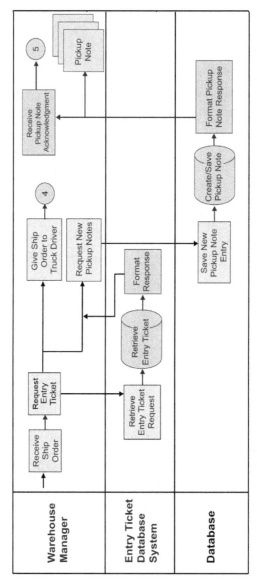

Figure 4.27. Corrected application and DB handoffs.

accurate. If the syntax (i.e., the icons and line connections) are not correct, then by definition, the drawing is wrong.

Figure 4.29 shows a corrected diagram for these errors. Of course, it seems obvious on a summary diagram such as this what the errors are, but on diagrams that can run 30 pages or more, the errors become insidious and difficult to track.

Misnumbered Connectors

Connectors come in pairs. If there is a "1" connector out of a process, there must then be a "1" connector into some other decision or process. Figures 4.28 and 4.29 show common connector errors. In Figure 4.28, the "1" connector is unmatched. This is the most common error—dangling connectors. This type of error often occurs when deferring some logic while developing the main logic path of the map. It is easily fixed during a group review when someone is given responsibility for monitoring that all connectors come in pairs.

The second common error is the use of sequential numbers—for example, assuming that the "1" connector out of a process is paired with a sequentially numbered "2" connector into a process or decision. This mistake in logic is usually made by novices who have not drawn many diagrams. It is easily corrected by remembering that every number used *out* of a process must be paired with the same number *into* a process or decision.

Sloppy Diagram Style

Novices tend to believe that any syntactically correct diagram is an acceptable one. However, diagrams that use different-sized icons, different length arrows, sloppy telecom arrows, unexplained lines, and incorrect icons are difficult to read. In addition, diagrams that do not separate swimlanes so that they are easily readable and those that use different-sized swimlanes not only look unkempt but also are also difficult to read.

In Figure 4.30, the top ("before") map has all of the errors mentioned previously and takes three pages to print legibly. The bottom ("after") map has the errors fixed and takes only two pages to print.

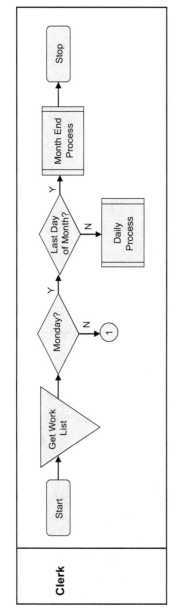

Figure 4.28. Dangling icons.

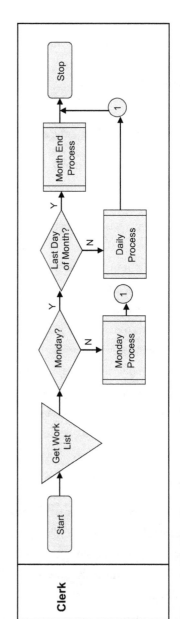

Figure 4.29. Dangling icons corrected.

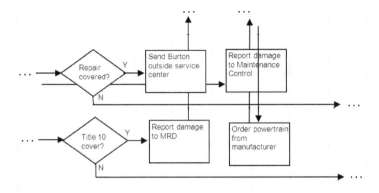

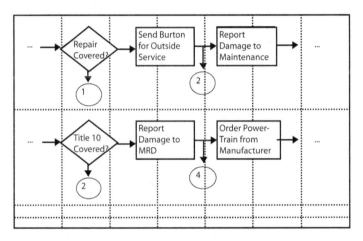

Figure 4.30. Before (top) and after (bottom) of fixes for sloppy mapping style.

Summary

Multiple inputs, outputs, or methods for conducting a process should all be clearly shown on the process map. In the case of multiple methods for conducting a process, either a decision diamond is shown to lead to the two paths, or, if the process differences relate to individuals—for example, a clerk and a manager—the swimlane is divided into sublanes to indicate the different flows.

A small, circular connector is used to show a change of process flow and to connect to the point where the flow continues. Connectors increase diagram clarity in situations where there are many possible paths through a process, minimize stop points for a process, or, in complex diagrams, minimize crossing lines.

Time, measurement points, goals, or other significant items can be shown by vertical lines through a map, when relevant.

Verifying and validating a process diagram are both important. First, diagrams should be reviewed with each interviewee and the people who do the work to confirm interview results. Inconsistencies or disagreements should be corrected or the alternatives shown on the diagram. Similarly, suspected errors should be highlighted on the diagram. Group walk-throughs complete the validation of diagrams. A walk-through is a formal group meeting with the goal of finding errors. A team member (not the author) reviews material with stakeholders, and project team members fill scribe and timekeeper roles. The stakeholders are the primary finders of errors.

In many ways, process mapping is more of an "art" than a "science." However, once the details of a process are known, maps by different people should be essentially the same, differing only in the level of detail shown on a diagram. When drawing maps, do not become a victim of the rules; for instance, do not expect to know all of the details. Use process map variations such as those in this chapter to explain processes more clearly. Process maps should make the process easier to understand rather than more difficult. Novice errors to avoid include incorrect role identification, arrow placement, handoffs, dangling icons, and sloppy style.

PART II

The Middle Game

The middle game in chess relies on the skill of the player to know the sequences of moves and combinations of approaches most likely to be effective. Similarly, a process improvement project team is required to have many skills and techniques available from which they choose those more likely to arrive at a successful project conclusion in the shortest amount of time. The middle game is "where the magic happens"—where expertise and know-how determine the quality of assessment, redesign, and project outcome. This part of the book begins the discussion of methods for analysis and change. In chapter 5, brainstorming techniques that are useful in many situations are discussed, along with techniques used to identify processes for change. In chapter 6, we discuss techniques to aid in removing non-value-adding process steps and other techniques for "leaning" the process. Chapter 7 is a review of analysis techniques for "cleaning" the remaining process steps to ensure that they also are lean and contain no unneeded actions. Chapter 8 addresses "greening" of the process to improve its environmental friendliness for your organization and to remove as much of the process from human hands as feasible. At the end of this part, the process and its problems will have been evaluated from many different perspectives, each of which adds value to the final recommendations.

Keep in mind that at the end of this part of the project, the outcome is not yet clear and that there may be conflicting or irreconcilable recommendations that come from the various analyses conducted. These issues are resolved in part III of the book.

CHAPTER 5

Problem Finding

Introduction

Many techniques are used in developing a view of an organization and its problems. The techniques presented in this chapter are a representative mix of idea generation, graphics, and diagramming and analysis techniques that can all be used on a single project in developing the organization view. These techniques are almost never used in isolation but are mixed and matched as the situation warrants. The techniques also have wider applicability than just problem finding, and they can be used during any phase of process analysis and improvement. The techniques can be combined in the development of a *baseline benchmark*, which is a self-assessment against which improvement efforts will be compared to determine their success.

Creative Problem-Solving Techniques

This section discusses group problem-solving techniques that differ in their conduct, setting, and outcomes. They all focus on groups because groups develop better decisions than individuals. In addition, through these exercises, a process improvement team can develop a congruent, shared understanding of the organization's issues. Thus group problem solving can lead to shared understanding of a problem or situation.

Brainstorming

Brainstorming is a group technique used to generate the largest number of ideas possible within a limited period. The group should comprise subject-matter experts (SMEs) who are instructed that the goal is idea generation and that there should be no comments on others' ideas until no one can think of new ideas. The process for conducting a brainstorming session includes the following steps:

1. Review the steps for brainstorming.
2. Clarify the objective of the session.
3. Take turns providing ideas.
4. Record each idea on a flip chart exactly as presented.
5. Pass to another member when an idea does not come to mind quickly.
6. Clarify the list as a team by discussing the ideas to assure all members have the same understanding of each idea after all ideas have been presented. Eliminate duplicate ideas in this step.
7. Rate each idea for practicality, importance, and accuracy.
8. Identify ideas that need investigation to rate.
9. Decide on ideas that require follow-up action:
   a. Further investigation
   b. Analysis and correction
   c. Tabling for lowest priority items

Ideas should be listed on a whiteboard or flip chart. Once ideas are exhausted, they are reviewed to consolidate similar ones or to revise or eliminate ideas that are not feasible. For instance, a suggestion might be to survey all customers. However, if there are millions of customers, then this suggestion is not practical. During discussion, the idea may be refined to survey a stratified sample of customers.

If some ideas need more investigation, then they are assigned dates by which additional information will be provided. Ideas should be rated in some way (e.g., by their potential for impact and their cost, as in hoping for high-impact, low-cost ideas). The most highly rated items are selected for action. The lower rated items could be tabled for future consideration.

Nominal Group Technique

Nominal group technique (NGT) is a technique to bring a small team that is in conflict to consensus. The conflict might be over some issue, problem, or priorities. NGT starts like brainstorming, except with written ideas relating to the target issue. The purposes of NGT are to organize more productive meetings—especially for problem identification, problem solving, and program planning—and to balance and increase participation and reduce errors in group decisions. NGT, like other idea-generation techniques, can be used for typical brainstorming sessions as well.

The process for conducting an NGT session is the following:

1. Silent generation of ideas in writing
2. Recorded round-robin listing of ideas on chart
3. Discussion and clarification of each idea on chart
4. Preliminary vote on priorities
5. Discussion of preliminary vote
6. Final vote on priorities

Written ideas provide time to focus on the issue in uninterrupted thought. In establishing the session, the moderator seeks to provide a creative setting that encourages each member to think of ideas. The written ideas avoid competition between participants, status differences, conformity pressure, evaluation, elimination of ideas because of criticism, and polarizing on ideas.

After idea generation, ideas are written on a flip chart, one at a time, going around the group until no additional ideas are identified. This process is one of equal time sharing and full group participation. Members are encouraged to build on each other's ideas, thus moving idea ownership from an individual to the group.

Once recorded, a consolidation and elimination process similar to brainstorming proceeds to reduce the set of ideas. The purpose is to clarify ideas and ensure further shared understanding of the proposed action. Further analysis, such as categorizing by cost and impact, as discussed in the brainstorming section, can be conducted as well.

Two rounds of written voting are conducted. First, an anonymous vote determines idea priorities. This avoids premature decisions and dominance by strong members of the group. The group discusses the preliminary vote to determine any ideas that might be eliminated due to lack of support.

The final vote decides the priorities, which are announced to the group. The final vote brings closure to the process, motivates future involvement with this activity, and provides a written record of the ideas generated and selected.

Brain Writing

Brain writing is similar to both brainstorming and NGT. It is essentially written brainstorming. Brain writing is used to generate ideas for solving several problems (rather than one) in a single meeting.

To initiate a brain-writing session, define the topic(s) needing a resolution, ideas, alternative courses of action, and so on, and write each on its own piece of paper. Participants sit in a circular arrangement. The papers are passed around the circle so that each person has only one piece of paper, that is, one issue to work on, at a time. Each participant adds his or her ideas, information, or comments on the idea before him or her. The papers then circulate around the circle until no more ideas are being generated. Participants discuss each idea, and the best among them are selected for follow-up by the person who posed the problem.

Brain Mapping

Brain mapping, also called mind mapping, is a method of arranging ideas for visual discrimination. Thus this technique can be used with all of the previously discussed techniques. The purpose of the technique is to group ideas in a way that is visually stimulating and clearly shows connections and interconnections. The main idea is placed in the center of a piece of paper (or computer screen). Then, items that relate to the main idea are drawn extending out from the main idea, separating unrelated ideas by a fair amount of space to allow for later addition of other ideas. Then ideas are reviewed and rearranged, creating branches, arrows, or groupings of some sort to show connections or relationships between ideas. Idea groupings can be color-coded for clarity.

Kartoo.com, which discontinued operation in January 2010, was a mind-mapping search engine that retrieves results and creates a mind map of them based on the number of words they have in common. Figure 5.1 shows the Kartoo.com map for "mind mapping." The size and shape of the dark area is symbolic of the number of related sites. When the dark areas are connected, the areas are related by connections to the

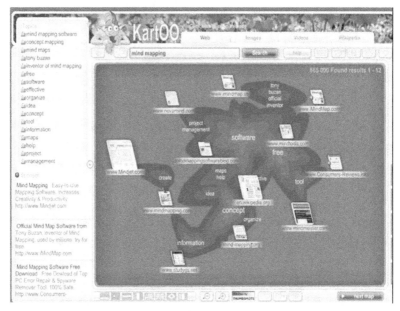

Figure 5.1. Kartoo.com on "mind mapping."

same sites. The different gradient colors of the Kartoo.com background indicate the relative number of related references.

The advantage of brain mapping is that the visual cues aid in gaining quick understanding of complexes of relationships. The disadvantage is that the mapping, unless generated automatically, such as on Kartoo.com, relies on the knowledge of the mappers and is subject to bias and error.

Delphi

Delphi is a technique through which SMEs determine relative importance of ideas, trends, issues, and so on through a written, multiround voting process. The purpose is to develop consensus without meetings. An example might be to identify five technology trends that will profoundly impact business in the next 5 years. There is no clear answer to this problem—only participants' informed opinions. Therefore, having SMEs who are qualified on the subject matter is often critical to the success of this technique.

The basic Delphi process is the following:

1. Develop the Delphi question (i.e., the initial broad concerns or topic).
2. Select and contact respondents.
3. Develop questionnaire #1 and send out.
4. Analyze questionnaire #1.
5. Develop questionnaire #2 and send out.
6. Analyze questionnaire #2.
7. Prepare final report.
8. Mail final report to clientele and respondents.

Using the previous example, a list of technologies expected to have an impact in the next 5 years might be developed. The stopping point is determined by some arbitrary criterion, for instance, the top 10 items or all items with 10 or more votes. The list might circulate among the experts to ensure formation of a list with the broadest scope. After the list is complete, it is sent to the experts for their voting. Votes are returned, electronically if possible, and tabulated or summarized. For the next round of voting, the list would be sorted top-down by number of votes, with number of votes shown. Again, voting is conducted, and votes are returned and tabulated. Once the final point is reached, a final report is developed and circulated to all participants as well as to the person or department requesting the exercise.

Advantages of Delphi are that no meetings are required, individuals and their votes are anonymous to the group, no single person dominates, and the aggregate judgment of experts should be superior to that of any individual. The disadvantage of Delphi is that it can take 30 to 60 days to identify and solicit experts, conduct the voting rounds, summarize the results, and conduct further voting rounds. Therefore, Delphi is not good for crisis management or even problems that need a decision in a short time unless the SMEs are internal to the company.

Graphics for Problem Finding

Graphics are pictorial summaries of numeric data that can greatly enhance understandability, especially when the data are voluminous. In this section, several uses of graphical forms are discussed. When developing graphics, be mindful to use consistent measures and axes, choose the right graphic for the information, and never intentionally alter the real meaning of the raw numeric data on which the graphic is based.

Graphics can be used to hide, misrepresent, or obscure data, thus reducing the effectiveness of any resulting decisions. For all graphics, the three "deadly sins" are ambiguity, distortion, and distraction.[1] *Ambiguous graphics* having multiple interpretations might take several forms. Incomplete labels are ambiguous—for instance, the number "22"—without telling what the measure is. Another form of ambiguity relates to visually misleading information, such as the small arrow in Figure 5.2, which implies that developmental assistance (ODA) has dropped dramatically when, in fact, it dropped 18 points, an insignificant drop relative to the other change depicted. There are two ambiguities in this diagram: the relative sizes of the arrows are not to scale and the starting level of ODA is unknown.

Distortion arises from inconsistent labels, inconsistent axis measures, choice of grouping factors in bar charts, untrue proportional size of graphics to depict differences between items, or use of three-dimensional pie charts, especially those that emphasize one slice. Avoid absolute numbers unless they tell a whole story. For instance, if you quote deaths of cattle from coyotes and compare Michigan and Montana, absolute numbers

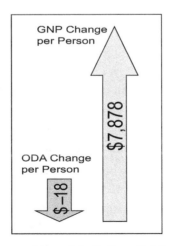

Figure 5.2. Growing wealth and declining official development assistance.

will show Montana a far more lethal place. However, as a percentage of all cattle deaths, Montana is twice as safe as Michigan. This is a distortion of facts by omitting critical explanatory information that provides a context for understanding the information.

Distraction comes from busy diagrams. Efficient graphical design minimizes the ratio of ink to data. Distraction may be inherent in super-imposed three-dimensional diagrams that measure different things, or in any three-dimensional diagram that does not clearly identify what and how it is presenting its data. One of the best multidimensional diagrams is Minard's diagram[2] of Napoleon's march to, and retreat from, Moscow; it is a rare exception to these statements.

Pie charts are omitted from this discussion because they are most amenable to all graphical problems and should be avoided unless they depict only one item and characteristics relative to it.

Next, we discuss several types of graphics: scatterplots, histograms, Pareto diagrams, line plots, and spider diagrams. In all cases, the tenets of good graphic design include the following:

- Use only needed lines; avoid grid lines if possible.
- Use color, line weight, and shading to organize the information.
- Clearly identify each axis and measure.
- Identify either the number for each item or percentage contri-
  bution to the whole, as appropriate.

Scatterplots

A *scatter diagram*, or *scatterplot*, is a nonmathematical, graphical approach to identifying relationships between two items. For example, a scatter diagram might be used to identify a correlation between a quality measure and number of man-hours of work per week. The scatter diagram approach is quick, easy to communicate to others, and generally easy to interpret.

For each observation, two pieces of information are required: The measure of the item having influence (X) and the measure of the item being influenced (Y). By convention, the observed variable, or depen-dent variable (Y), is plotted on the vertical axis, while the suspected cause, or independent variable (X), is plotted on the horizontal axis. In mathematical terms, Y is a function of X [Y = f(X)]. The point of intersection between the two axes is the average of each of the sets of data (i.e., the average of all the X values and the average of all the Y values). The collected data are not only for observing the performance characteristic under investigation but also for observing other factors or causes that might have an impact on the performance characteristic. For example, if we measure the surface finish of a machined part, measurements of other factors such as feed rate, tool condition, machinist work hours, and so on might also be taken and evaluated for their potential effect on the surface quality characteristic. In other words, do not look at two measures in isolation and expect them to tell a whole story. Competing and complementing relationships should also be evaluated.

Figure 5.3 shows three main types of relationships that scatterplots can surface. Figure 5.3a demonstrates a positive relationship such that an increase in the value of the X measure is accompanied by an increase in the value of the Y measure. Figure 5.3b shows no relationship, so that knowing the value of the X measure tells you nothing about the value of the Y measure. Figure 5.3c depicts a negative relationship in that an increase in the value of the X measure is accompanied by a decrease in the value of the Y measure.

The steps in creating a scatterplot are as follows:

1. Select the items you want to study. The results of a cause-and-effect diagram might be helpful in determining which items to select.
2. Collect the data—the more data, the more accurate the diagram. A minimum of 30 X-Y data point pairs should be collected.
3. Draw the axes of the scatter diagram. Label the performance characteristic on the Y-axis and the correlated factor on the X-axis.
4. Select the point of axis intersection as either (0, 0) or the average of each set of data (X,Y). Clearly identify the origin of the axes.
5. Plot each set of paired measures onto the graph, that is plot (X_o, Y_o), (X_1, Y_1), (X_2, Y_2), ... (X_n, Y_n), where n is the number of measured pairs.
6. Evaluate the presence or absence of a relationship between the X and Y items.

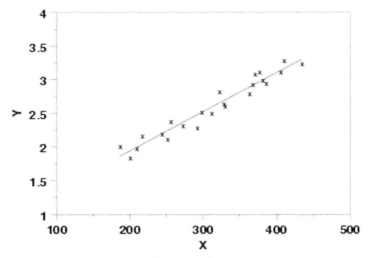

Figure 5.3a. Scatterplots show relationships: Positive relationship.

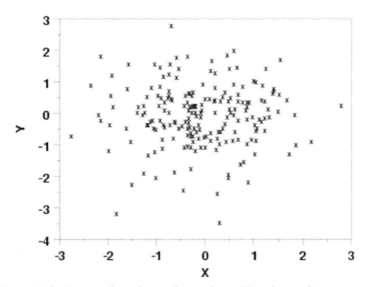

Figure 5.3b. Scatterplots show relationships: No relationship.

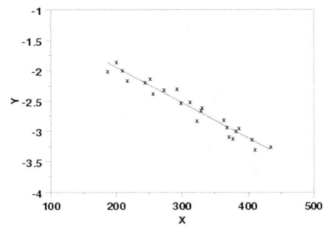

Figure 5.3c. Scatterplots show relationships: Negative relationship.

Histograms

A *histogram*, also called a *bar chart*, is a versatile tool for summarizing, analyzing, and displaying data to compare across items, time, or values of a single item. Histograms display the frequency of data in each category and the amount of variation in the set of data. A *line plot* shows only the top-most points of a bar on a histogram, connected by a line showing the direction of the relationship. Histogram observations are sorted into categories and can be plotted as vertical or horizontal bars.

Histograms show the distribution of data within the set of measured data points. There are many different types of distributions. A *normal distribution* is one in which the variation is distributed around the central mean (or average) according to the central limit theorem, which states that sums of random variables are approximately normally distributed if the number of observations is large (see Figure 5.4). Normal distributions occur most frequently in nature (e.g., grades, IQ, height, weight, and other common situations).

A *uniform distribution*, or *flat distribution*, is likely to arise from events that are of equal probability, such as the roll of a die (see Figure 5.5). With a die, there are six sides, and over time, each number should occur the same number of times.

Figure 5.6 shows an *exponential distribution,* which measures the time between independent events (e.g., death rate of an object) that happen at

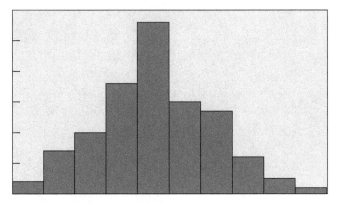

Figure 5.4. Normal distribution.

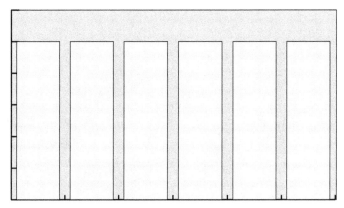

Figure 5.5. Uniform distribution.

a constant average rate through a Poisson process. A common distribution, exponential distributions describe object lifetimes for things such as a car, light bulb, appliance, tree, or other living or manufactured items.

A *Poisson distribution* is another common distribution based on the probability that an event will occur in a given period of time in a situation where the average event occurrence is known and events are independent of each other. Known for Siméon-Denis Poisson, who discovered properties that comprise Poisson distributions in the 1830s, Figure 5.7 shows a Poisson distribution, which predicts the life span of many manufactured items.

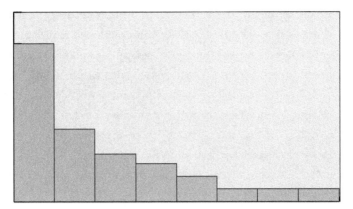

Figure 5.6. Exponential distribution.

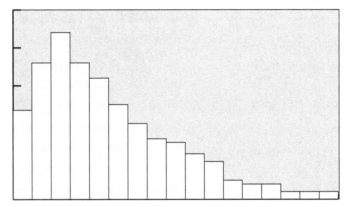

Figure 5.7. Poisson distribution.

To create a histogram, complete the following steps:

1. Collect the data. To ensure good results, a minimum of 50 data points, or samples, need to be collected.
2. Calculate the range of sample data as the difference between the largest and smallest data points (range = largest point – smallest point).

   The number of data points is then divided into classes to determine the X-axis intervals. This is a very important step because how you select the class interval size determines the accuracy of the histogram in interpreting the variation found in the data set. In general, interval size = range ÷ # intervals. One simple method is to pick the number of columns wanted (e.g., 10). With 50 data points, there will be 5 items in each interval. Then, compare this selection with the data to see how realistic it is. If, for instance, there are 9 data points with the same "x" measure, then a better number of classes would be 6. Selection of ranges determines the shape of the distribution, and the shape can change from normal to flat, depending on interval width. Several different intervals should be tried to ensure that the interval selected accurately reflects the data.

3. In any case, make sure the X-axis intervals are of equal length.
4. Draw the bars, showing the count of items in the interval on the Y-axis.
5. Label each interval on the X-axis with the minimum and maximum values of the range it encompasses. If possible, label the contents of the interval to show count or percentage of the total measures.

Pareto Diagrams

A *Pareto distribution* is a special form of distribution discovered by Vilfredo Pareto, who identified its properties. In general, 80% of the variation in many measured items is caused by 20% of the related events. Thus Pareto distributions are said to follow the 80-20 rule. The Pareto distribution has since been recognized to apply to a wide range of social, geophysical, and scientific problems.

Examples of business situations where the 80-20 rule applies include the following:

- sales revenue from number of customers (e.g., 80% revenue from 20% customers)
- error rates in software modules
- defect data in manufacturing work area
- cycle time in a service department
- errors committed during a transaction process
- design changes in software, architecture, or engineering diagrams

As Figure 5.8 shows for a defect analysis, 5, or 19%, of the error types explains 73% of the defects. These 5 defects would then be the focus of initial improvement processes. While the percentages are not exactly 80-20, they approximate the 80-20 rule.

The purpose of Pareto diagrams is to prioritize problems visually. The prioritized activities selected for action optimize the use of limited company resources by improving the problems with the greatest frequency of occurrence.

To create a Pareto diagram, complete the following steps:

1. Measure or count items to be compared.
2. Sort measures or counts from highest frequency to lowest frequency.
3. Place the items on the X-axis in the sorted order.
4. Identify item frequencies on the Y-axis.
5. On the right side of the diagram, draw another axis to show the cumulative percentage variation accounted for by each segment range.
6. Draw the cumulative percentage line to show where the 80% point is found.
7. If desired, color the 80% background area to identify the priority items clearly.

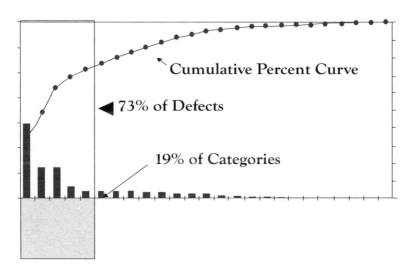

Figure 5.8. Pareto distribution showing the 80-20 rule.

Line Plots

Line plots are another form of histogram, such that only the dots representing paired X and Y coordinates and the line connecting them are plotted. During any self-assessment, one purpose for gathering measures of various aspects of an organization's functioning is to look for trends. A *trend* is a set of X and Y coordinates that shows a tendency or pattern over time, either moving up, down, or staying the same. *Trend analysis* is a technique used to predict the future based on past events and to identify problems in the trends. Trend analysis is popular because the plots are simple to create and are easily understood. Disadvantages of trend analysis are that choice of numeric intervals can alter the interpretation of results, the analysis may oversimplify a complex situation, and the analysis may not fit the context. Trend lines by themselves only indicate the direction of the trend—understanding the context is important in determining if a positive or negative trend is a cause for concern.

The major stumbling block in any decision-making process is uncertainty—that is, lack of knowledge over what the future will bring. We often speculate on the decision we would have made "if only we knew then what we know now." Hindsight is perfect, but what about foresight? The past may in fact not repeat, but it is not completely worthless.

Trend analysis is used to determine a need for management action. Simple trends are easy to track. For instance, in Figure 5.9, the line

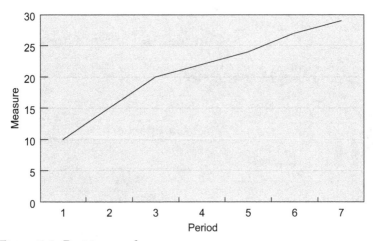

Figure 5.9. Positive trend.

moving from low to high shows a positive or rising trend. If the numbers were indicating increased error rates in a manufacturing facility—the positive trend—then the pattern shown in Figure 5.9 would be cause for concern. If the numbers in Figure 5.9 were revenues, then they would be cause for celebration. Figure 5.10 shows a negative, or dropping, trend. If these numbers were revenues, then the dropping trend would signify a need for problem analysis and resolution.

If you look at the set of numbers in Figure 5.11, it is difficult to find any trend. Diagrams give more information at a glance than long study of a table or voluminous report. In order to demonstrate this fact, Figure 5.11's information is graphically summarized in Figure 5.12. Further, if you only examine aggregated data for "all service," then the numbers do not indicate a need for further analysis. Disaggregated plots for cost components identify trends simply even though they may not be easily explained.

The data in Figure 5.12 show that in the early 1990s, most hospital costs dropped and entered a relatively stable period between 1995 and 1997. After 1997, a dramatic increase in costs was experienced, particularly for drugs, doctors, and outpatient expenses. By identifying the trends, the data point to three areas (drugs, doctors, and outpatient expenses) for additional analysis in order to explain their disproportionately higher cost increases.

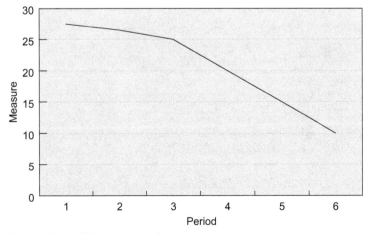

Figure 5.10. Negative trend.

Spending on type of health case service

Year	All Services	Hospital Inpacient	Hospital Outpatient	Physician	Drugs
1991	6.9%	3.5%	16.8%	5.4%	12.4%
1992	6.6%	2.8%	13.9%	5.9%	11.7%
1993	5.0%	4.8%	8.9%	3.3%	7.1%
1994	2.1%	−2.0%	8.7%	1.7%	5.2%
1995	2.2%	−3.5%	7.9%	1.9%	10.6%
1996	2.0%	−4.4%	7.7%	1.6%	11.0%
1997	3.3%	−5.3%	9.5%	3.4%	11.5%
1998	5.3%	−0.2%	7.5%	4.7%	14.1%
1999	7.1%	1.6%	10.2%	5.0%	18.4%
2000	7.8%	2.5%	11.5%	6.3%	14.5%
2001	10.0%	7.1%	16.3%	6.7%	13.8%
2002	9.6%	6.8%	14.6%	6.5%	13.2%

Figure 5.11. Table example of complex health care spending.

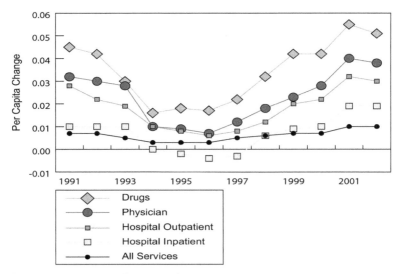

Figure 5.12. Hospital cost analysis.

To summarize, trend analysis is a graphical depiction of voluminous numeric data. By themselves, the trends often reveal relationship direction, not cause, and need further analysis to identify the causes.

Spider Diagrams

Spider diagrams, or spider charts, are another graphical method for visual comparisons of complex data. Spider diagrams are radial plots that display the magnitude of the different measures as connected points radiating from a central spot, usually drawn as the center of a circle. Strategic goals or comparisons are assigned to each radial line and each radial can have a different scale of measure. The information to be compared is plotted on the radial lines, with lines connecting the dots around the circle for two or more performance levels to be compared. The resulting diagram looks much like a spider's web. The advantages of spider diagrams are that they are easily understood and represent a good method for display of complex data. The disadvantage of spider diagrams is that the choice of intervals on each scale can affect the interpretation of the data. Figure 5.13 is the numeric basis for the spider diagrams discussed in this section.

One problem with developing meaningful spider diagrams is that the range of the numbers should be approximately the same so the diagram

Item for comparison	SCI	Company A	Industry average	Best practice
Hiring cost ($)	168	165	145	120
Training cost ($)	440	280	190	380
Average salary ($)	11	7	10	10
Training time in hours	40	40	20	40
Daily revenue, week 1 ($)	800	300	450	1200
Daily revenue, week 20 ($)	1200	800	800	1200
Average revenue ($)	900	600	700	1200
Average desk space (sq. ft.)	125	120	180	250
Hang-ups (%)	7.5	8.5	2.5	0.1
Turnover (%)	1.0	0.9	0.3	0.2

Figure 5.13. Call center benchmark analysis.

can be automatically generated by a program such as Microsoft Excel. If Figure 5.13 was used to generate a single automated diagram, then it would look like Figure 5.14 and would not be particularly meaningful.

When data are not to the same scale, you can change the scales, create multiple diagrams, or draw the diagram manually. One example is presented in Figure 5.15 for company revenues.

Figure 5.15 shows revenues by employee for average week, average week 1, and average week 20. As the diagram shows, the best practice has the highest numbers, but the performance of the company doing the analysis is competitive, with week 20 revenues matching the best practice amount. By contrast, Company A, a competitor, was lower on all measures. The target company revenues were all higher than the industry averages. This comparison might lead to complacency if managers were to focus only on revenue generation; however, the other analyses tell a different story.

An alternative to Microsoft Excel or other software-generated diagrams is to develop hand-drawn diagrams. Figure 5.16 compares a call center organization and industry averages—the dark line is the organization and light line is the industry average. The relationships between them are clearer because each scale is different and relates to the numbers in that category. In this analysis, it is clear that while revenues are

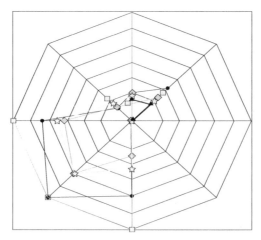

Figure 5.14. Spider diagram with auto scaling.

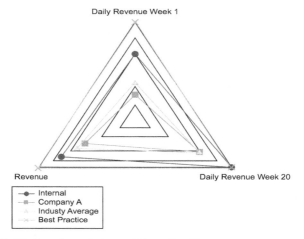

Figure 5.15. Benchmark financial spider diagram.

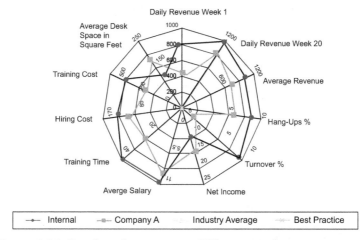

Figure 5.16. Benchmark comparison SCI versus industry average.

above the averages, the rest of the comparisons are unfavorable to the call center. The call center pays more yet experiences higher turnover, hang-ups, salaries, hiring costs, and training costs. Also, average desk space is a surrogate measure in the call center industry for "quality of life," which is unfavorable for the SCI call center. Thus a manually drawn spider diagram can clearly present complex sets of numbers for benchmark comparisons, each on its own scale.

Advantages and Disadvantages of Graphics

While a picture is worth many words, graphics need to be carefully designed for the intended use. The advantages and disadvantages of each are listed in Figure 5.17.

Other Methods of Problem Finding

While there are numerous other problem-finding methods, several frequently used ones are provided here: check sheets, cause-and-effect diagrams, critical incident analysis, and criterion analysis. All of these methods are for problem finding, but all also can be used in many other contexts.

Check Sheets

A *check sheet* is a customized form used to collect data about the frequency of error occurrence. The data can be input to other analysis tools, such as Pareto diagrams. While the format of a check sheet is usually a simple table with room for tick marks for the counts, more complex diagrams might be used to both locate and find errors that recur.

Advantages	Disadvantages
They are simple to create.	They may provide spurious correlations.
They are easily understood.	The more data, the more work and the longer to develop a graphic.
The provide simple correlation analyses.	Selection of intervals in histograms affects resulting distribution.
They are based on a small number of cases.	Three-dimensional pie charts are generally misleading, since the "slice" closest to the viewer appears larger than its true proportion.
They help prioritize problem areas.	Graphics can be chosen to hide information as easily as they simplify it.
Pareto diagrams identify how to get the most improvement with available resources.	

Figure 5.17. Advantages and disadvantages of graphics.

The following are the steps to creating and using a check sheet:

1. Outline (or map) the process.
2. Review each step of the process to determine possible defect areas.
3. Identify the events (i.e., application malfunction) or conditions (e.g., dents in a car) to be recorded.
4. Define the period for data recording.
5. Design the check sheet.
6. Record problems and defects on the check sheet for the required period.
7. Analyze the data and identify the problem areas for further analysis and correction.

Types of Check Sheets

There are five main types of check sheets:

- defect count
- defect location
- defect cause
- checkup confirmation
- problem finding

Defect-Count Check Sheet

The purpose of a defect-count check sheet is to determine the frequency with which types of known errors occur. To create such a check sheet, defects can be listed down the left margin or across the top of a table. In either case, tick marks are used to count the frequency of occurrence of each problem. By reviewing the counts, you can determine the extent to which the problems actually arise, focusing on those with high rates of occurrence.

Figure 5.18 is a check sheet used to detect the presence of different types of errors in a call center. As the figure shows, only the "credit-card process error" and "angry client" defects appear frequently. Frequency is not the only criterion for follow-up, though. For instance, a follow-up on the reasons why clients are angry enough to talk to a manager may be required. The other categories of error, both dealing with applications, probably also warrant follow-up because they have revenue implications.

Defect Type	Angry Client Requires Manager Intervention	System Error: Wrong Screen Display	System Error: Credit Card Payment Not Saved	Credit Card Process Error
Frequency	‖‖ ‖	‖	‖‖	‖‖ ‖‖ ‖‖‖
Total	7	2	3	14

Figure 5.18. Defective item identification check sheet.

The criteria for follow-up, then, are contextually defined and might include frequency, severity, or location of errors, as well as revenue-related errors or some other reason that is unique to the context.

Defect-Location Check Sheet

When the external appearance of a product is important, a defective-location check sheet can be used to identify the location of defects on a product. The method varies a bit, since instead of a check sheet listing problems, the check sheet is a picture of the product. Tick marks or other indicators are made on the picture to indicate where on the surface of the product the defect occurs.

For instance, Figure 5.19 shows a photo of the side of a car that might be the source of errors such as dents (A), dings (B), rust (C), and paint discoloration (D). The A, B, C, and D would be written on the car diagram to show where each occurred. Then, a count of each letter would summarize each error type, while the diagram shows the location of each.

Defect-Cause Check Sheet

A defective-cause check sheet is used to identify causes of a problem or a defect monitoring more than one variable. For example, data about the type of machine, operator, date, and time might all be collected on the same check sheet to help define the nature of the problem.

Multiple operators, spanning different days and shifts, would participate in the exercise. Then, the forms from all participants would be

A.	Dents – 3
B.	Dings – 1
C.	Rust – 1
D.	Paint – 2

Figure 5.19. Defect count and location together.

summarized on another check sheet (see Figure 5.20) in order to identify trends across the groupings. The afternoon seems most prone to error for workstation 2, regardless of operator. Follow-up on the lunchtime habits of the operators, plus a check of the differences in operating status for workstation 2, would be based on the figure. Ultimately, there may be several different problems relating to the issues with afternoons on workstation 2, but the check sheet reveals clues about where to look next for the root causes of the problems.

Checkup-Confirmation Check Sheet

A checkup-confirmation check sheet is used to ensure that proper procedures are being followed, and it may be part of a process audit. The check sheet lists the tasks to be accomplished and the steps taken to accomplish

Person	Time	Workstation 1	Workstation 2
Operator A	Morning	X	X
	Afternoon	XX	XXXXX
Operator B	Morning	X	XX
	Afternoon	XX	XXXXXXXXXX

Figure 5.20. Defective cause check sheet.

them. Alternatively, if some steps are considered mandatory and others optional, only mandatory steps might be checked. Tick marks are entered for these steps as they are completed. Over time, such check sheets show consistency rates for the task's performance.

Problem-Finding Check Sheet

Problem finding is similar to defective cause except that here the problems are determined on the basis of conjecture, and the check sheet is confirming the presence of the error. Often, during interviews, clients will comment on errors or problems in a process, leading you to believe that the problems occur frequently and obstruct work. Check sheets that confirm the presence of such an error are a useful triangulation technique.

Advantages and Disadvantages of Check Sheets

Figure 5.21 lists advantages and disadvantages of check sheets. Check sheets are a simple, cheap method of determining the presence, location, or frequency of defects in a process or product. Care must be taken not to rely on them as the only source of error or defect information, since they are not exhaustive. The data collected provide a rationale for actions taken to correct defects. Often, more analysis is needed to identify a root cause before corrective action can be planned.

Advantages	Disadvantages
They provide quick and simple analysis.	They may not be exhaustive in identifying all problems.
They are visually comprehended easily.	They require further investigation to determine error causes.
Data are recorded manually, so no cost.	
They are easily used with other tools.	
They are efficient means of data collection for problems that occur less than 100 times during the evaluation period.	

Figure 5.21. Advantages and disadvantages of check sheets.

Cause-and-Effect Diagrams

Also called *fishbone* and *Ishikawa diagrams*, the *cause-and-effect diagram* was developed by Kaoru Ishikawa in 1982 to support systematic identification and classification of different types of causes that might contribute to a problem. The graphic allows easy identification of possible errors and the relationships between them.

Development of cause-and-effect diagrams is a form of group brainstorming activity that combines the expertise of client representatives with the probing capabilities of the process improvement team. The group meets and identifies as many sources of errors as possible in the time allotted, categorizing them by type. Cause-and-effect diagramming exercises can lead to further data gathering using check sheets or some other method to determine the extent to which the causes occur in the problem environment.

Creating a Cause-and-Effect Diagram

The backbone of the diagram is a right-facing arrow for which the problem being analyzed is listed near the arrowhead (see Figure 5.22).

Lines creating the fishbone effect, "bones," branch off of the backbone, and each are named with a type of cause, such as the so-called 4 Ms (methods, man, machines, materials) or the 4 Ps (policy, procedure, people, plant) or equipment.[3] Alternatively, the main bones can

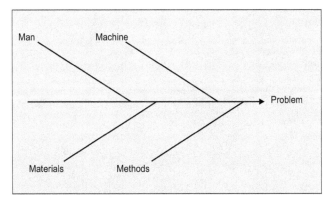

Figure 5.22. Basic cause-and-effect diagram components.

be customized to fit the context. However, when customizing categories, care must be taken not to bias the analysis. For instance, when analyzing a process map, the bones could be the steps of the process. The problem with this method is that with many bones or many process steps, the diagram can easily become overwhelmingly complicated, and rather than simplifying understanding of errors and relationships, it convolutes them. Therefore, this technique is best used on a single error where the total number of error branches is under about 30 and the number of causes (i.e., the main spines off of the center line) is 9 or less.

The final diagram has a series of ever-more-detailed bones off of the main cause bones, detailing the errors. Thus as the group discusses possible causes for an error, it identifies subcauses relating each to cause type. This, in effect, sorts the subcauses by type and allows discussion by cause type or by general cause. A sample diagram outcome might look like that depicted in Figure 5.23.

Eventually, each error or potential error is analyzed using other techniques that are discussed in the next three chapters to determine the root cause and remove, mitigate, or otherwise manage the problem.

Advantages and Disadvantages of Cause-and-Effect Diagrams

Cause-and-effect diagrams are a useful method for identifying potential causes of a problem with few serious disadvantages (see Figure 5.24). The

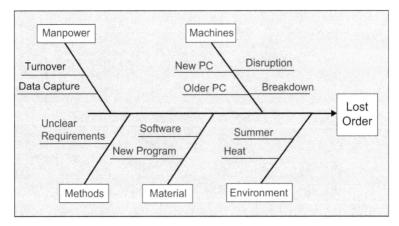

Figure 5.23. Cause-and-effect diagram.

Advantages	Disadvantages
They are useful for initial brainstorming.	As the diagram becomes more detailed, it may become so convoluted that it becomes difficult to read.
They focus attention on a specific problem or issue.	If the diagram is not detailed enough, then it may not identify the problem that should be the focus of improvement.
They organize and display potential root causes graphically.	Diagram might contain solutions rather than problems.
They depict relationships of factors influencing a problem.	They rely on recall and can be incomplete.
They help identify areas for further data collection and analysis.	They are prone to recency effects.

Figure 5.24. Advantages and disadvantages of cause-and-effect diagrams.

disadvantages require careful management of the group process to ensure that they are not present. The main disadvantage is diagram complexity, which may necessitate use of some other problem analysis or graphic depiction method.

Performance-Matrix Analysis

A *performance matrix* plots business processes on two dimensions, which, for change analysis, are typically "performance" and "importance to the corporate mission." However, other dimensions can be used. Performance matrices are popular because they are easy to understand and are simple to construct (given information availability).

A sample performance matrix is shown in Figure 5.25. Processes that have both high performance and high importance to the company are operating as expected and do not necessarily need change. Processes A and B are in this quadrant. If a process, such as "Process B" in Figure 5.25, is near the low performance area, it may be a candidate for improvement or for further analysis in deciding whether the process needs improvement. Processes C and D in the figure depict low performance but high importance and should be analyzed for improvement, possibly prioritizing them and improving both. In this example, "Process

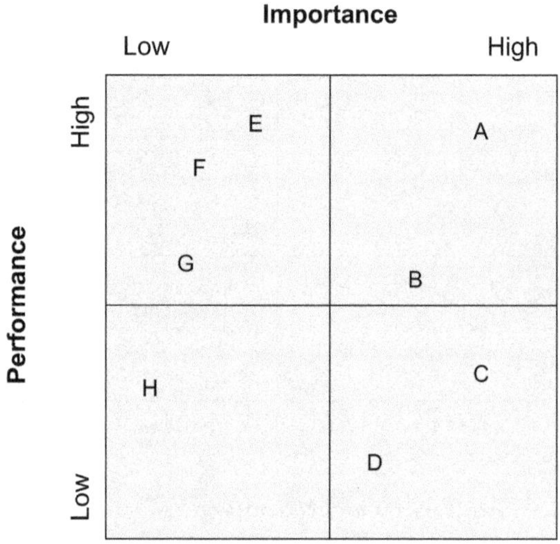

Importance

Figure 5.25. Matrix analysis.

C," being of more importance, would be the more likely candidate for immediate improvement.

Processes that are of low importance and high performance are, in marketing terms, "cash cows" and should not be improved, yet they should be continued because of their revenue-generating activity. This would include processes E, F, and G in the diagram. Finally, processes that are of low importance and low performance should be evaluated for discontinuation of the activity, since they are a drain on the company's resources. Process H falls into this category.

In this discussion, the comparison was concerning processes for improvement. Matrix analysis might use the same matrix, but the entities can be based on some other criteria. For instance, critical incidents or processes might be plotted. In the case of process plotting, the criteria for "importance" might shift from revenue generation to importance in meeting customer expectations.

There is nothing sacred about the two dimensions used, so the terms can be modified to provide the most appropriate analysis. If incidents are plotted, their importance to the business might be evaluated in terms of customer visibility, lost opportunities, or lost revenue. The incident-performance dimension might be evaluated in terms of dimensions for disruptiveness to the business or extent of business affected.

Figure 5.26 shows a plot of the cost and importance of each of six critical incidents. Each incident is plotted in terms of both its importance and cost, but in addition, the dots used for each incident are sized to show their relative cost and risk to the organization compared to the others.

The analysis illustrated in Figure 5.26 highlights the importance of problems with the electrical outage at a distribution center as clearly representing the most risk to the organization. The electrical outage, the data center, and the website failure are important but do not represent the same amount of cost risk to the organization. Each perspective gives a different answer in terms of the most "important" outage to remedy.

The advantages and disadvantages of matrix analysis are presented in Figure 5.27.

Critical-Incident Analysis

Critical-incident analysis (CIA) defines the who, what, where, when, why, and how of problems in an organization. An *incident* is any event or business feature that causes an interruption to, or a reduction in, the quality of the service or product. The incident may not be part of the standard design or operation for the service or product. *Critical-incident analysis* is a technique for identifying a process, subprocess, or problem

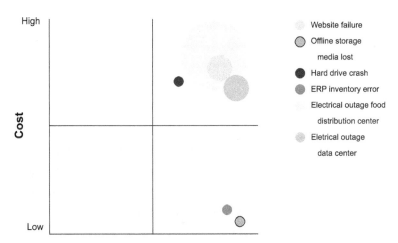

Figure 5.26. Matrix analysis showing relative cost and importance.

Advantages	Disadvantages
They focus attention on a specific problem or issue.	Dimensions may not be defined to depict the analysis most appropriate to the decision.
They depict relationships of factors influencing a problem.	They are subject to opinion and subjective judgment.
They help identify areas for further data collections.	

Figure 5.27. Advantages and disadvantages of matrix analysis.

area to be improved based on some selection criteria, such as cost or scope of the outage. The goal is to fix the underlying cause of an incident to ensure that it does not happen again. The word "critical" is important in this technique. The amount of effort and funds spent on CIA means that it should be used sparingly for situations in which significant failures have threatened the viability of the organization or its computing resources.

One way CIA is initiated is through a standing cross-functional team that chooses incidents to work on by selecting from all incidents that occurred in the period since the last meeting. Another CIA initiation method is for all senior executives to be authorized to convene an ad hoc CIA team for remediation of an incident they define as critical. Both methods are used, but the standing committee that looks at all incidents in an organization is recommended for compliance and certifications such as ISO 20000. In any case, recurring incidents or incidents that have a significant organizational impact are subject to problem analysis and resolution.

Other techniques are often used with CIA to identify some small set of truly critical incidents for problem resolution. In such a case, techniques such as matrix analysis, cause-and-effect diagrams, or Pareto analysis might be used to select or prioritize incidents for further inquiry.

The team evaluates the set of incidents and selects one for analysis based on difficulty, frequency, expense, damages, customer visibility, or organizational disruption. From all incidents, those that meet the criteria are set aside for further analysis and remedy. Each incident is ranked on the importance of its correction, and its process is identified as already mapped or slated to be mapped as a prelude to remediation.

Next, the problem is defined as completely as possible in order to provide the clearest understanding of its nature. Events leading to the incident are recalled and documented, and all background information is documented. SMEs are convened as part of the group; group members may also research and attend classes to become experts in the topic area being analyzed.

An example of critical-incident analysis occurred in a food delivery company, which had empowered managers to determine incidents requiring remediation. An example of the problems the company encountered follows, with the initial incident-analysis estimate of cost to the company:

- Offline storage shipment was lost, with an estimated cost of $10,000; appears to have been a handoff failure between data center personnel and off-site storage company. Shipment was recovered 2 days later and properly handled.
- Hard-drive crash of the main database at one site, with an estimated cost of $50,000; appears to have been a random failure.
- Electrical outage at the main data center; outage lasted 42 hours, with an estimated cost of $2 million; possibly caused by an electrical-storm lightning hit.
- Electrical outage at a regional food distribution center; outage lasted 38 hours in 90-degree weather, estimated cost was $12 million; appears to have been a transformer failure.
- Failure of implemented modules in the enterprise resource planning system, with an estimated cost of $45,000; appears to have been a testing failure for all variations required in accounting modules for warehouse-inventory accounting.

These issues all occurred within a 2-week period and were used to convene an ad hoc critical incident team to determine whether the issues listed were severe enough to require more attention.

Figure 5.28 shows a matrix analysis of the cost and importance of each of the six incidents described in the critical-incident discussion. This analysis highlights the importance of the distribution center electrical outage as clearly representing the most risk to the organization. Both the electrical, data center, and website outages were important but did not represent the same amount of financial risk to the organization. Other factors that

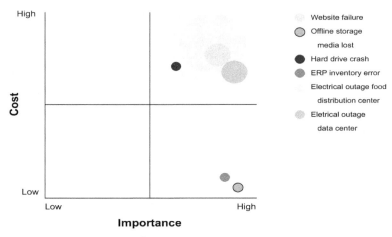

Figure 5.28. Matrix analysis.

might have been taken into consideration include good-will impact to the company (e.g., the distribution center outage actually gained the company goodwill when, because of the inability of the electric company to find a transformer on a holiday weekend, the company found the part, trucked it to the location, and paid the overtime for the electric company to install the part), visibility of the problem by the customers (e.g., the website and distribution-center outages were visible; the others were not), customer impact from the problem (e.g., low for hard-drive crash, very high for website failure), and so on. Each perspective gives a different interpretation regarding the most "important" outage to remedy.

A Pareto analysis of the CIA incidents summarizes each incident by cost to the company. Since some problems cause multiple incident types, the percentages could be greater than 100%, although in the example in Figure 5.29, this is not the case. Figure 5.29 shows that more than 80% of the cost is accounted for by the distribution-center outage. Therefore, that error would become the first problem needing resolution.

The CIA found that the local electrical company had incorrectly sized the transformer for the warehouse. Because of the severity, every warehouse location was subsequently rechecked to ensure transformer adequacy. Two other warehouses were identified as having been incorrectly sized. As a result, remediation included both fixing the problems and also

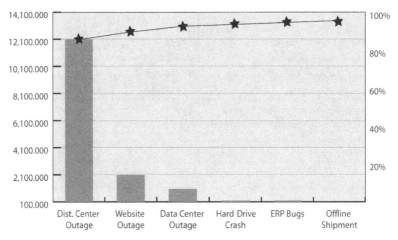

Figure 5.29. Pareto analysis of outage cost.

developing an algorithm to size transformers that no longer relied on the local electrical company.

CIA, then, is used to identify and define incidents for resolution, and then other techniques are used to identify the cause of a problem.

Advantages and Disadvantages of Critical Incident Analysis

The advantages and disadvantages of critical incident analysis are listed in Figure 5.30.

Criterion Testing

A *criterion*[4] is a condition or rule that enables a choice and upon which a decision or judgment can be based. In testing a criterion, there is a defined cutoff point to which the criterion is compared and considered a "pass" or a "fail." An example of this idea can be applied in evaluating an organization against its industry. For instance, industry "best practice" says that, with 3 days of training, a collections agent should average $30,000 per week in collections after 4 weeks of work. The industry-average collection amount after 4 weeks of work is the criterion being tested. Call center customer service representatives' (CSRs')

Advantages	Disadvantages
They are relatively inexpensive and provides rich information.	They rely on remembered events and truthfulness of reporting.
They emphasize analysis of vulnerabilities in a process.	They may focus on rare, rather than common, events.
They are appropriate for identifying unusual events, which may not be identified by other techniques that rely on everyday activity reporting.	They may overemphasize incidents with negative outcomes.
There is no need for CIA team members to have had direct observation of the event.	They are resource intensive in training observers and collecting data on a large number of incidents.
They focus on observable, measurable behaviors in real situations.	They may require CIA participants to become experts on areas not ordinarily part of their expertise and, therefore, require intelligent participants who are able to effectively find and assimilate complex information.

Figure 5.30. Advantages and disadvantages of critical incident management.

average collections would be evaluated to determine whether the training is better or worse than the industry average.

Another alternative is to compare two groups on one or more criteria to determine a preferred method of behavior. For instance, for call-center training, the industry average is three 8-hour days, and we believe that to produce better collectors than the average, the company should train for five 8-hour days, and thus we can test that criterion.

Two groups of people are trained—one group for 3 days, and one group for 5 days. The content of the training should be essentially the same but may have a longer on-the-job training component in the 5-day group. Then, the two equally matched groups are tested on their knowledge of (a) the process of collections, (b) different applications used in the collections process, and (c) their actual collections outcomes for week 2, week 5, and week 10 of their work. Figure 5.31 summarizes the measures involved in comparing the two groups.

As Figure 5.31 shows, the two groups have five criteria on which they are evaluated. In all cases, Group B, the group with 5 days of training, has superior performance to Group A. If the results were mixed, the evidence may not be sufficient to conclude that 5 days of training is superior. However, in this example, five different criteria are applied, and all support 5 days of training. Therefore, the criteria support the hypothesis.

The objective of criteria testing, then, is to evaluate some behavior or practice against a standard, measure, or defined cutoff point to determine the quality of the behavior or practice.

Advantages and Disadvantages of Criteria Testing

The advantages and disadvantages of criteria testing are listed in Figure 5.32.

This section discussed several methods of identifying, prioritizing, and analyzing errors. Each technique can be used alone or in concert with other techniques to develop the basis for process change.

Baseline Benchmarking

Self-assessment is a snapshot of some aspect of organizational performance used to form an overall impression of the organization's key processes, identifying likely candidates for improvement. The snapshot defines measures that will have lasting use as the process undergoes several rounds of improvements. The current use of measures is to aid in determining, first, which process(es) to improve and, second, what problem areas to improve within that process.

Self-assessment, in general, encompasses the techniques for evaluating performance levels of an organization and its processes. Self-assessment differs from other performance measures in time, focus, and use (see Figure 5.33).

Self-assessments provide a coherent view of core organizational processes or of processes that are candidates for improvement projects. All critical business processes should be measured throughout the day. The purpose of performance measures, after their use in determining candidates for improvement, is to monitor and manage daily conduct of work. The self-assessment benchmark is different in that it is a starting point for developing a longer term focus on how the process should be conducted and how much time is required for each process step.

Several tools aid in the development of a self-assessment. First, a baseline benchmark should be taken and declared the *baseline* against which

Group	Process knowledge	Applications knowledge	Week 2 collections ($)	Week 5 collections ($)	Week 10 collections ($)
A	82.6	70.2	26,000	36,000	35,000
B	86.7	80.0	36,000	48,000	38,000

Figure 5.31. Criterion testing.

Advantages	Disadvantages
They focus on observable, measurable behaviors in real situations.	They rely on remembered events and truthfulness of reporting.
	They may focus on rare, rather than common, events.
	They are resource intensive in training observers and collecting data on a large number of incidents.

Figure 5.32. Advantages and disadvantages of criterion testing.

	Self-assessment	Normal performance measures
Time	Snapshot	Ongoing
Focus	Provide an overall, coherent organizational view of "core processes" or processes being evaluated for improvement.	Measure most, if not all, processes.
Use	Develop a baseline benchmark for long-term focus.	Manage day-to-day activities; define areas for continuous improvement.

Figure 5.33. Self-assessment versus performance metrics.

all other measures of the activity will be made. The *baseline benchmark* is the set of initial measures that define the starting point for an improvement process. The baseline benchmark is the standard against which the improvements are evaluated to determine if the change has reduced cycle time, reduced error rates, or attained other goals of the process.

Types of Baseline Benchmarks

There are many different ways of measuring organizational functions. The most common methods relate to cycle time and financial analysis, which are used to develop a basic process understanding. Other methods relate to assessments of efficiency, effectiveness, or quality cost. All of these are discussed in this section. Keep in mind that many other types of benchmarks can be taken.

Cycle-Time Baseline

Cycle time is the elapsed time from start to completion of a process or process step. Measures of cycle time are highly dependent on accurate definition of the process scope and are the sum of the process time and the opportunity time. *Process time* is the time applied to process conduct. *Opportunity time* is the rest of the time that includes, for instance, wait time, rework time, and so on. The *opportunity cycle*, then, is the nonapplied time within the process that is the focus for improvement.

Consider the following example. A machine parts manufacturer receives an order at 9:00 a.m. on day 1 for delivery on day 30, with 160 hours of machine time to complete the work. The manufacturer has previously missed several deadlines and wants to determine the cause of the "problem" using this order to track issues. Manufacturing workdays are 16 hours (consisting of two shifts); therefore, for a 30-day commitment, there are 60 man-days to meet the commitment. All other departments in the company work an 8-hour day. The task is to analyze cycle time (see Figure 5.34). During interviews and observations, the company finds that there are more tasks for new customers than for repeat customers and decides to analyze the entire process. New-customer tasks are prefaced with "NC."

Once all of the tasks and their timing have been recorded, it is possible to begin drawing some conclusions about the problems. If this were the first of such measures taken, then this table would become the baseline benchmark. If not the first measure, then the numbers can be compared to a past benchmark, or some ideal or goal in order to further analyze the problems. That ideal or goal can be created internally or can be set against an industry (or some other company) average. Before continuing, take a few minutes to study Figure 5.34, and develop your own conclusions.

The total time for all departments is misleading, since one group has an 8-hour workday, while manufacturing has a 16-hour workday, so the totals for nonmanufacturing and manufacturing should be used. These numbers are then converted into workdays for each group. For new customers, the cycle time in actual days ranges from 29.5 to 39 workdays, while the actual process time is 14.1 to 21.8 workdays. For return customers or new customers for which a part mold exists, the cycle time is 11.1 to 18.1 workdays and process time is 12.4 to 16.3 workdays.

Thus for returning customers or customers for whom a part mold exists, the 30-day estimate appears realistic. However, for new customer orders that require creation of a mold, even if minimum times are met for all groups, the minimum time of 18 nonmanufacturing days plus 11.5 manufacturing days is 29.5 days, thus resulting in a new order being late. If maximum times are taken on a new customer order, then a total of 39 days is required. Further analysis shows that manufacturing is not the problem but that the times taken for scheduling and meeting appear to be the major sources of delay.

Task	Department	Total time (hours)	Process time (hours)
Enter order	Sales	1–8	1
Move order to engineering or manufacturing	Sales app	1	1
NC—Is part mold(s) available?	Engineering	16–32	2–4
NC—Make new mold		80	16–32

NC—Create machine setup and manufacturing instructions:
 Meeting setup
 Meeting:
   Draft instructions
   Draft manufacturing instructions
   Draft quality assessment (QA) criteria
	Engineering and manufacturing	
		
		16
		8–24
			
			1
			1–8

NC—Test all instructions and QA	Engineering, manufacturing, and QA	16	1–8
NC—Revise all instructions or QA as required	Engineering, manufacturing, and QA	8	0–3
Schedule production	Manufacturing	8–24	2–4
Production	Manufacturing	160–200	160–200
QA	QA	8–16	8–16
Rework	Manufacturing	8–16	8–16
NC total—all departments	Total hours Total 8-hr. days	330–441 41–55	201–293 25.3–37
NC total—nonmanufacturing departments	Total hours Total 8-hr. days	146–185 18–23	23–57 3–7
NC total—manufacturing/ QA only (schedule production, production, QA, rework)	Total hours Total 8-hr. days Total 16-hr. days	184–256 23–32 11.5–16	178–236 22.3–29.5 11.1–14.8
NC total physical days		29.5–39	14.1–21.8
Returning customer or no mold—total physical days	Non-Mftg Time Mftg Time Total 8-hr. days	1–25 176–240 11.1–18.1	10–18 178–224 12.4–16.3

Figure 5.34. Cycle-time example.

Overall opportunity time for this example is 16 to 22 eight-hour days (derived from the row titled "NC Total Time—All Departments" by computing the problems "41 − 25" and "55 − 37"), but the most opportunity is in premanufacturing activities leading up to "Testing of instructions and QA" because there is a wider gap between their total and process times (16 to 18 days) than that between manufacturing and rework.

Cycle-time definition is imperative for obtaining an accurate interpretation of an organization's operation. As the example demonstrates, there can be multiple differing cycles within a single cycle, and all must be defined accurately for their context.

Financial Cost Baseline

Financial cost is the amount of expenditure allocated to a work unit. A work unit may be some defined product, the detail of which depends on the granularity of analysis. To compute the financial costs of a work unit, both the work unit and a "model," or description of each cost component and its percentage contribution to total cost, are defined.

In "pure" environments, such as manufacturing, which can be analyzed at the machine or product level, or project services, which can be analyzed at the project or task level, developing a financial cost model is straightforward. In a "blended" environment, such as a call center, developing a cost model is less straightforward. If we were to analyze only first-party collections, given the way the Davox works, each person might be working different campaigns for every phone call. The software serves up the proper company script with the information to be read by the CSR. To develop a cost model would require separation of campaigns, using at least 10 hours of analysis to develop a cost baseline. In blended environments, simplification to get some measure of cost may be required. For instance, for a call center, a financial goal might be to define the cost of a single collection.

Components of a cost baseline should be customized for the work environment, but in general, it can include the following:

- machine-hours
- man-hours (which should be clarified as with and without overhead)

- resources (plant, equipment, raw materials, all other materials)
- rework cost (scrap and machine, man-hours, resources, bad will)
- quality assurance cost
- customer support cost
- customer satisfaction cost
- training cost
- turnover cost

The heuristic, or rule of thumb, is to define costs as simply as possible to allow consistency of definition across organizational environments. For instance, all of the measures, assuming availability of information, might be applied to all aspects of a call center—manufacturing activity, service activity, accounting, and so on.

Continuing the manufacturing example, to develop a financial-cost baseline benchmark, identify all of the cost components for the task, and then apply average costs to each component. Figure 5.35 summarizes the example's financial information, simplifying to man-hours, machine time, and raw materials.

Cost models are useful in many types of organizational analyses. For instance, when deciding whether to outsource production work, a cost model of in-house and outsourced production costs would be compared. In seeking to manage any activity or its components, a financial cost model is fundamental to understanding where the money goes. The financial model demonstrates where money is being spent; a process model shows where money and time might be saved.

Efficiency Baseline

Efficiency is the ratio of inputs to outputs expressed as a percentage. Again, typical inputs include money, time, people, and materials. To improve efficiency, one of three outcomes is possible:

1. The productivity ratio must be improved—that is, the number of inputs should be decreased to generate the same number of units.
2. Production must be increased at the same cost, therefore, product quality is decreased.
3. The number of units produced must be decreased.

Cost component	Department	No. of units	Average cost ($)/unit	Total cost ($)
Enter order	Sales	1 hour	50	50
Move order to engineering/manufacturing	Sales app	0.1 hour	85	8.50
NC—Create, test, revise machine setup and manufacturing instructions—man-hours	Engineering, manufacturing, and QA	2–8 hours	65	130–520
NC—Create new mold—man-hours	Engineering	18–36 hours	65	1,170–2,340
NC—Create new mold—machine time	Engineering	16–32 hours	130	2,080–4,160
NC—Machine time	Manufacturing and QA	1–8 hours	130	130–1,040
Schedule production—man-hours	Manufacturing	2–4 hours	65	130–260
Schedule production—computer time	Manufacturing	2–4 hours	85	170–340
Production—man-hours	Manufacturing	160–200 hours	22	3,520–4,400
Production—machine time	Manufacturing	160–200 hours	130	20,800–26,000
QA—man-hours	QA	8–16 hour	30	240–480
QA—machine time	QA	8–16 hour	220	1,760–3,520
Rework—man-hours	Manufacturing	8–16 hour	22	176–352
Rework—machine time	Manufacturing	8–16 hour	130	1,040–2,080
Total process cost			Min. cost $31,463	Max. cost $45,551

Figure 5.35. Cost-model example.

Understanding cost components is important for increasing efficiency because it is important to know where money can be squeezed out of a process. In companies with overhead assessed as a "tax," the tax per product and how it affects the cost of each unit must be known to determine if efficiency increases are possible. Often, companies confuse reducing quality with increasing efficiency. In such a case, the cost of quality should be evaluated in order to determine the most cost-effective action. Cost of quality is a topic covered later in this book.

A zero-scrap or zero-waste organization would be 100% efficient. However, even white-collar workers do not work every minute of their workday. Daydreaming, phone calls, personal e-mails, or social interactions with coworkers all reduce efficiency of a person's workday. Add in downtime from, for example, computer viruses, software malfunctions, and other technology glitches, and office worker productivity or efficiency is further eroded.

To measure efficiency, exact measures of every input and every output of a product or process are monetized and divided by the total product or process cost. Ideally, efficiency percentages should be equal to, or near, 100%; however, on the average, unmanaged organizational efficiency is closer to 40%.

Effectiveness Baseline

From the company's perspective, *effectiveness* determines the value obtained from each dollar expended. Effectiveness, from a customer's perspective, is a measure of the extent to which customers are satisfied with a company's products. People sometimes talk of efficiency as "doing things right," while effectiveness is "doing the right things." Again, typical inputs include money, time, people, and materials. To improve effectiveness, enhancements to product characteristics, product quality, or support services could be increased for the same amount of money.

There are many different ways of measuring effectiveness depending on how it is defined in a given context. The most popular method is customer surveys that are conducted by a survey organization. Another method is to determine the percentage of products that meet quality standards (e.g., a conforming product, as defined in the next section). The resulting percentage is a simple measure of effectiveness. In the manufacturing example, the company defined a 10% rework percentage; this is the obverse is the effectiveness ratio, which would be 90%.

Quality Baseline

Philip Crosby developed *cost of quality* in his book *Quality Is Free.*[5] Cost of quality is characterized by two main components: cost of conformance and cost of nonconformance. *Conformance cost* is the amount of money spent on ensuring that products fall within an accepted specification range. This includes costs of quality-assurance activities, such as standards, training, and process management, and costs of quality control activities, such as reviews, audits, inspections, and testing.

Cost of nonconformance is the amount of money spent on reworking, correcting, or replacing products that are outside the accepted range. Components include rework machine time, materials, work time, and reinspection time but may also include such items as legal fees, customer-support fees, product-return shipping fees, and other similar items.

Creating the Baseline Benchmark

Before change recommendations are developed, a *quantified snapshot*, or *baseline benchmark*, of the organization's current process components should be developed. A *benchmark* is a point of reference against which other measures at different points in time are compared or measured. Benchmarks can be categorized as one of the following categories.

1. *Internal.* Measures of internal processes or process steps that are compared to each other. For instance, appropriate comparisons in a collections call center might be of an individual collector against others, an individual collector against the group, one group against another group, one day's collections against another day, first-party CSRs against third-party CSRs, and so on. Then, within a category, the times evaluated might be talk time, collection ratio, downtime, and so on.

2. *External.* Measures of a process compared to those of other organizations. The process comparisons may be of the same processes or different processes that provide a similar service or product. For

instance, a service consulting company that specializes in HIPAA-IT[6] consulting might compare, for example, average daily revenue per person, average project duration, average project profit, and so on to those of a company in the same business, a company that specializes in generic IT consulting, or a company that specializes in SOX-IT[7] consulting. All of these comparisons will generate slightly different results, but they all should approximate those of the HIPAA-IT consulting firm.

3. *Best practice.* Measures an industry to create average, minimum, and optimum measures for a variety of situations and process areas. Best-practice measures are usually within an industry, for example, "collection agency" is characterized by a North American Industrial Classification System code (NAICS) of 1867-56144, assigned by the U.S. government,[8] that identifies it as part of the "Services-Consumer Credit Reporting, Collection Agencies" industry. Industry associations are the best source of industry best practices, although a company must usually become a member of the association to have access to its best-practice benchmarks.

All three types of benchmarks might be created in the development of the initial baseline. Ideally, all three types of benchmarks should be compared in order to support optimal decisions.

Useful benchmarks yield the following information:

- total process cycle time
- a measure or product and process quality
- number, cost, or type of resources needed to perform the process
- a measure of staff skill levels
- measures of equipment and staff productivity

There is no one way to measure, and there is no one right set of measures. If measurement is new to the organization, then some guidelines for selecting measurement points in a process are to develop measures for the following items:

- handoffs
- monetary transactions

- monetary processing
- customer-user interactions and touch points with individuals within the organization (e.g., to develop customer survey questions, to analyze the number and type of interactions and handoffs, to determine up-sell opportunities, to determine areas for improvement)
- application transaction processing (e.g., to determine that transactions have been processed fully and correctly, that error messages are appropriate, and that the process fits the business)
- known bottlenecks
- queues and waiting times, such as in-box, e-mail, transmission, mail, and so on
- overall cycle time, including the time to process each step

One assessment is to determine if the measures taken are "good enough" for their intended purpose of supporting the decision about which process to improve. Some questions to answer in evaluating the worth of measures are as follows:

- Do the measures together give a complete and accurate view of the process?
- Do the measures identify bottlenecks, waiting time, and actual work time?
- Do the measures quantify handoff timings?
- Do the measures identify incoming and outgoing data and the timing of each?
- Do the measures evaluate all products and services within the overall process under review?
- Do the measures quantify events and demands relating to completion of customer-facing process steps?
- Do the measures improve the understanding of the process when compared to any current measures?
- Do we have timely access to alternative or more accurate measures?

When developing measures, it is important to determine what the scope of the measures should be. For example, in a company with 2,000 customers and no prior measures, it may not make sense to measure work relating to all customers. The first step, then, is to determine which measures apply to each customer set. The Pareto method, or 80-20 rule, can be used for this analysis. According to Pareto analysis, roughly 80% of income, errors, customer activity, and so on is initiated by 20% of the customers. If you find that the rule holds for the situation under review, then apply it to the measures developed. For instance, develop all of the measures but apply them to the top 20% of customers. This action results in (a) focusing on the important information and (b) a minimal set of numbers to be generated.

In addition to applying the Pareto rule to the data, it is important to decide the timing of the measures. If a company is in crisis, then revenue-generation activities might be measured daily along with an overall summary of revenues and expenses. Some reports should be daily, with weekly, monthly, and other periodic summaries. The different formats and contents of the reports need to be developed with the managers who regularly use the reports.

If measures are new to the organization, then decisions regarding which processes to improve might be based on as little as a week's activity. Applying Pareto principles, about 80% of the issues should be identifiable in about 20% of the time. So, roughly 10 weeks are needed to identify about 80% of the problems occurring annually. The question that should be asked is whether having more information would necessarily change the decision or action contemplated. If the answer is no, then the time can be considerably shortened; hence, the suggestion of decisions based on a week's activity.

The first set of benchmark measures is the baseline against which all other measures of the changed process will be compared. However, defining when the "first set of measures" is complete is a judgment call. The baseline should be complete before any recommendations or changes are made.

In summary, baseline benchmarks are developed in order to define the starting point for comparisons that determine process improvement success. At a minimum, an internal baseline is defined. Baselines may be internal, external, or best practice. A best practice is to use all three types.

Summary

The techniques discussed in this chapter include problem identification, problem finding, graphical data presentation, and benchmarking. Each of these presents a different perspective on the current state of an organization with the primary purpose of identifying processes for change. Keep in mind that each method has other uses and that there are many other methods for analyzing a situation when identifying processes for change.

The chapter began with several idea-generation techniques. Brainstorming can generate a large number of alternative ideas in a fixed amount of time. While most commonly used for problem solving or marketing-idea generation, brainstorming can be used in any situation that calls for the development of alternatives. This method is not best for highly political situations or situations in which participants have wide divergence in their organizational powers and positions. Nominal group technique (NGT) can be used for problem identification, problem solving, and program planning. Because NGT begins with written idea generation, it is useful for political situations, but it takes more time than brainstorming due to its use of written sessions. Delphi is a gathering of SMEs on the topic of interest to generate a list of related ideas or alternatives, which are then voted on several times until some preestablished criterion is met. Delphi relies on expertise in developing trends or ideas, and because experts may be remote, this may take a considerable amount of time. Brain writing and mind maps are variations on idea generation. Brain writing combines brainstorming and NGT by having several problems circulating during the writing down of ideas. It then proceeds like a brainstorming session. Mind maps are a method for arranging ideas or topics, once generated, to show their relationship to the central ideal or problem. Ideas are evaluated and grouped. Each "leg" of the map is color-coded to make it visually distinguishable.

Graphics provide simplicity and easy understanding of complex data, simple correlation analysis, and prioritization of problem areas. Care must be taken not to obscure the meaning of the data through ambiguity, distortion, or distraction in graphics design. Scatterplots provide a graphical tool for plotting data collected from two measures, one of which is suspected to have an influence on the value of the other. The shape of the dot plots identifies whether or not a relationship exists.

Histograms and line plots are used to summarize data across items, time, or values of a single item. Histograms display the frequency of data in each category and depict the amount of variation within the set of data. The range of data is used to determine the set of equally sized intervals for presentation in a histogram. This is important because interpretation and distribution vary depending on interval selection. Line plots simply show the X and Y coordinates rather than the area under the dots. Line plots depict a set of numbers that are meaningful to the organization and show whether there is a positive or negative trend.

Pareto distributions are a special form of exponential distribution that applies to a wide range of situations, measuring a variety of independent categories relating to a single area. Pareto distributions have the characteristic that approximately 80% of the variation is explained by approximately 20% of the data. To create the diagram, a count of the categories is sorted highest to lowest and plotted as a simple histogram. On the right side of the diagram, the axis shows the cumulative percentage of categories up to 100%.

Spider diagrams are snapshot comparisons of multiple measures for several organizations on a radial plot that looks like a spiderweb. Spider diagrams show the magnitude of differences on each radius and, by connecting the dots for a given company, depict a measure of relative "success" or "failure."

The disadvantages of graphics are that they may identify spurious correlations, take a long time to develop with voluminous data, and may depict the problem areas of ambiguity, distortion, and distraction.

Performance matrices plot some items to be evaluated, such as business processes, on two dimensions, such as their importance to organizational success and their performance. The more important and the lower the performance of an item is, the higher its priority for improvement.

Cause-and-effect diagrams are useful for identifying and classifying different types of causes and their interrelationships that might contribute to a single topic area. Also called a fishbone diagram, the diagram is created by identifying the topic area or problem on a horizontal "backbone" line, and then by labeling diagonal lines off of the backbone for the major contributing cause types. The 4 Ms (methods, man, machines, and materials) and the 4 Ps (policy, procedure, people, and plant/equipment) are commonly used as starting causes; however, causes may be customized to the problem context. Branches are added to each main cause type for issues relating to that type. Cause-and-effect diagrams are good for initial brainstorming, focusing attention on a problem, organizing potential problem causes, depicting relationships between factors relating to a problem, and identifying areas for further analysis. Disadvantages of cause-and-effect diagrams are that they may be convoluted and difficult to read, may not identify enough problems, or might contain solutions rather than causes of the problem.

Check sheets are customized forms used to collect data about the frequency of error occurrences. Check sheets are classified into the four following categories: defect count, defect cause, confirmation, or problem finding. Check sheets provide quick and simple analysis of potential problems, are visually simple to comprehend, cost virtually nothing to develop or use, are an efficient means of data collection for errors that occur in the tens (not thousands), and can be used easily with other techniques. The disadvantage of check sheets is that they may not provide an exhaustive evaluation of all problems, thus necessitating further analysis in order to determine the root cause.

A criterion test is the evaluation of some particular measure to determine its importance to an organization's function. If all items evaluated are considered equally important, then evaluating them on several criteria might help in prioritizing them for improvement.

A baseline benchmark is a set of initial measures of different aspects of an organization that are used for comparison against change efforts in order to determine if they are improving organizational functioning. Cycle time is the elapsed time from the start of a process to its completion and is a key metric that organizations seek to reduce. Cycle time evaluates the actual process time and all other time (opportunity time), seeking to reduce this "other" time. Financial cost is also a focus of improvements and is the amount of expenditure allocated to a work unit.

There are different types of baseline benchmarks—efficiency, effectiveness, and quality. Efficiency is measured as the ratio of inputs to outputs, and the goal is usually to decrease the ratio, that is, to use fewer inputs to produce the same number of outputs. Efficiency efforts focus on reducing reworks and waste as well as finding more efficient means of production.

Effectiveness baselines evaluate the value obtained from each dollar spent, although there are many ways and perspectives from which effectiveness can be evaluated. Most commonly, companies use customer satisfaction ratings as a measure of their effectiveness.

Quality baselines rely on standardized processing to define guidelines on conformance. Any products or processes falling outside the conformance guidelines become targets for improvements.

While there are many types of benchmarks, they fall into three categories: internal, external, and best practice. Internal benchmarks compare similar processes within a company, external benchmarks compare similar processes across companies, and best-practice benchmarks compare a company's performance to industry best practices. All benchmarks seek to determine how competitive an organization or process is relative to its standard for comparison.

Benchmarks can be used to identify areas for improvement. A special form of benchmark, the baseline, is a snapshot against which the process improvements will be compared in order to determine their success.

CHAPTER 6

Process Leaning

Introduction

In the 1950s, W. Edwards Deming, who popularized the notion that continuous process improvement leads to quality production, developed many modern quality programs in Japan. Today, the practice *genba kanri*,[1] which loosely translates as "workshop management," is a movement to error-proof processes. The "5 Zs" provide the guiding principles. The Japanese word for "do not"—*zu*—ends each of the 5 "Z" words:

- *uketorazu*: do not accept defects.
- *tsukurazu*: do not make defects.
- *baratsukasazu*: do not create variation.
- *kurikaesazu*: do not repeat mistakes.
- *nagasazu*: do not supply defects.

Six Sigma is an error-proofing movement that was started at Motorola in the 1980s, borrowing from the Japanese, with the specific goal of allowing no more than 3.4 errors per million opportunities. A *sigma* is a standard deviation from a population mean. Six Sigma practice strives for 99.9997% accuracy in the process. *Lean Six Sigma* combines lean manufacturing discipline with Six Sigma's low defect goal. Leaning is the removal of waste from processes. Thus Six Sigma and lean are compatible with *genba kanri*.

In this chapter, we begin with the *uketorazu* stage by seeking to eliminate steps that do not contribute to organization profit or customer satisfaction. The first technique, value-added analysis, evaluates a process and "leans" out superfluous activities in preparation for developing proposed changes. Then we evaluate how to improve processes by eliminating defects and variations from processes—the *uketorazu, tsukurazu,* and *nagasazu* stages. Finally, we introduce quality function deployment (QFD) as a tool to identify and choose between means for making changes. The other stages are discussed in the next chapter.

Value-Added Analysis

Value-added analysis (VAA) is a technique for removing nonessential process steps. There are four types of *event-driven processes*: customer affecting, management, primary, and support. A single process can have elements of more than one process type within it, and when analysis is done, part of the task is to tease out which type of process each step is conducting.

Customer-affecting processes are those for which a customer would pay. It forces one to think about what the customer actually is paying for. Management processes are those required for the organization to control and guarantee quality of its processes. Primary processes are those that are needed to allow the process to take place. For instance, in manufacturing, machines might need to be set up or calibrated before the manufacturing process takes place. Even though a customer would not want to pay for setup, it is still necessary. Secondary processes are those that are not germane to the process, such as moving raw materials from inventory. Both the inventory and the movement are secondary.

In conducting value-added analysis, we seek to identify each step as one of the four process types, keeping customer-affecting processes and evaluating all others to determine their real value to the organization. Then, after stripping all nonessential or non-value-adding process steps, the process is redesigned to perform in the most efficient way. Thus VAA is a prelude to the improvement process. It is a form of "leaning out" process steps that are of little organizational value. That is, according to lean Six Sigma tenets, waste removal is performed before perfecting performance of the remaining process steps.

A typical process by some estimates will have only 5% of its steps value adding (VA).[2] To be value adding, a customer must be willing to pay for the activity, and the step must in some way affect the service or product with 100% accuracy. Thus value adding and customer facing are the same thing. Flawed (non-100% accuracy) VA steps are also evaluated for their necessity and, if required, are then forwarded for root-cause (or other) analysis of defects. An example of value-adding steps in a law firm, for example, are "analyzing case papers to develop a line of defense," or, in manufacturing, "rust-proof painting of a car's underside."

The remaining 95% of process steps are either non-value adding (NVA) or do not contribute to enhancing the customer experience. NVA steps can be further analyzed by type as management, primary, or support. Some activities of each of these types will be "necessary waste," as they respond to legal, regulatory, or other required activities to deliver a product to a customer. However, in each NVA category, it is possible to identify steps that are not necessary. Occasionally, there are steps that are considered "the way we've always done things" or that are responses to special requests from a manager or are of unknown origin. These steps should all be evaluated for elimination. Compliance actions that would otherwise not be conducted are an example of an NVA activity.

As waste analysis is performed, some activities will be identified that can be, or should be, completely eliminated. These are called non-value-adding, unneeded (NVAU) activities. In general, any activity that is not VA, not required by law, or not needed to maintain the organization as a going concern are NVAUs. Examples of NVAU activities in a law firm are "moving boxes of documents from one place to another," or, in manufacturing, "moving raw materials to the manufacturing floor."

To the extent possible, NVA and NVAU activities should be eliminated. One common acronym for the seven elements of waste is TIMWOOD (time, inventory, motion, wait time, overproduction, overprocessing, defect rework), but an easier one to remember is DOWNTIM[e], developed by Taiichi Ohno for Toyota,[3] DOWNTIM[e] includes the following items:

- *D*efects: anything not done according to specifications and correctly the first time
- *O*verproduction: making product faster, sooner, or more than needed. According to Ohno, overproduction leads to most of the other types of waste
- *W*aiting: time lost when people, material, or machines are waiting
- *N*onutilized talent: not fully utilizing the workers involved

in the process; not using the people closest to the actions and their knowledge

- *T*ransportation: any movement of parts, materials, employees, or customers creates waste
- *I*nventory: any material in excess is classified as one of three types—raw material, work-in-progress (WIP), and finished goods
- *M*otion: movement of people, product, materials, or machines that does not directly add value to the final product

When these activities are eliminated, they are replaced by improved processes, automated metrics, and controls. Since some NVA and NVAU activities may still be required, they are evaluated to minimize their impact on process time and cost. Minimizing may take the form of the following:

- minimizing time of item or process movement between people by moving the participants physically closer
- combining steps
- reassigning work done by several people to one person
- coproduction activities
- automating the task, thereby eliminating human activity
- outsourcing

To conduct value-added analysis, the following steps are conducted:

1. Map the process.
2. List all process steps and place them in a table with five other columns for duration, DOWNTIMe, and identification as value adding activities (VA), non-value-adding, but required, activities (NVA), or unnecessary non-value-adding activities (NVAU).
3. Review each process step, asking the following questions:
   A. Does this activity meet any of the DOWNTIMe definitions?
      i. If yes,
         a. Could this activity be eliminated if some prior activity were done differently or correctly? (If yes, then NVA)

  b. Could this activity be eliminated without impacting the form, fit, or function of the customer's "product"? (If yes, then NVAU)
  ii. If no, then VA
4. Evaluate all NVA activities for the potential to automate them.
5. Evaluate all NVAU activities for elimination or automation.
6. For NVA and NVAU activities that do not appear able to be automated or eliminated, mark them for further analysis for cleaning (chapter 7), for greening (chapter 9), or some other replacement with VA activities.

Figure 6.1 describes the steps in a simple process flow to create cabinet doors through only two manufacturing operations with the activities defined as VA, NVA, and NVAU.

As the figure shows, only two activities are actually required: cutting pieces and machining the doors. If all other activities could be eliminated or automated, the time could be substantially reduced. For instance, if just NVAU activities were eliminated, the process would be reduced by 96%, or by 152.75 hours, to 5.5 hours. The NVA activities are materials handling or machine setups, both of which are required even though they are not directly aiding the customer experience. Therefore, efforts would focus on the NVAU activities and their elimination.

In the example in Figure 6.1, the NVA activities might be improved as follows:

- Outsource raw materials management to the vendor and change to just-in-time management so there is no materials handling.
- Improve the manufacturing planning process to minimize setups for both operations, allowing, for instance, no more than one per shift.
- Move cut pieces directory to the CNC process area.

Value-added analysis, then, seeks to identify any process steps that delay, interrupt, reduce efficiency of, or duplicate other process steps. These are all non-value-added categories and are unnecessary steps. Once the NVAU steps are identified, the goal is to remove, automate, or at least

Activity	Description	Duration	VA	NVA	NVAU	DOWNTIMe
Material handling	Get panel stock	15 minutes			X	Move
Set up	Set up saw	15 minutes		X		Control
Saw	Cut pieces as required	30 minutes	X			
Queue	Store cut pieces	6 hours			X	Wait
Material handling	Move cut pieces to CNC	15 minutes			X	Move
Set up	Set up CNC machine	15 minutes		X		Control
Machine	Machine cabinet doors	4 hours	X			
Queue	Store machined pieces	2 days, 30 minutes			X	Wait

Figure 6.1. Value-added analysis for two-step manufacturing process.

handle those steps outside of the process, thus removing impediments to the process's speediest execution.

Advantages and Disadvantages of Value-Added Analysis

Value-added analysis seeks to drive wasted effort from processes. It is a useful technique with more advantages than disadvantages (see Figure 6.2).

Cost-of-Quality Analysis

According to the American Society for Quality, the *cost of quality* (COQ) is "the difference between the actual cost of a product or service and what the reduced cost would be if there were no possibility of substandard service, failure of products or defects in their manufacture."[4] Cost of quality comprises several components:

- *prevention costs*—the cost of all activities designed to prevent or provide on-the-spot remediation of defects or insufficient quality in products or services
- *appraisal costs*—the cost of measuring, evaluating, or auditing products or services for conformance to required quality standards or for required process performance
- *failure costs*—the cost of nonconformance to standards in either product or process performance

Advantages	Disadvantages
It identifies the minimal set of process steps needed to accomplish the process.	It can be time-consuming for complex processes.
It supports ISO, military, and other compliance efforts.	It may identify problem areas that an organization does not want to confront.
It can identify opportunities for automation.	
It is inexpensive.	
It is a useful precursor to strategy, resource, and policy realignment.	

Figure 6.2. Advantages and disadvantages of value-added analysis.

- ○ *internal failure costs*—the failure costs incurred if the defects or failures are found before being shipped or provided to the customer
- ○ *external failure costs*—the failure costs incurred if the customer discovers the defects or failures

In the ideal world, a company would not experience failure costs. The company would have provided sufficient attention to preventing errors such that minor appraisal, with even more minor failure remediation, would be required. Many companies adopting COQ tenets move from a position of weakness and many failures to one that is less than ideal but that approaches the ideal. The outcome of COQ management is to reduce the overall money spent on quality and to greatly reduce the amount of money spent on failure remediation, thus making cost of quality a desirable outcome to most companies. The following are examples of each of these types of costs:

- failure prevention
  - ○ new product review
  - ○ planning
  - ○ training
  - ○ preventive maintenance
  - ○ quality improvement projects
- appraisal
  - ○ raw materials inspection
  - ○ in-process and final product inspection
  - ○ audit
  - ○ test and measurement
  - ○ calibration
- internal failure
  - ○ scrap
  - ○ rework
  - ○ downtime
  - ○ concessions
  - ○ overtime
  - ○ corrective actions
  - ○ retesting

- ○ reinspection
- • external failure
  - ○ customer dissatisfaction
  - ○ customer complaints
  - ○ customer returns
  - ○ loss of goodwill
  - ○ administrative cost of dealing with a failure[5]

The worst outcome from low product quality comes from costs incurred to recover lost reputation, make concessions to dissatisfied customers, or to repay customers for losses incurred from low product quality. Ideally, through prevention programs, quality can be raised to a level that reduces overall cost (the size of the ideal circle in Figure 6.3 is smaller to indicate lower costs) and where most costs are preventive.

There is no one method of appraisal for quality improvement. In general, quality experts perform the appraisals. The experts are usually engineers who are able to analyze manufacturing processes to automate metrics, analyze all aspects of machine-human interaction, and improve equipment functioning. Similarly, there is no one way to accomplish prevention. For highly complex (e.g., computer chip or nano-sized manufacturing) or numerous step processes (e.g., telecommunications equipment), statistical process control is used. Other preventions are

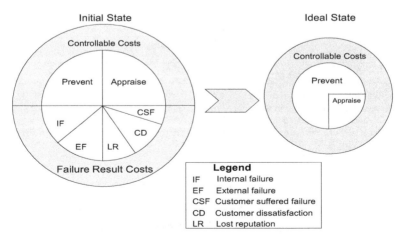

Figure 6.3. COQ initial and ideal states.

accomplished by perfecting every aspect of each step. These activities are more fully discussed in the next chapter.

Many companies do not believe that low quality reduces customer goodwill and that, in some captive markets, the impact may not be felt initially. But when alternatives become available, a dissatisfied customer will move to the alternative source. Open-source software, now a multibillion-dollar industry with thousands of products, was founded in response to shoddy quality of vendor software. The advantages and disadvantages of COQ analysis are listed in Figure 6.4.

Quality Function Deployment

Sometimes in process analysis, the lack of a current process or a high number of changes is such that complete rethinking of the process is warranted. *Quality function deployment* (QFD)[6] supports both design and redesign of processes. QFD is a technique for translating customer needs, requirements, and expectations into detailed product and process specifications. Therefore, while it can be used to analyze existing products, QFD is often applied to the analysis of new needs and requirements that determine the nature of a new product. QFD is very good for summarizing complex thought processes and competing analyses of a given situation. One disadvantage is that the data can be very complex to interpret because the diagram can actually present too much information. Another disadvantage is that many items require subjective judgments that can

Advantages	Disadvantages
Over time, overall cost of quality improvement management is less than the cost of failure management.	It usually requires engineering and quality training.
It can result in lower expenses, lower turnover, increase productivity, increase quality of service and product, and contribute to many other quality improvements.	It is time-consuming and expensive to implement.

Figure 6.4. Advantages and disadvantages of cost-of-quality management.

alter the outcome. By attending to the possible disadvantages, however, they can be managed.

QFD can provide the continuity of thought and process required to bring a product to market. Figure 6.5 shows how QFD can be used from defining a product concept through defining production documentation with the output of each step becoming the input to the next step. QFD, then, can be used for any part of a product development process, with its input either from a previous QFD analysis or from an existing product or process.

Thus QFD is a tool for translating customer needs, requirements, and expectations into detailed product and process specifications. Some uses for QFD are the following:

- customer requirements
- product concept
- product and process design
- idealizing process and product redevelopment
- prioritization of change process requirements

First, we discuss the mechanics of developing a QFD analysis, and then we discuss the process of developing the QFD. QFD builds a

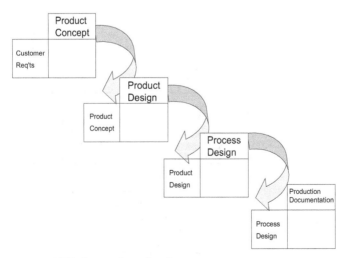

Figure 6.5. QFD for product development.

"house of quality" matrix (see Figure 6.6), with project goals ("what") in rows, means to reach the goals ("how") in columns, and the priority or quantity of each ("how much") in each cell. Each of these items—goals, means, and priority or quantity—are entered on a matrix such as the one shown in Figure 6.6. As appropriate, a goal may have multiple competing means. For instance, if you were analyzing alternative houses to purchase, the needs might be monthly payment, down-payment percentage, points, mortgage rate, duration, rate duration, maximum rate, and so on. The alternative means might be types of mortgages you have been offered, such as fixed 30-year, adjustable-rate 15-year, family loan with 15-year fixed rate, and so on. The cells would contain the specifics of each mortgage.

The next set of information completes the "house," as shown by the shaded areas in Figure 6.7. First, each need is prioritized or weighted in the "importance" section. Priorities can be a simple sequential ranking from 1 to *n*, where *n* is the number of needs, a portion of 100%, some percentage that need not add to 100%, or an integer that has meaning within the organization. In any case, the method of assigning importance should be defined and provided in any reports so that the reading audience understands its rationale. In general, since rankings are subjective, simple is better because it is more defensible and understandable.

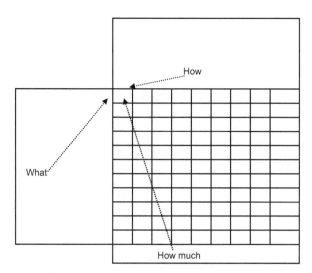

Figure 6.6. QFD basic relational matrix.

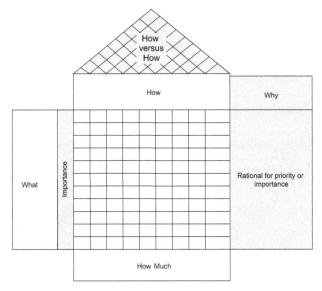

Figure 6.7. QFD house of quality.

Priority assignment is subjective, so it is important that the criteria be clearly defined for each need and entered on the right side of the QFD matrix. Criteria examples include cost of materials, process complexity, environmental impact, customer preference, and so on.

Next, the methods of implementing the requirements being analyzed (the "how") are listed across the top. Then, a simple visual method that includes the symbols suggested in Figure 6.8 is used to identify the relationships of methods to requirements in each need-mean cell. Notice that the number assignments for relationship strengths in Figure 6.8 are significantly different. This is to ensure that strong relationships are accorded the importance they should have. Not all symbols are used in all analyses. For instance, not every analysis will have negative relationships.

Above the means ("how") and below the "roof" is an area that shows the type of measure, or amount of the means, that is desired. The three possibilities are absolute—that a specific amount of the item is needed, or minimized; that the least possible amount is desired, or maximized; or that the maximum possible amount of the means is needed. These possibilities are identified by arrows or a circle, as shown in Figure 6.9. These entries provide information in the QFD but are useful later when the metrics for determining process success are developed. Absolute measures

Symbol	Relationship	Relationship Strength
⭕	Strong	9
◯	Positive	3
△	Weak Positive	1
✕	Negative	–3
✖	Strong Negative	–9

Figure 6.8. Relationship symbols.

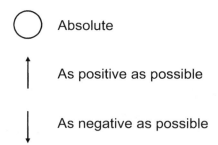

◯	Absolute
↑	As positive as possible
↓	As negative as possible

Figure 6.9. Measurement symbols.

require count-type metrics, where minimal or maximal type measures require continuous metrics. These are discussed more fully in chapter 10.

The cells of the triangular "roof" of the house compare means of meeting needs. For instance, in the mortgage example, the roof analysis would compare the different mortgage types to identify which benefits could be combined to provide a "perfect" mortgage.

The symbols used in the roof seek to identify the impacts of the product. Impacts can be color coded and relate to more than one entity (e.g., one set might identify environmental impacts, while another set might identify capital-budget impacts). Symbols used for impact analysis can be the same as those used in the body of the QFD analysis; however, because they are often not sufficient, other commonly used symbols for the roof are shown in Figure 6.10.

Another area of the house of quality is the right side of the diagram, which seeks to answer "why" questions about the entries. This area also can be used for several types of information. Two common uses follow. First, in developing marketing plans or products, the right side can provide columns for benchmark information of this company versus its competition, industry average, or best practice. The use of benchmark data provides an instant check on the importance of each need. Second, the area is also used in product development QFDs to identify the rational for priority definition, with a rationale provided on each row's "need" entry. This is useful for deflecting any political discussion that might relate to how needs are prioritized.

The last area is the "basement" of the house, which seeks to answer questions of "how much" in terms of the means entries. This area may also contain several types of information, including raw materials costs or amounts, financial contribution or margin for a product feature, or other supply chain or financial information.

To begin developing the QFD "house of quality," the following steps should be taken:

1. Define the needs for the analysis down the left side. This is the "what" information being analyzed.
2. Develop the priority system, and rate each need.
3. Define the means, sometimes called quality characteristics, to reach the needs across the top. This is the "how" information in terms of how the needs will be accomplished. More than one means may be

✓ ✓ Strong positive impact

✓ Moderate positive impact

X Moderate negative impact

XX Strong negative impact

Figure 6.10. Technical impact symbols.

entered for each need so that analysis of costs and interrelationships between means can be conducted. Eventually, the best method for accomplishing each need is developed.

4. Define the ranking system for strength of relationships between the needs and the means (e.g., similar to Figure 6.8).

5. Compare each need or means pair, and enter the symbols for the relationship strength in the corresponding matrix cell. In performing this analysis, think of the means as the only method of meeting the need. If it were the only method, the strength is the extent to which it could fully achieve the need. If there is no relationship, the cell is left blank.

6. In a horizontal row above the means, enter the type measure to determine success for that means. There are three measures—absolute, as positive as possible, and as negative as possible. Figure 6.9 depicts the symbols used for these entries.

7. As appropriate, analyze the extent to which means are competing or cooperating for producing each good in the crosshatched "roof" area of the "house." The entries in the crosshatch cells represent relationships between different means of accomplishing all needs. Cooperative, positive relationships are defined as means that— as they are met—facilitate the use of another mean. Competing, negative relationships are identified when one means impedes the use of some other mean. For instance, in building a house, added BTUs to an air conditioner will increase the weight-bearing needs of the location in which it is placed. Technical impacts can use the same symbols as in Figure 6.8; however, some authors[7] recommend other symbols, such as those in Figure 6.10. In addition to using the symbols, there is the option of identifying the direction of impact—from the left means to the right or vice versa—by including an arrow above the symbol in the cell. If there is no relationship, the cell is left blank.

8. Compute the total numeric value for needs relating to means by summing across the row, and then multiplying the sum by the priority rating for each need in order to derive the weighted importance of each need.

9. Evaluate the roof impacts to develop the best set of means for accomplishing the needs with the fewest negative impacts.

10. To develop organizational impacts of the entire set of needs and means, a responsibility matrix can be developed to show each organizational role by means and who should have primary or supporting responsibilities and who should be informed. The same symbols used for the cell–means matrix can be used for this matrix.

Other analyses can be added to a QFD, but every addition decreases its understandability. Some analyses include, for instance, customer ratings of goals, compliance goals and their importance, raw materials needed to accomplish each means, competitive engineering assessment for raw materials conversion, or various measures of importance of means to a project and difficulty in implementing each means.

QFD Analysis

An example of a QFD analyzes alternative solutions for problems found in a call center. The company suffered from inconsistent processing by service representatives, errors in recording call outcomes, nonstandardized contracts, and contract information that was verbally transmitted to the dialer administrator responsible for setting the equipment to meet contractual agreements. As a result of these issues, the company's billings were decreasing. The "needs" in the QFD analysis in this case were recommendations to remedy these issues, with one goal of prioritizing recommended changes for implementation. The main purpose of the QFD was to develop recommendations about how to accomplish the needed changes. During the discussions, responsible parties for each change were also identified.

The first step was to list the needs, as shown in Figure 6.11. For each goal, a priority is defined. The prioritizing method used assignment of priorities such that the sum of all priorities equals 1.0. In the call center example, only two goals—accurate payment and accurate billing—were considered more important than the others. These two goals are assigned priorities of 0.2, while all other goals are assigned priorities of 0.1.

Discussion regarding which goals to list mainly focused on whether or not to include "increased customer satisfaction" as a goal. The three main call-center customers were solicited about what aspects of call-center capabilities they valued most. Their answers were very uniform and specifically

Direction of Improvement	
Customer Requirements/Solutions	Priority
Accurate Contract Information	0.1
Accurate Campaign Information	0.1
Accurate Collection Information	0.1
Accurate CSR Information	0.1
Accurate Payment Information	0.2
Accurate Termination Code Processing	0.1
Accurate Management Reporting	0.1
Accurate Billing	0.2

Figure 6.11. QFD goals.

addressed "meeting contractual agreements," "proving that contracts were met," and "providing accurate collection and billing information." As a result of the discussion and these customer requirements, the overall goal of increased customer satisfaction was omitted.

Discussion about goal priorities centered around which goals were most important. Accurate collection information was viewed as at least as important as accurate payment information. But the group decided that if accurate payment information was necessary, the related need for accurate collection information was also required. Therefore, the more important goal was accurate payment information. Similarly, accurate billing information was considered a higher priority because it was the true measure, available to clients, of the call center's compliance with contractual agreements. All other goals were viewed as relating this goal.

The next step was to develop the means for meeting the goals. To keep this analysis reasonable, not every method of meeting a goal was provided. The recommended changes include the following:

1. Standardize contracts.
2. Develop a quality review of contracts.
3. Standardize campaigns and campaign information.

4. Develop a quality review for campaigns.

5. Develop a form to convey campaign information (and make it available on an intranet).

6. E-mail contract and campaign information to customer service, IT, and the call center as they are completed.

7. Develop a dual-write capability to provide backup for the Davox dialer-resident collection database. This recommendation also included the discontinuation of the dual-write capability on a second IBM AS/400 computer system.

8. Create custom software to error-proof collection software and process.

9. Create custom software to error-proof customer service representative (CSR) logon.

10. Create custom software to error-proof dialer admin campaign handling.

11. Develop a capability to reconcile collections (called "sales") on the diagram daily.

12. Develop procedures to improve quality controls on billing information.

13. Standardize and create new management reports for the call center. To the extent allowed by contracts, discontinue customer reports for each customer unless paid for by the client.

It was decided that in-house development of all needed software would be recommended. Further, all goals would be analyzed and prioritized based on this assessment, with the highest priorities developed first but with all changes to be implemented eventually. The means are listed across the top of the QFD; then, an analysis of which means relate to which goals is conducted and entered into the cells. As Figure 6.12 shows, most of the means relate to providing accurate management reporting and billing. The most important single goal is providing accurate payment information.

To complete the QFD, several other analyses are conducted (see Figure 6.13). The relationships between means are analyzed in order to define which relationships should provide synergistic positive impacts when implemented. The direction of improvement was added under the "roof." At a minimum, absolute measures for contracts, campaigns, forms and e-mail, Davox double-writes, daily reconciliation, and standardized

Legend:

Symbol	Numeric Value
●	9.0
○	3.0
◁	1.0

Direction of Improvement	Standardize Contact	Contact Quality Review	Standardize Campaign	Campaign Quality Review	Form to Convey Campaign Information	E-mail Contact Announcement	Double-Write on Davox Collection Files	Error-Proof Collection Software and Process	Error-Proof CSR Logon	Error-Proof CSR Payment Process	Error-Proof Dialer Admin Campaign Handling	Daily Reconciliation of Sales	Improve QC on Billing	Standardize Management Reports	Total Numeric Value	Weighted Importance
Customers Requirements/Solutions		←		←				←	←	←	←		←			
Accurate Contact Information	●	●			◁									○	25	0
Accurate Campaign Information			●	●	○							○		○	51	0
Accurate Collection Information					●			●						○	21	0
Accurate CSR Information								○	●	●	●	●		○	30	0
Accurate Payment Information							●	●	◁	●	●			○	49	0
Accurate Termination Code Processing								●	◁	●	◁			○	16	0
Accurate Management Reporting	○	◁	○	◁	○	○	○	○			○	●	●	●	50	0
Accurate Billing	○	○	○	○	○	○	◁	○		○	○	●	●	○	46	0

Figure 6.12. Goals and means relationship assessment.

Legend:

Symbol	Numeric Value
◉	9.0
◯	3.0
△	1.0

Customers Requirements/ Solutions	Priority	Standardize Contract	Contract Quality Review	Standardize Campaigns	Campaign Quality Review	Form to Convey Campaign Information	E-mail Contract Announcement	Double-Write on Davox Collection Files	Error-Proof Collection Software and Process	Error-Proof CSR Logon	Error-Proof CSR Payment Process	Error-Proof Dialer Admin Campaign Handling	Daily Reconciliation of Sales	Improve QC on Billing	Standardize Management Reports	Total Numeric Value	Weighted Importance
Accurate Contact Information	0.1	◉	◉	◯	◯	△									◯	25	2.5
Accurate Campaign Information	0.1			◉	◉	◉	◯					◉	◉		◯	51	5.1
Accurate Collection Information	0.1				◉			◉							◯	21	2.1
Accurate CSR Information	0.2							◉	◉	◉					◯	30	3
Accurate Payment Information	0.1						◉	◉	△	◉	◉	◉			◯	49	9.8
Accurate Termination Code Processing	0.1									△	◉	△			◯	16	1.6
Accurate Management Reporting	0.1	◯	△	◯	△	◯		◯	◯		◯	◯	◉	◉	◉	50	5
Accurate Billing	0.2	◯	◯	◯	◯	◯		△	◯		◯	◯	◉	◉	◯	46	9.2

Figure 6.13. Completed QFD.

management reports all require "count" measures, while the others require measures that show the extent to which the item is present. All means need baseline measures against which improvements will be compared.

The numeric entries on the right side of the QFD show the total and weighted value of each goal in terms of impacts across the means. This measure supports development of priorities for implementation. With the highest rating of 9.8, providing accurate payment information is the highest priority goal. This goal has a strong positive relationship with the Davox dual-write, all error-proofing activities, and daily reconciliation recommendations. These tasks then become the highest priorities for development.

The final analysis in this section is development of the responsibilities matrix shown in Figure 6.14. This matrix shows organizational responsibility for the changes to be made to call-center support software and related organizational processes. The marketing organization is tasked with the standardization of contracts and campaigns. In assigning this responsibility, the executive committee charged the marketing group to assume no customizing except for the contracts of the largest customers.

One recommendation for the customizing of contracts might require approval of the chief operating officer. Further, it was recommended that the marketing, call center, and customer service departments be jointly charged with developing a form for campaign information that would be generally available for use within the company. Only terms of contracts tied to the call center or service support departments would be made public.

It was also recommended that the chief information officer (CIO) and IT organization take responsibility for all of the software changes, making decisions concerning whether the development was insourced or outsourced. Another recommendation was that responsibility for daily reconciliation and improved quality control for billing should move from the IT operations manager to the accounting department. Errors found because of missing records, for instance, would be referred to the CIO for tracking of bugs and software fixes. While this reduces the responsibility of the IT operations manager, it was also expected to increase the quality of information on which billings were produced and therefore should also increase the quality of information provided to clients.

Legend:

● Primary   ○ Support   △ Inform

Tasks/ Organization	CIO	Operations	Call Center	Customer Service	Marketing	Accounting	Finance	Executive	HR
Standardize contacts					●			●	
Develop contract QC procedure					●			○	
Standardize campaigns and campaign information		○	○	○	●			○	
Develop campaign QC procedure				○	●			△	
Develop campaign form			●	●	●			△	
Develop intranet	●	●	○			○		○	○
Develop procedure for e-mail contract and campaign information		○	○	●	○			△	
Set up e-mail for all employees	●	○	△	△	△	△	△	△	△
Develop Davox dual-write capability	●	○	△					△	
Create software to error-proof collections	●	○	○					△	
Create software to error-proof CSR logon	●	○	○					△	
Create software to error-proof campaign handling	●	○	○					△	
Develop daily reconcilliation capability	△		●	△		●	○	○	
Develop QC for billing information	△		△			●	○	△	
Standardize new management reports	●	○	●	○	○	△		○	

Figure 6.14. Responsibility matrix.

Advantages and Disadvantages of QFD

QFD is a complex but value-adding analysis for evaluating competing alternatives. The QFD advantages and disadvantages are listed in Figure 6.15.

Summary

Value-added analysis is a method of documenting the steps of a process and defining the type of activity it is: customer-facing, support, administrative, or other. All "other" steps are further analyzed to determine whether needed, and the steps are eliminated when feasible. Similarly, support and administrative steps are analyzed to ensure they are as efficient as possible and required for this process. For non-value-adding steps that are still required, preferred outcomes include either removing the steps from having an impact on the process or automating the steps. Any activities that are not required are removed as a prelude to process redesign.

COQ analysis determines the difference between actual cost of a product or service and the cost of the product or service if there were no failures or defects. COQ seeks to move all or most costs of quality into prevention and appraisal and to remove all failure costs relating to

Advantages	Disadvantages
It can result in products that tie all features and functions directly to customer requirements.	It is time-consuming and expensive to implement
It can show benchmark, supply chain, financial, and trade-off information in a single place.	It requires practice and expertise to properly develop a QFD analysis.
It supports the thinking required to develop a complete summary or decisions relating to product concept definition, product design, process design, engineering design, and production documentation.	Information can be complex to interpret.
	Many subjective judgments are required during QFD that can alter the outcome.

Figure 6.15. Advantages and disadvantages of quality function deployment.

internal failures, such as scrap, rework, downtime, and so on, as well as external failures found by customers, such as complaints, returns, and dissatisfaction.

QFD is useful for requirements, concepts, designs, idealized processes, and many other analyses. By matching business goals to alternative prioritized means, an organization can develop an analysis of effects of means on each other. Outcomes include prioritized goal actions and means of meeting the goals, as well as raw materials, costs, and many other details. The use of symbols to depict relationships creates an easily digested presentation of the information. Symbols are also used to describe the effects of different means on each other and the direction of success for using a means. Another useful outcome of QFD analysis is responsibility matrices, which delineate tasks and responsibility assignments.

CHAPTER 7

Process Cleaning

Introduction

At this point, all current mapping is complete, and waste or non-value-adding steps have been removed from the process to the extent possible. In this chapter, cleaning techniques are applied to remaining process steps in order to improve their efficiency and effectiveness. Cleaning can be thought of as the difference between the Japanese and American views of process improvement. Americans say, "If it ain't broke, don't fix it." The Japanese say, "If it isn't perfect, perfect it." This chapter's techniques all relate to perfecting otherwise operational process steps.

To begin this discussion, we add two techniques critical in complex process control: statistical process control, which is discussed in terms of its use in surfacing areas for improvement, and root cause analysis, a technique used to determine all possible causes of an error or outage incident. We then turn to several simple "cleaning" techniques that improve the functioning of individual process steps.

Statistical Process Control

Statistical Process Control (SPC) is a collection of strategies, techniques, and actions taken by an organization to determine and remove sources of errors for optimal quality performance. SPC assumes that each attribute throughout the planning, procurement, and production processes contributes to the overall quality of the product or service, and therefore, each may be amenable to some type of SPC control.

The basic notions behind statistical process control are that automated process control is desired and that any process that is executed a sufficient number of times is amenable to SPC. SPC requires normally distributed errors that are due to *assignable variance* rather than random variance. SPC begins at the product-planning stage, when attributes of a product or service are specified, and continues with monitoring and control of production and quality assurance in order to manage the production process.

As product specifications are developed during planning and design, measurable attributes for SPC are defined. Then, as products move into production, the machines on which they are produced (or processes by which they are executed by humans) are programmed to take measures of the attributes throughout the process day. Diagrams of the measurement data are developed to show the changes in output quality over time. SPC charts are monitored to find variations in manufacturing that are outside tolerance limits. Once that happens, the machine (or human) exhibiting problems is recalibrated or otherwise maintained.

SPC is essential to total quality programs such as Six Sigma. While most often applied to manufacturing, SPC can be applied to knowledge work in engineering, software bugs, or problems in IT operations.

In this chapter, we are interested in using SPC charts to determine whether variations in a process are significant enough to continue analysis of the underlying process, machine, or measured entity.

To understand SPC charts, it is necessary to be familiar with five terms: population, sample, mean, variance, and standard deviation. A *population* consists of an entire collection of an item under consideration. A *sample* is a subset of a population used to estimate the population characteristics. Ordinarily, in SPC, samples are used because the population volume may be enormous, and if the sample is properly selected, then it will tell us the same information that the population would. A *mean* is the average of a measure for the group. The sample mean is computed using the formula shown in Figure 7.1. This formula indicates that all of the observations from each item in the sample are added, ΣX, and then divided by the number in the sample (n) to get x-bar, the sample mean or average.

The *variance* is the mean of the squared deviations from the mean. The formula for the variance, shown in Figure 7.2, assumes that the expected

$$\overline{X} = \frac{\Sigma X}{n}$$

Figure 7.1. Sample mean formula.

$$\text{var}(X) = E((X - \mu)^2)$$

Figure 7.2. Variance formula.

value of X, an observation, is known and described as E(x). And mu, μ, is equal to E(X). The formula says that the variance of an observation is equal to the difference between the observation and its expected value. So for a single observation, a measure of three is expected, but a measure of two is obtained—the variance of that measure is one ($1 = 3 - 2$).

The *standard deviation* is the positive square root of the variance and is designated by the Greek letter sigma σ (see Figure 7.3). The expected value of a measure, the population mean μ, can have X-bar, the sample mean, substituted for it. Therefore, conceptually, we compute σ as the square root of the sum of deviations from the mean squared and divided by n – 1.

Once we know the standard deviation of a sample, we can make some inferences about it depending on quality goals. Figure 7.4 shows the sigma levels and their corresponding error rates per million units. This table is adapted from the website http://www.isixsigma.com.

Now you have the basics of the statistics behind a control chart. Figure 7.5 shows a sample control chart for analysis. The components of a control chart are the centerline, upper and lower limits, and performance data. The *centerline* is the mean of all samples plotted and is shown on Figure 7.5 as the gray line at 10% on the Y-axis. The *upper and lower statistical control limits* define the acceptable limits of variation in the process involved. The limits are usually expressed in standard deviations and are

$$\text{Conceptual Formula} = s = \sqrt{\frac{\Sigma(X - \overline{X})^2}{n-1}}$$

$$\text{Computational Formula} = s = \sqrt{\frac{\Sigma X^2 - \frac{(\Sigma X)^2}{n}}{n-1}}$$

Figure 7.3. Formulas for standard deviation.

Σ level	Error rate (rounded)
1σ	690,000 per million units (69% error rate)
2σ	308,000 per million units (30.8%)
3σ	66,800 per million units (6.7%)
4σ	6,210 per million units (.62%)
5σ	230 per million units (.02%)
6σ	3.4 per million units (.00003%)

Figure 7.4. Six Sigma errors and error rates.

Source: Copyright © 2000–2006 iSixSigma LLC. All Rights Reserved. Reproduced with Permission of iSixSigma.com.

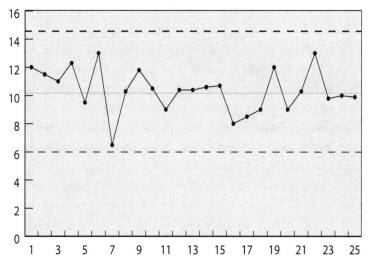

Figure 7.5. Example control chart.

shown in the figure as dotted lines. If an organization is embarking on a new SPC program, control limits typically are set at 3-sigma, allowing a 6.7% error rate.[2] *Performance data* are measures taken throughout the process and plotted as connected dots according to a schedule that shows the variation (Y axis) over time (X axis).

There are two types of control charts: variable control and attribute control. A *variable control chart* portrays arithmetic measures such as time, quantity, or cost, which are measured on a continuous scale and are highly accurate. An *attribute control chart* classifies characteristics that tend to have binary measures, such as acceptable versus unacceptable, brown versus red, or assembled correctly versus assembled incorrectly. The reported counts are of how many items exhibit the characteristic at a point in time.

SPC Process for Chart Analysis

SPC chart analysis uses the following process:

1. Collect all appropriate data and display it in the form of an SPC control chart.
2. Compute sigma levels and draw lines on the chart, as needed, to show them. In automated SPC, these first two steps should be completely automated.
3. Analyze the diagram for areas for further investigation and possible improvement (see discussion below).
4. Investigate each deviation. For any unexplainable variation, perform a root cause or other analysis to determine the variance cause.
5. Design changes to the process (or measures) to alleviate the source of variance.
6. Verify that the changed process has resolved the problem by starting again at step 1.

Notice that this is a continuous process. Now imagine a manufacturing facility with 800 machines, running 3 shifts, and creating at least 2,400 control charts per day. Clearly it is a very labor-intensive task to stay current with both analysis of the need for intervention and the review of ongoing production. In addition, facilities usually take different types of measures, so the facility mentioned previously might actually create as many at 10,000 charts for every day's activities. Thus the people reviewing SPC charts quickly become very expert at identifying needs and can review diagrams at a glance. Some chart analyses may also be automated.

SPC Analysis of Variance

Investigation of assignable variance should be taken any time a control chart contains one or more the following issues out of 100 points plotted:

- any points outside the ±3σ control limits
- 4 of 5 successive points ±1σ on the same side of the centerline
- 6 successive points that increase or decrease
- 8 successive points on the same side of the centerline
- 14 points on the same side of the centerline

The example control chart (Figure 7.6) is designed so the highest and lowest horizontal lines indicate 3σ, the dotted lines indicate 1σ, and the dashed lines indicate 2σ. The chart identifies two issues:

- One point is slightly above the +3σ line and therefore requires investigation. To the extent that the variation is not explainable, it would undergo root-cause analysis or some other problem evaluation and remediation step.
- Both the positive and negatives sides of the centerline have more than 14 points on the side of the line. These variations need investigation and may indicate different settings by different operators, operator variation, issues with environmental controls, or similar problems.

SPC is not only used in many types of manufacturing but also in less obvious ways such as determining optimal engine performance for racing

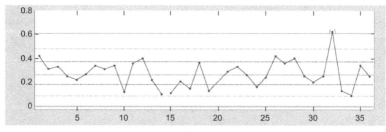

Figure 7.6. Control chart limits example.

cars, interest rate fluctuations relative to stock market fluctuations, occurrence of errors in software, and many other applications.

False errors are an issue in statistics. The two types of false error are Type I and Type II. *Type I* errors are false positives that show an error where none exists. Incorrectly following Type I errors leads to a waste of time and money used to fix problems that do not exist.

Type II errors are false negatives that show no error where one actually does exist. Type II errors can occur when the wrong characteristic is measured or when the equipment doing the measurements is not calibrated properly or not sensitive enough to detect the condition. Incorrectly following Type II errors—by measuring an area where no error exists—also wastes money.

There is no way to determine either type of error just by looking at a control chart. Rather, someone would actually monitor the machine or process creating the measures and make sure that readings are accurately taken and that the errors do in fact exist.

The reason that 3-sigma control limits balance the risk of error is that, for normally distributed data, data points will fall inside 3-sigma limits 99.7% of the time when a process is in control. This makes Type I error witch hunts infrequent while still ensuring that unusual causes of variation are likely to be detected.

Forms of SPC can be used in nonmanufacturing situations. For instance, help-desk problem reports might be used to determine application deployment quality, as shown in Figure 7.7. The company tracked

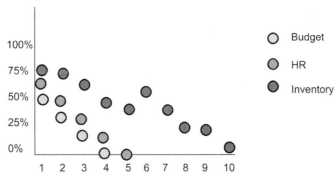

Figure 7.7. Implementation error control chart.

enterprise resource planning process and software implementations, which occurred monthly in each of 37 locations over an 18-month period. The diagram shows a 10-week period. Tracking involved evaluating each implementation's counts of help-desk support calls. For this company, a 20% drop in calls per week, until the percentage of calls approached zero, was considered "normal" behavior. Knowing normal patterns of problem incidence is required when interpreting the diagram.

Figure 7.7 tracks error reports for three modules over a 10-week period. The inventory module did not show the same drop in incidents reported as other implementations. Further, the increase in calls in the inventory module at week 6 was a cause for concern. The inventory module clearly violated the 20%-per-week drop expectation and was therefore deemed an issue for follow-up.

Advantages and Disadvantages of SPC Control Charts

SPC control charts are useful summaries of processing over time when voluminous data are collected. The advantages and disadvantages of control charts (not SPC in general, which is covered later in the book) are listed in Figure 7.8.

Root-Cause Analysis

Taking as input incidents identified through SPC control chart, matrix, Pareto, cause and effect, or some other analysis method, an organization then seeks to determine the underlying cause of an incident in order to

Advantages	Disadvantages
They summarize complex information in such a way to show variation and patterns in variation.	They are expensive to develop.
They simplify error finding.	Poor measures result in poor control charts.
Problem finding and diagnosis are based on fact.	

Figure 7.8. Advantages and disadvantages of SPC control charts.

take remedial action to ultimately prevent its recurrence. *Root-cause analysis (RCA)* is used to find the most fundamental reason(s) a problem or incident has occurred such that performance does not meet expectations. The goal of RCA is to answer the following questions:

- What happened?
- Why did it happen?
- How did it happen?
- How do you prevent it from happening again?

RCA can be used during process redesign to ensure that all aspects of lean process steps are free of error-producing defects. RCA is especially effective for services analysis.

"Root" cause means to find the *true* or most fundamental cause(s) of "events" or "mishaps." The process is used to identify the true cause and the ways to prevent its recurrence. This technique also called a "why-why chart" or the "five whys." Usually, five levels are sufficient for uncovering the root cause, but any number of levels might be evaluated in dealing with a complex problem. Frequently, team research into potential causes requires them to become expert in areas beyond their immediate responsibilities.

A team doing RCA should be interdisciplinary and involve subject matter experts (SMEs) who are part of the process under review, as well as those involved in resolving the incident(s) from which the problem arose. A detailed RCA is developed for a call-center example.

Call Center RCA

First, RCA was used to evaluate check-processing inconsistencies in a call center. That analysis is presented next. When there are compound answers to a question, each of the answers is analyzed in sequence. The analysis may look repetitive because, often, the problems have the same causes; however, each question analyzed is unique and traced to its source. Root causes are shaded. To assist in readability, compound answers are repeated, with the area being analyzed italicized. The entire analysis is approximately 10 single-spaced pages.

Background to the Problem

The call center has 140 mostly part-time customer service representatives (CSRs). A process improvement initiative found that check processing led to a series of different problems. Some of the problems included inconsistent representative processes, wrong termination codes, suspected software errors in some check recording, supervisors who did not supervise, and training that was not always completed or consistent. Most of the errors are revealed in the following analysis, and many of them share common causes.

RCA

Q. Why is check processing (CP) problematic?
A. Because agents do it differently.
  Q. Why do agents do CP differently?
  A. *Supervisor issues*, turnover, and lack of training.
    Q. Why is supervision an issue?
    A. Not enough agent observation and feedback, little direction, and no training.
    Q. Why is there insufficient agent observation?
    A. Equipment lacking, supervisor training, and no time.
      Q. Why is *equipment lacking*?
      A. *Not enough equipment to go around*; software does not cover all environments; and observation only allows audio surveillance not visual, that is, what is done on screens.
        Q. Why is there *not enough equipment* to go around?
        A. The headsets and software are expensive; call center pays for 5 seats but has 3 quality assurance (QA) people and 8 supervisors, so there are 11 people who need the 5 seats of software. Everyone has his or her own headset.
      Refer to call center manager and COO.
      A. Not enough equipment to go around; *software does not cover all environments*; and observation only allows audio surveillance not visual, that is, what is done on screens.
        Q. Why does *software not cover all environments*?

A.   There is no software to monitor all of the environments the CSRs interact with—Davox, Lyricall, AS/400, scripts, and sometimes PCs.

Q.   Why is there no software to monitor all environments?

A.   There is no evaluation software to monitors all environments; there is software that allows monitoring of screens.

Q.   Why has no one evaluated software that allows monitoring of all screen activity?

A.   They have. Software to allow looking at screens as well as audio is over $10,000, and call center does not want to spend the money.

Q.   Why does call center not want to spend money for audio and video monitoring?

A.   They feel the return would not justify the expense.

Refer to call center manager and COO.

A.   Not enough equipment to go around; software does not cover all environments; and *observation only allows audio surveillance not visual, that is, what is done on screens.*

Q.   Why does *observation software only support audio?*

A.   Software to allow looking at screens as well as audio is over $10,000 and call center does not want to spend it.

Q.   Why does call center not want to spend money for audio and video?

A.   They feel the return would not justify the expense.

Refer to call center manager and COO.

A.   Equipment lacking, supervisor training, and no time.

Q.   Why is *supervisor training* an issue?

A.   *Not enough supervisor training*, no one to train, the supervisors usually learn from each other, not enough time, and no follow-up on on-the-job training (OJT).

Q.   Why is *there not enough supervisor training?*

A.   Time pressure on the job; CSRs slack off if not monitored.

Refer to call center manager.

Q. Why is there *too much time pressure* on the job?

A. First-party clients have contractual commitments about % collection by # agents in Y time. Since collections have the highest priority, call center loses money on agents, time, or both if needed to comply with client contracts.

> Q. Why do clients have these assurances?
>
> A. According to marketing, "That's the way contracts have always been done."
>
> Refer to marketing, call center manager, and COO.

A. Time pressure on the job; CSRs slack off if not monitored.

> Q. Why do *CSRs slack off* if not monitored?
>
> A. According to supervisors, monitoring motivates people to work. According to the process improvement team, in over 30 hours of observation, with and without supervisors around, CSRs did not slack off.
>
> Refer to call center manager.

A. Not enough supervisor training, *no one to train*, the supervisors usually learn from each other, not enough time, and no follow up on OJT.

> Q. Why is *there no one to train supervisors*?
>
> A. The trainer has never been a supervisor and does not know enough about the job to develop and deliver training; supervisors do not trust the trainer.
>
> Q. Why is the trainer not trained?
>
> A. She does not know supervisor jobs.
>
> Refer to call center manager.
>
> Q. Why do supervisors not trust the trainer?
>
> A. Supervisors perceive the trainer as a gossip and "spy for management."
>
> Refer to call center manager.

A. Not enough supervisor training, no one to train, *the supervisors usually learn from each other*, not enough time, and no follow up on OJT.

Q.   Why is *a supervisor learning from other supervisors a problem?*

A.   Some supervisors refuse to help people they do not like or do not think should be supervisors and no one tells them to stop this behavior.

   Q.   Why are supervisors allowed to choose whom they will help?

   A.   It seems to have fallen through the cracks relating to high manager turnover in the call center.

Refer to call center manager.

A.   Not enough supervisor training, no one to train, the supervisors usually learn from each other, *not enough time,* and no follow up on OJT.

Q.   Why is there *not enough time to train supervisors?*

A.   First-party clients have contractual commitments about % collection by # agents in Y time. Since collections has a higher priority, call center loses money on agents, time, or both if needed to comply with client contracts.

   Q.   Why do clients have these assurances?

   A.   According to marketing, "That's the way contracts have always been done."

Refer to marketing and COO.

A.   Not enough supervisor training, no one to train, the supervisors usually learn from each other, not enough time, and *no follow up on OJT.*

Q.   Why is there *no follow-up on supervisor OJT training?*

A.   Management turnover in the call center and poor follow-up.

   Q.   Why is management turnover so high?

   A.   One call center manager falsified his resume and was fired; one call center manager stole equipment and was fired; and call-center manager is the third call center manager in 6 months.

Refer to call center manager and COO.

Q.   Why is management follow-up so poor?

    A.   It seems to have fallen through the cracks relating to high manager turnover in the call center.

Refer to call center manager.

A.   Equipment lacking, supervisor training, and no time.

    Q.   Why is *supervisor not having enough time* an issue?

    A.   First-party clients have contractual commitments about % collection by # agents in Y time. Since collection activity is the highest priority, call center loses money on agents, time, or both if needed to comply with client contracts.

    Q.   Why do clients have these assurances?

    A.   According to marketing, "That's the way contracts have always been done."

Refer to marketing and COO.

    A.   Supervisor issues, *turnover*, and lack of training.

    Q.   Why is *turnover* an issue?

    A.   Turnover is currently running at about 180% per year and the churn causes supervisors to spend time helping people get started rather than longer term people to improve or follow the standards.

    Q.   Why is there *180% turnover per year*?

    A.   HR policy is to hire 90% part-time employees with an average age of 18 years. This demographic has a high turnover rate. Call center's turnover is double that of other call centers in the same metro area.

Refer to call center manager and HR.

    A.   HR policy is to hire 90% part-time employees with an average age of 18 years. This demographic has a high turnover rate. Call center's turnover is double that of other call centers in the same metro area.

    Q.   Why is Call Center's *turnover so high*?

    A.   *Firing for petty offenses is used to keep people motivated,* call center is not perceived as having good salaries, and having many managers has led to many policy changes in the call center. Turnover doubled in the last year.

    Q.   Why is *firing used as a motivator*?

    A.   It is management policy.

Refer to call center manager and HR.

A.   Firing for petty offences is used to keep people motivated, *call center is not perceived as having good salaries*, and having many managers has led to many policy changes in the call center. Turnover doubled in the last year.

Q.   Why is *call center not perceived as having good salaries*?

A.   Poor internal communications and recent changes to the commission structure.

Q.   Why are internal communications poor?

A.   Call center base salaries are the highest in the metro area. The commission structure is comparable to the competition. Changes were made without any discussion or public announcement. CSRs found out about the changes via memos.

Refer to call center manager and COO.

Q.   Why did the *commission structure* change?

A.   Analysis of financial strength of the company led the COO to recommend changing the commission structure. The changes lead to similar payouts but require higher base collections to begin receiving bonuses.

Refer to call center manager and COO.

A.   Firing for petty offences is used to keep people motivated, call center is not perceived as having good salaries, *and having many managers has led to many policy changes in the call center*. Turnover doubled in the last year.

Q.   Why have there been *so many call center managers*?

A.   One call center manager falsified his resume and was fired; one call center manager stole equipment and was fired; and call center manager is the third call center manager in 6 months.

Refer to call center manager and COO.

A. Firing for petty offenses is used to keep people motivated, call center is not perceived as having good salaries, and having many managers has led to many policy changes in the call center. *Turnover doubled in the last year.*

Q. Why *has turnover doubled?*

A. Firing for petty offenses is used to keep people motivated, call center is not perceived as having good salaries, and having many managers has led to many policy changes in the call center. Turnover doubled in the last year.

Q. Why is *firing used as a motivator?*

A. It is management policy.

Refer to HR and call center manager.

A. Supervisor issues, turnover, and *lack of training.*

Q. Why is lack of training an issue?

A. CSR training sessions are inconsistent from one group to another; training sessions have technology problems and are sometimes cut short. Not everyone gets the same training (OJT and in class)

Q. Why are *CSR training sessions inconsistent?*

A. One individual who has never had teaching training does training, time and job pressure on the trainer, and technology problems during training.

Q. Why is the *trainer untrained?*

A. Previous to having a trainer, OJT was the only method of training. Call center promoted a CSR who wanted to do training for the position when they realized that people could not walk in off the street and start the job, since OJT was too inconsistent. The trainer took the job materials and successfully created training modules, so the call center manager had not given the trainer any other training.

Refer to call center manager.

A. Training sessions are inconsistent from one group to another; *training sessions have technology problems and sometimes are cut short.* Not everyone gets the same training (OJT and in class).

Q. Why are there *technology problems during training?*

A. Special test customer files need to be loaded on the Davox, related AS/400 customer records need to be "reset," and test logons and passwords need to be activated. These setups require coordination between the trainer and dialer administration for the Davox and the operations manager in IT. They are usually given 2 days notice, via e-mail sent from the trainer, for setups. Occasionally, one or more of the setups are not timely. The trainer does not test the setup until it is needed. If one or both of the required people are away from their desks when a problem is noticed, then the class is cut short.

Q. Why are dialer administrator and the operations manager not notified automatically when training is scheduled?

A. This would require HR involvement.

Refer to call center manager and HR.

Q. Why does the trainer not test the setup before the training?

A. No known reason.

Refer to call center manager and trainer.

A. Training sessions are inconsistent from one group to another; training sessions have technology problems and sometimes are cut short. *Not everyone gets the same training (OJT and in class).*

Q. Why are *training sessions inconsistent?*

A. Training is usually 1 full day in the classroom and one full day of OJT, listening to a CSR for half of the day and talking with the CSR, and listening and offering suggestions for improvements. When a new account opens or turnover has been particularly high, there is pressure to get new CSRs "on the phones," collecting or selling. Therefore, the class-room training becomes half a day (or less if there are technical problems), and the OJT is half a day. Agents trained in half the time are not as familiar with termination and error codes or with payment processing, resulting in inconsistent performance.

Q.   Who authorizes the 1-day training?

A.   This is not clear. It appears that HR and a previous call center manager initiated this practice. Then, as call center managers turned over, whenever the conditions recurred, the trainer continued the practice on his or her own.

Refer to call center manager.

Root-Cause Issue Summary

Once RCA is complete, a summary of issues is created and presented to the people charged with remedying the situation. In some cases, that may be the RCA group, but for the call center, that means giving issues back to the various managers, as identified previously. The root causes are summarized as follows for each person or department:

Call Center Manager

- CSRs are thought to require supervision, which leads to no or inadequate training for supervisors.
- The trainer is not trained and does not know supervisor jobs, so she is not qualified to train them.
- Supervisor OJT is selective, with some supervisors refusing to help others.
- Supervisors perceive the trainer as a "gossip" and "spy for management."
- There has been no follow-up on (lack of) supervisor training.

Trainer

- The trainer has never been formally trained on how to create or deliver training.
- The trainer does not test training setup before sessions begin.
- A practice to cut training to ensure contract performance was initiated by a prior manager. The trainer has continued this practice automatically whenever there is a new client.

Call Center Manager and COO

- Software for monitoring CSR calls is not adequate. Call center pays for 5 seats but has 11 people who need to use the software.
- Audio-video monitoring costs $10,000.
- Failures in communicating to CSRs about commission restructuring are causing perceptions of call center having poor salaries.
- The need for higher base collections to receive bonuses is causing perceptions of call center having poor salaries.
- Management turnover in the call center is partially responsible for lack of poor supervisor training.

Call Center Manager and HR

- High turnover may partly relate to use of firing as a motivator.
- Automatic notice to dialer admin and operations manager when training is scheduled may cut down on technical problems with training.
- High turnover may partly relate to policy on hiring part-time young people.

Call Center Manager, Marketing, and COO

- Supervisors are not trained because of collections pressures relating to contracts.

Call Center Manager

- Testing for training setups should be conducted the day prior to training to allow for any missing setup or technology fixes to be completed.

Two analyses are conducted for the call center: a change analysis using analytical hierarchic process (discussed later) and a cleaning analysis using the techniques discussed in this section.

RCA Process

There are two types of RCA: one that relates to a specific incident or problem and one that relates to perfecting of a process or process step. Both types follow the same basic processes:

1. RCA is initiated when the need for analysis is recognized through some means (e.g., as a result of quality function deployment analysis [QFD], cause and effect, critical incident, etc.).
2. The problem background is described as fully as possible, including internal and external environments, as needed. Sometimes, the need for external environmental analysis is not obvious and is added later in the process as internal causes are eliminated or as questions extend beyond the organization's boundaries.
3. The fundamental question to be resolved is described as specifically as possible. The question usually takes the form of "Why did [this event] occur?"
4. All possible answers to the question are developed. Multipart answers are common and indicate *paths of investigation.*

    At each level of analysis, attention is drawn to all possible contributing factors, including the following, taken from the "5 Whys Methodology":[3]

    a. Technology, industrial infrastructure, engineering constraints
    b. Skills, training, experience, human capital, psychological factors
    c. Constitutional framework, legal institutions, markets, property rights
    d. Tradition, heritage, myths, culture, anthropological issues

    e. Natural resources, environment, climate issues, disasters

    f. Discipline, commitment, leadership, will, spiritual issues

    Examine each path of investigation in order to reframe it as a question to ask at the next level of "why." Use words that clearly tie the question to a path of investigation.

5. Answer each question in turn with as complete an answer as possible. Repeat steps 4 and 5 until root causes are revealed. The cycle continues until the answers become circular in that the cause is the question is the cause (e.g., when the root cause is managerial neglect or policy or when the answer no longer results in divisible questions as to its cause). Figure 7.9, a simple sequence of questions and answers, shows the nature of questions and paths of investigation that turn into questions.

6. Once all possible causes have been identified for all issues, the next step of analysis is performed to determine why and how each root cause was allowed to occur and what its contribution to the problem is.

The result of this analysis is usually recommendations to management for changes in policy, procedure, process, or work instructions. Each change should include metrics to prove that the problem no longer occurs or to identify it if it should recur.

In specific problem remediation, only those potential causes that actually contributed, and their related contributing factors, continue to the next step of questioning and evaluation.

Question	Paths of investigation (answer)
Why did A happen?	B
Why did B happen?	C
Why did C happen?	D
Why did D happen?	E
Why did E happen?	Root cause error to be fixed

Figure 7.9. Sample root cause questions.

RCA Common Errors

The two most common errors in RCA are the assumption that 5 questions are sufficient and the assumption that 5 causes should be found. Both of these assumptions are incorrect. Further, there is no *right* number of questions for an RCA, nor is there a *right* number of levels of questioning. Rather, RCA continues until there are no more details of causes possible (i.e., the root causes are found). In actuality, an RCA of any complexity can result in hundreds of questions. Similarly, there is no one *right* number of root causes. For analysis of a specific incident, one cause may be found, but more often, there are many contributing factors.

Advantages and Disadvantages of RCA

RCA is a powerful technique that can identify unanticipated needs for improvement and find the absolute cause(s)—rather than only symptoms—of a specific problem. The advantages and disadvantages of RCA are summarized in Figure 7.10.

Process Cleaning

To *optimize* means "to make as perfect or effective as possible" or, in computing, "to increase the computing speed and efficiency of (a program)."[4] By optimizing, we adjust a process to obtain a cost-effective and efficient

Advantages	Disadvantages
It separates real causes of problems from symptoms.	It is time-consuming.
It is inexpensive.	It may require special training for participants.
Problem finding and diagnosis are based on fact,	It may identify areas of problems that an organization does not want to confront.
It can identify potential solutions to problems.	Participant bias may prevent real causes from surfacing.
	Skills learned from one analysis may not apply to other problem areas.

Figure 7.10. Advantages and disadvantages of root-cause analysis.

design. In performing the optimizing techniques, the process components evaluated include the equipment and controls used in the conduct of the process. At this point, since we have removed unneeded non-value-added and non-value-added, unessential steps from the process, we can now concentrate on the remaining required process steps. However, we still may remove or replace process steps through some of the techniques.

Optimizing does not mean exhaustive evaluation of all possible alternatives to find a *perfect* solution for a problem. Humans make decisions within a bounded rationality for which the bounds might include time, cost, practicality, operability, and so on. What we seek in optimizing is a balance between *satisficing*—a term coined by Herbert Simon to define the acceptance of an answer that satisfies the need without evaluating many alternatives—and perfection, avoiding analysis paralysis that leads to a search for a utopian perfection that is unlikely to be found within the constraints of budget, time, and human resource commitments in most business settings. The goal, then, is to find 3 to 5 alternatives that can each provide the basic needs of a solution. From this, evaluation and selection are feasible within project constraints. This need to balance between any solution and the perfect solution applies to all seek-and-search behaviors, including decisions relating to, for instance, outsourcing, negotiations, benchmarking criteria, benchmarking partners, and so on.

This section describes techniques for perfecting all aspects of processes and process steps. All of the techniques can be viewed as "cleaning" single process steps.

Streamlining

Streamlining originally described the process of shaping a body to minimize resistance when traveling through air or water. *Streamlining*, as applied to processes, means to eliminate waste and increase efficiency. The process of streamlining includes review of process steps and removal of unnecessary administrative tasks, approvals, and paperwork.

Since value-added analysis does not remove all NVA tasks, the streamlining review seeks to further evaluate the necessity of retaining administrative tasks and the form in which they are conducted. The goal is to remove approvals, or to move approval down in an organizational hierarchy, in order to speed a process or to remove, reduce, or simplify paperwork, forms completion, data-entry needs, manually generated reports, and so on. The other goal is to recommend automation or reautomation of some tasks.

To perform streamlining, evaluate each aspect of how a process, or process step, is conducted against alternatives to do the same function but better, faster, or cheaper. If an alternative is found, then note this possible change and continue the cleaning activities.

This idea is not new and can have radical monetary results. A New York–based insurance company decided to stop producing 30,000 pages of computer-generated accounting reports every month. Their motivation was partly frustration and partly cost cutting. The company was frustrated because they generated a small room full of paper reports every month. People needing the data first received authorization (if not already authorized) and then visited the room to choose the reports they needed. Most people needed only a subset of data in any one report, so people tore out the parts of reports they needed. This process was repeated in several remote locations of the organization. The result was that about half of the paper was scrapped every month. And they still had complaints from all over the organization that people who needed various accounting information did not have access and therefore could not easily do their jobs. Further, once authorized, there was no way of policing the taking of data by employees who were not authorized to enter the report room.

The company installed a query application that allowed everyone needing access to get their own information online, printing only what they needed. Within 4 months of the application's implementation, the authorized-user population increased from 800 to over 4,000, with improved control over access. This streamlining-with-automation solution increased the company's efficiency, saved them money, and improved morale, all with one change.

Not all streamlining will have such dramatic results, nor does all streamlining imply automation as the solution. Nevertheless, using creative methods to remove waste, reduce paperwork, and streamline approvals can improve company functioning.

Eliminating Bureaucracy

The term *red tape* is a derisive term for excessive regulation or mindless attention to rules that accompany excessive, redundant paperwork and lack of action or decisions. Governments are particularly affected by the problems of bureaucracy in that laws are passed without regard to reporting or compliance burdens. For example, in February of 2007, the European Union (EU) announced a bureaucracy reduction initiative to remove "administrative burdens on businesses resulting from EU legislation."[5] This initiative improved European companies' profitability by 2 billion Euros the first year and saved the EU economy over 25 billion Euros.[6]

Bureaucracy is characterized by standardized procedures and rule following, division of responsibilities that are organized hierarchically, and impersonal relationships. Therefore, *bureaucracy elimination* removes inefficient or unnecessary administrative steps, work products, and organizational hierarchy.

Bureaucracy elimination is applied to non-value-adding administrative steps in processes. The evaluation is to reduce paperwork, to eliminate steps that only serve the service delivery organization, and to make efficient such tasks as waiting in line.

The process is to evaluate all forms, web-page templates, and so on for elimination, consolidation, or other forms of activity. For instance, many jobs require access to multiple applications with similar information requirements. All of the applications may require data entry for the same information, thus duplicating the data entry function. Providing software that automatically copies information from one form to another decreases errors, time, staff aggravation, and money.

The first question to be asked is, if this process step were to disappear, who would suffer? If no one would notice, including the providing organization, then removing the process step completely should be investigated. If the process is required, then different delivery methods, such as the Internet, should be evaluated for their ability to reduce consumer or customer time spent dealing with the process.

Automation is frequently one means for reducing bureaucracy. An example of bureaucracy elimination is the problem in developing countries where the populace overwhelms the government's ability to cope. In

India in the 1990s, some states still required payment of bills for water and electricity in person, requiring the payer to stand in line for as long as 6 hours. This clearly cut into personal productivity and was an onerous burden on the paying public.

One innovation provided for payment of electrical bills via a bank drop-box. This effort, while resisted by the local government, which no longer "controlled" the payment process, was very successful with the general public. Soon, banks and other organizations extended payments to Internet websites. This initiative was so successful that many cell phone, telephone, water, and insurance payments can now be made via the Internet. The government experienced less stealing by employees, a happier public that no longer stands in long lines, and more accurate accounting of payments. This example demonstrates that bureaucracy elimination or reduction can provide direct improvements both for the delivering organization and for the customers.

Eliminating Duplication

Duplication of duties in an organization frequently has its origin in the need to separate responsibilities in response to audit requirements. Just as in double-entry accounting, where each transaction has two entries—a debit and a credit—functions dealing with fiduciary responsibilities or finances of organizations frequently build in duplication of responsibilities as a way of minimizing the potential for stealing or false dealings. As automation has taken over the actions of humans, the separation of duties has moved to other areas of responsibility (e.g., the person doing programming code changes must be different from the person testing them and the person approving them). As duties in new areas arise, however, organizations frequently forget to dismantle duplications based on the old methods of work.

Duplication elimination, then, is the process of evaluating the organization, its compliance, fiduciary, and security responsibilities, and, to the extent possible, removing all duplicated work from an organization. The removal of duplicate work frequently results in the design and implementation of controls that still monitor the work in question but remove or reduce human involvement with the process.

The Harley-Davidson Motor Company evolved its systems over a period of time with a focus on product improvement and sales rather than organizational efficiency. Many applications had few controls, so the organization maintained such responsibilities as duplication of accounting entry responsibilities within the accounting organization.

In response to compliance requirements of the Sarbanes-Oxley Act of 2002, Harley-Davidson instituted an internal compliance office that sought both better application controls and reduced human effort in the bargain. By eliminating duplication of duties by humans and adding controls to applications to flag issues for human resolution, the company was able to meet its compliance requirements and improve its organizational functioning as well.

The process is to evaluate every role on a process map that uses or accesses the same information as another role. First, determine that the actions taken are required. If they are not, then eliminate the unneeded actions. Then, determine that the actions require different skill sets or are required to be separate for compliance reasons. If not, then consolidate the tasks into a single role.

Finally, evaluate the extent to which each task is automated. If not automated or not extensively automated, then evaluate the potential to replace the process through automation. If, for instance, two roles are required for compliance, then automation of the compliance approval process can facilitate and speed the e-signature process and track the tasks to ensure that they are completed.

Simplifying

Simplification relies on the concept that if the final product is not dependent on some process step then the process step is not needed and should be eliminated. Simplification evaluates non-value-adding tasks from a different perspective—that of the final product rather than that of the customer.

An example of simplification is evaluation of a management in-process report produced as a result of a particular error, resulting in reworks. The process was automated 4 years ago, and the report incorporated, even though the automated production system does not produce the specific error any more. The report and all related work should be removed from the process.

Simplification requires analysis of interprocess-step relationships between users, contents of reports, and process step conduct in order to asses how the step can be more easily completed and whether the data, report, screen, form, or other item is *really* used and optimized for its purpose. Any time the answer is no, simplify the entity's design.

Reducing Cycle Time

Cycle time measures the time from initiation of a process to its end. In 2006, *Business Week* asked the question, "Is Your Company Fast Enough?" raising notions of cycle time and agility to change as key indicators of business success. With the bywords being "better, faster, cheaper, and more," companies seek to remain competitive by compressing their process cycle times to meet or exceed those of their competition. In manufacturing, one key process is the product development cycle that is called "time to market" cycle time.

Time-to-market cycle time begins when resources are assigned to assess a product's feasibility and ends when the first production unit is delivered. New cars go from concept to showroom in about 24 months in the United States, while in Japan, Nissan Motor Co., Ltd.'s development cycle has been cut to 10.5 months. With that kind of competitive edge, Nissan has lower development costs to recoup and has a significant lead over its competition. Reductions might come from incorporating computer-aided design (CAD) tools that automate both design and much design testing. In addition, CAD allows a 24-hour workday with global collaboration to work-share around the globe, thus cutting design times by as much as one third. Often, cycle time reductions, such as those of Nissan's design cycle, are partially due to the use of standardized materials. For instance, the steering wheels, tires, nuts, bolts, screws, seats, electronics, window wipers, door handles, and so on might all be reusable, thus a new model requires less engineering.

Cycle-time reductions concentrate on both removing unneeded steps and reducing the time each step and each necessary delay takes. Manufacturing is not the only cycle time on which companies focus. The *quote-to-cash* cycle for sales fulfillment is also crucial to most businesses. Similarly, in service businesses, service delivery processes such as application design, program coding, and process improvement are subjected to life-cycle methods oriented toward managing time while ensuring product quality.

There are many key components of successful cycle-time improvement. First, an intimate understanding of every step in the current process is required to ensure that no crucial, but little understood, activities are omitted. Second, measures in the form of both baseline benchmarks and competitive benchmarks should be used to determine targets for improvement, with definition of the durations of improvement. Finally, measures of each human touch point in a process should be taken to provide for daily process monitoring, with regular reporting to identify trends or problems for improvement. Efforts to reduce cycle times usually result in reducing both direct and indirect activities, establishing a link between manufacturing cycle time and manufacturing cost.

Federal Express (FedEx), an organization obsessed with improving its cycle times, has a 40-year history of innovation and cycle-time reduction with subsequent business improvement. FedEx launched the first regional automated call center in 1979, a digitally assisted dispatch system in 1980, a money-back guarantee on package delivery in 1982, the first PC-based shipping system in 1984 (IBM announced its first PC in 1983), the first bar-coded labeling system in 1985, the first bar-code scanner to capture package information along its route in 1986, Express-Clear to speed customer clearance in 1993, the first online package status tracking in 1994, and the first customer package shipment registration via the Internet in 1996.[7] In addition, FedEx was the first service company to win the Malcolm Baldrige National Quality Award in 1990, was the first in its industry to attain ISO 9001 certification globally, and was the company chosen to deliver 250,000 Harry Potter books on the day of its release to preorder customers.[8]

In addition to its innovations, during each process upgrade, FedEx seeks to reduce cycle times, with measurable results. Projects not meeting expectations are reviewed and reengineered until results are met.

Cycle-time reduction requires doing a value-added analysis on each step of a process. Some companies do time-motion studies to analyze how a task is accomplished and the time each movement takes. Similar to the leaning of whole processes, each movement is analyzed to identify specific aspects for improvement. For instance, call-center collections activity could decrease the average time for every phone call by 15 or more seconds simply by populating payment screens with payee data.

Upgrading

Upgrading is the improvement of a process or product through an increase in quality of some aspect of the process or product. Upgrades might be improvements within the process, training, technology, software, support, raw materials, materials handling, skills, and so on.

The following is a list of steps for conducting an upgrading assessment:

1. Assess all resources used in the delivery of the product or process.
2. Evaluate alternative methods, technology, materials, training, skills, and so on of preparing for, accomplishing, or following up on process steps.
3. Upgrade any steps that
   a. would result in cheaper or faster production;
   b. result in better quality output with fewer current resources at no more than the current cost;
   c. result in higher skilled staff, resulting in fewer reworks and better overall product or process quality;
   d. can avoid adding resources in the future.

Upgrading should be constant in some industries, particularly those with life-sustaining responsibilities, such as health care. In 1999, a disturbing study reported that between 2000 and 2002, 195,000 deaths in the United States were attributed to in-hospital human error,[9] causing the launch of an initiative to develop more "reliable organizations." One aspect of the initiative was to institute continuing education and constant upgrading of hospital staff skills to help them cope with increasingly complex equipment and medical delivery systems. In addition, upgrading of technology infrastructure to support in-hospital communications was recommended. The report recommended linking applications to strategic goals of the organization, including life preservation, to remind the organization of the importance of all support infrastructures.

Using Simple Language

Anyone who has read legal documents has evidence of complex, arcane language that confuses even the simplest of concepts. *Simple language* initiatives seek to use a reduced vocabulary to produce easily understood documents for children, students, nonnative speakers, or cognitively disabled audiences. While it is impossible to meet the target simplicity for every paragraph of every document, the results still produce simple language documents that most people, regardless of education, can understand.

Simple language tenets apply a reduced language set to produce documents that contain all required information and *nothing else*. To obtain simple language, every document used in, produced by, or describing a process or product is reviewed and rewritten to provide a clear, simple document structure that uses clear, simple language. When technical, complex, or uncommon language is required, a dictionary is created for the document to provide simple explanations of those terms. The result of simple language documents is more effective communication and more satisfied customers of the written product, whether they are internal or external to the organization.

Common errors in writing, listed in Figure 7.11, are from *A Plain English Handbook* by the Office of Investor Education and Assistance of the Securities Exchange Commission (SEC). In addition to avoiding these errors, the handbook recommends the preparation of documents that are visually appealing and logically organized. Visual appeal includes layout of text to enhance its readability, suggesting bulleted items where possible, and judicious use of "white space," as well as enhancing documents with color, font selection (provided it is easily read), and boxed, highlighted text.

An example of a complex sentence and the steps in the simplified version is presented in Figure 7.12.

The English used should avoid legalistic phrases, "boilerplates," unneeded repetition, and passive tense. Sentences should use a short, declarative, active voice complemented by tables and graphics but avoiding pie charts (as they are too misleading). Simple language is crucial in conveying meaning. The more complex the topic and the more diverse the audience, the more important simple language is.

Writing complexity causes
Long sentences
Passive voice
Weak verbs
Superfluous words
Legal jargon
Financial jargon
Numerous defined terms
Abstract words
Unnecessary detail
Unreadable design
Unreadable layout

Figure 7.11. Common errors to avoid in simple English.[10]

Before: *At this time, the machine should be recalibrated despite the fact that it may not appear to need recalibration.*	
1.	Strip out the legal sounding words to simplify the sentence.
Intermediate: *Now, the machine should be recalibrated though it may not appear to need it.*	
2.	Analyze the words to determine whether they convey meaning in the context of the sentence. "Now" is vague and not exact. Unless the preceding sentence gives the time, replace "now" with time. The fact that the machine may not appear to need recalibration is not needed if the rule is to recalibrate.
After 1: *The machine should be recalibrated every four hours.*	
3.	This sentence is simple, direct and clearly stated; however, the word "recalibrate" may be unknown by many people. Recalibrate means to "readjust" or "reset within tolerance limits," with recalibrate being the correct term. The sentence might be further improved by providing a contextual definition for recalibrated as follows:
After 2: *The machine should be recalibrated (reset within its tolerance limits) every four hours.*	
4.	The term "recalibrate" should be in a dictionary created to accompany the document.

Figure 7.12. Example of simple language changes.

Standardizing

When we talk about process improvement, we are talking about standardizing the work steps to conduct the process. *Standardization* defines a context to be maintained in one or more locations, including explicit definition of the relationships between resources, people, technology, and processes. Standardization of information technology (IT) and its related processes allows complete portability and virtual IT organization management. Data center standards for—for instance—hardware, operating systems (OS), OS management software, librarian software, configuration management software, help-desk support, processes for supplier relationships, licensing agreements, client contracts, and so on can provide built-in portability for disaster recoverability. Similarly, manufacturing companies that can duplicate standardized environments provide a global vocabulary for work processes and build in career growth opportunities through enhanced personnel portability at the least cost to the organization.

Standardization is everywhere and is being legislated with increasing regularity. The International Organization for Standardization (ISO) is charged with creating and promoting industrial and commercial standards. The International Electrotechnical Commission (IEC) and the Institute of Electrical and Electronics Engineers (IEEE) are organizations charged with creating and promoting technical and electronic standards. Other common standards organizations include the European Telecommunications Standards Institute (ETSI) and the American National Standards Institute (ANSI), both of which coordinate voluntary standards development, and the World Wide Web Consortium (W3C), which develops the standards for HyperText Markup Language (HTML), Cascading Style Sheets (CSS), Extensible Markup Language (XML), Web Ontology Language (OWL), and other languages used on the Internet. Plus, each country has its own standards organizations.

If the process under review is used in multiple locations, then standardization is more highly desirable because, in addition to recoverability, there is then one set of policies, one set of processes, one (or a limited set of) supporting technology, one vocabulary, and consistency of reporting that allows more efficient, simpler management decision making.

Standards are usually dictated from a centralized controlling organization (see Figure 7.13). The central organization sets policies relating to standards, working with the approval of an executive management committee. Typically, a steering committee develops the policies relating to the subject area. Then, some other group—for instance, a SME committee—develops standardized processes for discussion, review, and implementation throughout the organization. Each process then has standardized procedures for describing the process steps, metrics and reporting, and management structure. Finally, work practices allow for local definition of exceptions or additions to the procedures. This process infrastructure accommodates global thinking and local action while guaranteeing portability of process, vocabulary, and work. The more global the organization, the more standardization becomes a necessity in efficient management.

Standards should extend to inputs and outputs of the process. Clients who receive the process output (i.e., product or service), vendors and raw materials providers who provide process inputs, and internal suppliers should all operate under some sort of service level agreement (SLA) or operating level agreement (OLA). SLAs and OLAs are types of contracts describing the services or products to be provided, handoffs required, quality requirements, and actions and penalties for noncompliance.

By formalizing the handoffs between customers, vendors, and internal suppliers, there is less likelihood of error and more opportunity to

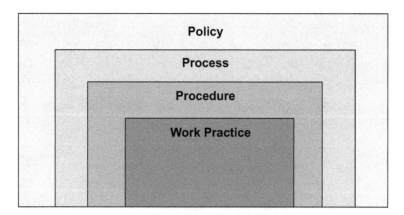

Figure 7.13. ISO/IEC 20000 structure for standards.

recognize opportunities for improvement. Further, the quality of products expected from every supplying organization is specified and measured, with nonperformance penalties and contractual default arrangements defined before they are needed. When a problem occurs, the parties simply invoke contractual agreements and act on them. This does not imply that nonperformance always ends a relationship; however, it does mean that any negotiation for a nonperforming partner has a starting point, with penalties that are generally not negotiable. This type of arrangement helps keep all parties honest.

The regular reporting of key process indicators (KPIs) is part of standardized processes and standardized relationship management. *KPIs* are summary statistics that report performance of some critical component of a business agreement. Typically, every control point has a measure, but the detailed measures are meaningless in the context of many contracts and require summarization for reporting. Client KPIs should provide the summary definition that relates to some aspect of strategy attainment for the client organization.

An example of this is a client of a data center who contracts for e-mail service to be provided 24 hours per day, 7 days a week. The individual components of providing e-mail include, at a minimum, hardware, e-mail software, OS, a local network, an Internet connection, security and privacy standards, procedures, software, and staff for monitoring and support. Each component will have one or more KPIs to measure its function. The customer is not interested in components though, but only in the availability of e-mail, which will have a KPI defined for e-mail service availability. Therefore, reporting within the providing IT organization for e-mail might include both component-level and summary-level measures, while reporting to the customer would only include the summary measures of e-mail service availability.

In summary, standardization is the written definition of relationships between people, procedures, information, tasks, and management. Standards apply to both work processes and relationships between the focal organization and its customers, vendors, and internal suppliers. Measurement, reporting, and continuous improvement based on KPIs are critical components of standardization.

Optimal Improvement

Once other efforts to remove waste from a process and to maximize automation of non-value-adding process steps are complete, the process improvement team knows enough about both what not to do and what to do to develop optimal scenarios for conducting the process. In developing the ideal scenario for conduct of a process, optimal improvement analysis assumes an unlimited budget, unlimited resources, and unlimited managerial support for radical change. Keep in mind, though, that an ideal scenario is unlikely to be accepted unless the company is failing and likely to go out of business.

There is no one best way to develop an optimal process. Rather, many techniques can be combined to develop ideas that can be used to define the optimal process. Idealizing starts with *brainstorming*, or getting as many ideas about the potential process as possible, and then analyzing how they apply in defining how the process might best be conducted. *Out-of-the-box thinking*—coined by Michael Hammer, one of the early proponents of business process reengineering—is a similar technique for describing the type of thinking that is used when an old method is discarded and a new one is being developed. The goal of both techniques in process redesign is to find the "best" method, assuming a blank check and a blank slate in terms of how the process is conducted. "Best" may be defined as fastest cycle time, lowest cost, or other overall goal for the ideal environment.

Analysis can be simple, starting with a time-motion study of the work and analyzing required actions to set target times for completion. Then, by adding automation analysis, tasks can be more fully automated or reautomated in order to integrate previously disparate databases or applications.

More complex analysis might include QFD analysis of customer requirements mapped to methods for meeting those requirements. Or the process improvement team might work with user stakeholders to redesign the process to comply with industry best practices. Activity-based costing (ABC) might be used to identify cost drivers for each process step and minimize the cost of conducting each process step.

Another alternative is to apply *analytical hierarchic process* (AHP) analysis,[11] through which the goal or final product of the process is identified (see Figure 7.14). Then, to create the hierarchy, subgoals required to meet the final goal are identified. Using this type of analysis, much like the five-whys analysis, each subgoal is divided into further subgoals that must be met for it to be successful until no subgoals are left. Then, each subgoal is optimally defined for its setup and conduct with the expectation that by optimally defining each subgoal, the final goal will also be met. Once the alternatives are defined, they are given weights of importance, and in a complex environment, a series of matrix algebra analyses are conducted to determine the best overall outcomes.[12]

AHP can be combined with ABC, matrix analysis, automation analysis, and many other techniques to develop ideas about how best to design each subgoal.

In short, many types of analyses can result in ideal process design, accommodating best practices and all customer requirements at the same time as preventing errors in the process.

At some point in any of these analyses, the following steps should be taken:

- Define starting and ending points for each process step and for each point of customer contact or activity.
- Seek methods of coproduction that move work out of the target process and into customer control.
- Verify that website, intranet site, and other opportunities to make information generally available and searchable both externally by vendors and clients—and also internally by staff—are exploited.
- Define jobs, payment recommendations, and reward systems to optimize changed process quality.

Process for Cleaning

There are several methods for applying the cleaning processes discussed in this chapter. One method is to actually perform each as if the others have not been done. The rationale for treating each as separate is that by reviewing the post-VAA process seven or eight times, it should be as clean as possible at the end. Using this method, recommended changes from each analysis are noted and compared in order to develop an integrated set of

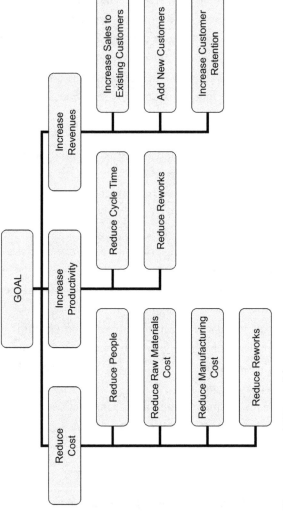

Figure 7.14. AHP analysis summary.

recommendations. The other method is to combine them so that one pass through the post-VAA steps is made. The rationale for this approach is to provide the optimal improvement by thoroughly analyzing each process step once through eight or nine lenses. This method will surface conflicts or alternative approaches faster than performing each analysis singly and should force an ongoing discussion of which potential changes are "best" for the particular situation.

In reality, the two methods should end up at the same place with approximately the same amount of work. The first, disaggregated method should result in more postanalysis to rationalize all of the suggested changes, while the second method should result in an ongoing analysis that rationalizes the changes in an ongoing manner.

Summary

Statistical process control charts identify the need for problem analysis. Reports use 3 sigma limits as a guide to all problems needing resolution. Depending on the number of reference points in a sample of 100 reported measures and the relative distances of points from the 1-sigma and 2-sigma lines, other issues might be identified for analysis. Large manufacturing facilities that measure thousands of points in their production processes will generate thousands of reports per day, requiring expertise in automated analysis and resolution.

RCA is a method for identifying the original cause of an incident or problem. Once the original cause is found and either fixed or removed, the incident should no longer occur. By performing RCA, then, companies become more effective in using the time of support people who are involved in recovery from the incidents that prompted the analysis.

Once problems are known, the problems and the processes in which they are embedded need further analysis in order to remove them from the area under review. Techniques for removal of problem areas use both logical and idealizing techniques. The logical techniques include duplication reduction, streamlining, bureaucracy reduction, cycle time reduction, upgrading, language simplification, and standardization.

Streamlining seeks to eliminate waste and increase efficiency by removing non-value-adding work, unneeded steps, approvals, and paperwork.

Bureaucracy reduction removes red tape in the form of wasteful administrative hierarchy, process steps, or paperwork through analysis of each document, report, piece of data generated, decision location, and so on by determining whether the item would be missed if eliminated.

Duplication elimination evaluates the organization's compliance, fiduciary, and security responsibilities, removing any duplicated work or work products while ensuring that required controls and monitoring are provided.

Cycle time reduction is applied to a company's defined key cycles, such as time to market or quote to cash. Each step of the cycle's process is measured and benchmarked to identify targets for improvement. Measures of each touch point in the process are taken to allow monitoring of the process.

Upgrading is the improvement of a process or product through an increase in quality in aspects such as training, technology, software, support, raw materials quality, and so on. Resources used in the process are listed and evaluated in order to assess the potential for alternatives that would be cheaper, faster, or both.

Simple-language initiatives seek to simplify the language used in documents to ensure their understanding by limited-vocabulary audiences. All documents, such as user manuals, are rewritten, omitting adjectives and adverbs while restricting the vocabulary to simple, common words. Jargon, passive voice, weak verbs, abstract terms, and unnecessary words are omitted. Further, any uncommon word that is required is defined using simple language in a dictionary that becomes part of each document.

Standardization revises processes by defining relationships between people, procedures, information, operating environments, tasks, and management that are replicated across many organizations. A typical structure for standardization is for policy, process, and procedures to be standardized, while work practices allow for local customizations that add steps to procedures.

These cleaning techniques are relatively simple to conduct but can result in significant improvements in expenses, turnover, productivity, and quality of service or product delivery. The disadvantages are that recommendations might be attributed to opinion and that important, value-adding steps might be cut.

Optimal improvement, also called idealizing, is conducted to determine the best possible process assuming no budget, managerial, or technical limitations. Many techniques can be applied in developing an ideal solution, including brainstorming, QFD, AHP, and others. The outcome of the idealizing design is an optimal process, with job and pay systems that can be used as an alternative to incremental changes.

CHAPTER 8

Process Greening

Introduction

Once the process is lean and clean, the next step is to decide on the following factors: whether to outsource, how to engage customers to do the work for you, the extent to which automation can speed and reduce the cost of the process, and finally, the extent to which the process can become environmentally safer without adding to its cost. Once this analysis is complete, the process is ready to be reconstructed with consideration of all recommended changes.

Outsourcing

Outsourcing is the movement of a function or related automated support to another company. It is an emotionally charged topic because it means that the people who formerly held the outsourced jobs often lose their jobs. However, outsourcing can benefit companies in terms of increased access to innovative practices, upgrades in technology, reduced operating costs, and increased quality of work.[1] These outcomes can occur in a company that manages the outsourcing process well and oversees the outsourced work as if it were still within the business.

Outsourcing Variations

While outsourcing typically refers to physical movement of some process or manufacturing activity to another physical location, some outsourcing can be done within a factory or business site. Toyota Motor Company has long been known for trying to reduce inventory for just-in-time car manufacturing. When Toyota Motor Sales, U.S.A., Inc. built a plant in the United States, they embedded miniplants in it so that, for instance, when seats are required, the order is sent to the manufacturer 80 minutes before the seats are to be installed in a car. The manufacturer makes the seats to order and places them on a hook-and-pulley system to move them from their minisite to the main production floor, where they are installed in the vehicle. The Toyota production floor was designed to minimize the distance manufacturers move their goods. Similarly, other vehicle subassemblies are made to order within the plant. This allows Toyota to hold virtually no inventory for assembled parts. The manufacturers maintain their own inventories and manufacture every item for Toyota. The outcome of this arrangement is better financial management for all companies. The outsourced goods are ready when needed with no transportation, little movement, and minimal wait-time costs for either party. A similar type of outsourcing is practiced by Wal-Mart for IT services. Thus while most outsourcing is offshore or nearshore, some can be "off-the-floor" and near enough to circumvent language or cultural problems.

The Outsourcing Request-for-Proposal Process

Before selecting an outsourcer, a request for proposal (RFP) should be developed to document requirements for the engagement and to provide a response format for the RFP. Once responses are received, they are evaluated using a matrix of the requirements to compare the proposals, much like the process for evaluating hardware or software discussed later in this chapter. The offering with the most favorable overall assessment is selected and contracts are negotiated. In many ways, outsourcing is like marriage in that consideration of all aspects of the relationship and its future needs are assessed. The switching costs of a bad outsourcing agreement can negate any benefits that might be gained and can damage a company for the outsourced function for several years.

Outsourcing Contracts

In addition to careful outsourcer selection, contracts must be carefully crafted to provide all of the "who, what, where, when, why, and how" information needed to conduct the work for, and by, both sides of the contract. The following is a list of the critical information that should be included in the contract. Keep in mind that this list is partial and that every outsourcing relationship requires detailed analysis of all needs for both sides:

- Include the work to be done and all of its circumstances and details. Ideally, the policy, procedures, process, and work instructions that are recommended for all processes should be available for use by the outsourcer. To the extent related to the outsourced activity, process, hardware, software, and data architectures should be provided as part of the RFP process so the extent of requirements is clear. Number of users, PCs, geographic locations, hours of operations, and minutes for response for outages are all critical information requirements. Further, growth rates should be estimated for the coming 3 to 5 years and periodically adjusted so both parties are clear on expected resource needs.
- In addition to the work, the extent to which the work is subjected to audit, compliance, or other legal obligations is an important disclosure. The outsourcer is required to follow the same legalities as the client, and the outsourcer is subject to audit by the client's auditors (or government auditors) as if they were the client. Therefore, any compliance issues need specific, detailed revelation.
- Similarly, the needs for security, privacy, user access and authentication controls, and so on should be defined in detail. Further, outsourcer arrangements for providing security, privacy, and so on should be important to the selection process. An outsourcer's policies, procedures, work practices, and past security or privacy audits should be presented as evidence of their ability to provide these capabilities to the extent needed.
- Project management and who is to provide that function should be specified. Methods to be used for resource estimations, costing, project planning, tracking, and control are all needed.
- The extent to which mergers or other acquisitions are expected, or to which different means of work are expected, should be detailed.
- Detail the method and means of work coordination and reporting outages, problems, and changes. This includes

help-desk capabilities for operational aspects of the outsourcing agreement as well as business issues that need addressing. Therefore, there may be several different types of interface needs—one for technology-related issues and one for business relationship issues. If either company follows a framework for managing work, such as Information Technology Infrastructure Library (ITIL), Capability Maturity Model Integration (CMMI), Control Objectives for Information and related Technology (COBIT),[2] or something else, they should be disclosed and discussed. In general, the greater the extent to which the same framework is used by both sides, the smoother the relationship between the parties will likely be. A no-fit situation, where one side is disciplined and the other is not, is a recipe for disaster or at least contract renegotiation. It is better that these issues be revealed during the contracting process and that expectations be set at the beginning, rather than having them come to light later and at a higher cost.

- One or more service level agreements (SLAs) should be crafted by the outsourcer to document their commitment to the activity in terms of computing and human resources supplied, response times, uptime, acceptable downtime, actions for errors or outages, noncompliance penalties, and so on.[3]
- Reports should be negotiated that detail the processing and financial aspects of the work. This requirement means that the metrics of different steps of the process should be developed and reported on, as are the details of billings. Ideally, reporting is through an Internet dashboard that has drill-down capabilities with downloadable detailed reports.
- The client organization should periodically benchmark service costs to ensure that the charges are reasonable.
- The extent to which innovation is required should be defined and, to the extent possible, the nature of the innovation.
- The contract should provide provisions for periodic review of contract terms as companies can drift apart in their goals and delivery quality, thereby making a prior attractive arrangement a costly disaster.

The items in this list all discuss requirements from the client perspective. Nevertheless, there are requirements the outsourcer should also pursue so as not to be held accountable for someone else's problems. For instance, client company litigation, history of bill-paying delinquency, business reputation, commitment to the success of the outsourcing arrangement, assignment of permanent liaisons, and the extent to which client needs are thorough and completely articulated are all key indicators of the potential for a successful continuing relationship.

Outsourcing Problems

Outsourcing is not without its problems. Some of the major issues include the following:

- Companies may not think through their decisions with sufficient care and may outsource core capabilities that define their company's distinctive competency. Yet outsourcing works best when it is custodial rather than strategic. When core capabilities move into a custodial process, the kind of rapid change needed in response to changing industry events may be compromised.
- Outsourcing displaces people and thus makes for unhappy remaining staff members. This unhappiness can result in staff members who try to subvert the outsourcers or otherwise ensure that they suffer problems.
- Many companies that think they can provide a 2-day turnover of people and processes, often unwritten, get negative outcomes. There is usually a 4- to 6-month turnover period when phasing in outsourced work. During this time, costs are often substantially increased over the normal costs.[4]
- Many companies also assume that once outsourced, the workload for continuing the relationship is minimal. In fact, this is not true. While the relationship cost should decrease significantly, there is an ongoing relationship need. Companies that outsource application development, for instance, often find that they needed to move staff to the outsourcer's geographic location to provide interpretation of specifications. It

should be no surprise that without contextual understanding, the outsourcer is forced to take a literal translation of words on a page, yet many multinational companies make this mistake. Thus the cost of maintaining a staff in, for example, India may become an added, unanticipated cost that cuts into the savings from outsourcing arrangements.

- Spoken English can be an issue. Companies that move work to India and Latin America and require language skills wrongly assume that English is English, not accounting for accents. When customers encounter Indian-English accents, many complain of not being able to understand. To address such situations, many companies invest heavily in accent-reduction training for anyone employed in telephone jobs.

Outsourcing Relationships

Successful outsourcing requires knowledge of the four types of exchanges that are involved in developing and sustaining a successful outsourcing relationship: product or service, information, financial, and social.[5] As a customer-facing activity, it is crucial that the outsourcer be aware of the four types of exchanges and how to exploit them to the best advantage. The most common services outsourced are help desks and call centers, so these are used as the examples.

The *product or service exchange* is the actual work taken over by the outsourcer (hereafter, "Outsourcer"). Normally, work arrives in some form from the client organization (hereafter, "Client"). Typically, this is an Internet transaction exchange of some sort. In the example, customers of the Outsourcer contact the help desk (e.g., via phone, e-mail, or Internet form), requesting assistance or support. Help-desk products and services are relatively self-explanatory, but the service provided becomes the Outsourcer's responsibility. The Client relies completely on the Outsourcer to provide quality interface services to its customers, often without any means of verifying that quality. The ideal situation is for the Client to provide random monitoring of help-desk representatives and periodic customer satisfaction surveys of help-desk users. Metrics are critical in monitoring outsourced processes and therefore require development attention.

The *information exchanges* in the outsourcing relationship include formal and informal discussions about the nature of the work, report exchanges, and the like. As much as contracts might try to clarify and routinize information exchanges, much of this activity is informal and not likely to be amenable to contractual specification. Most of the information exchange depends on the incumbents in the interface positions of the Outsourcer and Client companies.

Information exchange relies on, and is related to, social exchanges. *Social exchanges* relate to non-job-related discussions that lead to the development of trust, friendship, and cordiality. Job incumbents need to know each other well enough so that bad news or problems can be reported without fear of reprisal and with constructive conversations that lead to useful solutions. A form of trust is required that allows open exchange of information without one party becoming dependent on the other, as might happen when relations become too close. Also, more than two people should participate in the Outsourcer-Client relationships to prevent the development of two key people who alone know the situation, events, issues, problems, and other issues in the relationship.

To best develop the social exchange, it needs to be explicitly recognized and managed. For instance, regular face-to-face meetings, one or two times per year, facilitate the social interchanges necessary to the outsourcing relationship. While this is not unlike other forms of business relationships, outsourcing is unique in that the Outsourcer must become a committed partner to the greatest extent possible. This implies that the Client representative is committed to Outsourcer success as well. Without a cordial, constructive, and cooperative social relationship, the outsourcing relationship can deteriorate into one of Client commands and reluctant, literal Outsourcer responses that are not personally satisfying to the participants even though they might meet the contract terms.

Financial exchanges relating to payments, billing, margins, and the like are also important in managing the outsourcing relationship. Financial transparency in terms of meeting Client goals is required. Most Clients enter an outsourcing arrangement with some expectation of cost reduction. Further, the expectation of a relatively stable financial future with respect to the outsourced business must also be managed. Most information technology (IT) organizations, for instance, grow their data storage 100% or more every year or so. This usually entails added costs.

In such a situation, the Outsourcer must provide transparency on architectural and infrastructure planning as it relates to the Client organization's outsourced activities in order to ensure that those goals are met. As an inducement to further decrease costs, Outsourcer incentives for cost reductions can be offered as the contract progresses. Common financial activities in outsourcing arrangements include open-book accounting, competitive benchmarking relative to service costs, and monthly reports on costs.[6]

Outsourcing Summary

Outsourcing can be beneficial when conducted for noncore activities, with full disclosure of all pertinent information by both parties and management of the types of exchanges required for products and services, finances, information, and social aspects of the relationships. Service-level agreements are, at best, clear articulations of expectations that the Outsourcer should meet in order to comply with the contract. Many issues require discussion for inclusion in an SLA, and some of the more important ones relate to the product or service provided, the needs of the customer, compliance and privacy requirements, project management, growth, methods of work, methods of reporting, and metrics for measuring success.

Coproduction

One method of improving process cycle time and, therefore, efficiency is to remove some steps from the process. Elimination of processes via, for instance, value-added analysis is one method for removing steps. However, this type of removal usually means complete elimination of the step. Frequently, non-value-adding activities are still required for good business practice, compliance, management needs, and the like such that elimination is not an option. In such cases, coproduction might be a useful option to consider for removing steps from a process.

Coproduction has more than one conceptualization. *Coproduction* means to produce something in collaboration. In business, *coproduction* means off-loading work to the customer, vendor, or outsourcer. A more recent conceptualization of *coproduction* is that it is leading to an economy where value is related to social impact rather than monetary accumulation.[7] All three of these notions are explored briefly with the implications for process improvement.

Coproduction as Collaboration

An early conceptualization of coproduction from the 1970s[8] defines it as a collaborative work effort between clients and social service producers (but it could be any type of vendor) to actively engage clients in the work of the organization. The desired outcome is an improvement in the delivery of services at a reduced cost.

One purpose of the coproductive effort is to develop a community of clients that band together to help coproduce the desired outcome. Examples are from social services, such as education in Brazil, waste treatment in Nigeria, and neighborhood patrols in several countries.[9] The idea is to turn otherwise passive receivers and critics of an initiative into partners who coproduce the effort.

While described in terms of social settings, this notion can be carried into the other types of coproduction and can lead to the notions of coproduction today, which not only serve a business purpose but also build social capital for those participating in the effort. These notions are explored more fully in the next section.

Coproduction as the Off-Loading of Work

In the business sense, coproduction off-loads work to customers or outsourcers, transferring the cost of the activity to some other entity or individual. One example is shipment tracking capability, through which customers can track their own packages. By providing this service, customer satisfaction soared, as customers no longer wait for call center pick-up, wait while the package is tracked, and wait to get an answer that they must rely on without seeing the results. Shippers also profit by avoiding the millions of dollars to increase their call center to deal with the increasing volume as their delivery services gained market share.

Another example of business coproduction relates to Amazon.com. In its early days, Amazon had an online monopoly that allowed it double-digit growth with virtually no competition. As Barnes and Noble, Borders, and other booksellers developed web-selling capabilities, price became the chief method of competition, and with already thin margins, Amazon's viability was challenged. Therefore, as an Internet-only company, Amazon has had to constantly improve its services or face extinction. One innovation was allowing readers to provide reviews of books on the website, thereby providing would-be purchasers with more information about a product than that offered by the publisher. This has been a winning proposition for both book buyers and Amazon—happy customers return *because* of this capability.

Another Amazon innovation is the ability of small booksellers who cannot afford their own website to sell books through Amazon. Through this arrangement, in exchange for a small fee on items sold, booksellers get an audience of millions that they would otherwise not have.

As Amazon branched into other selling areas, it extended its coproduction arrangements into those areas as well. Customer loyalty to Amazon still relies on the right product at the right price, but buyers are more likely to return because of successful results with previous coproduced activities.

Coproduction as Social-Capital Development

The third outcome of coproduction is the development of the importance of social capital at the expense of monetary accumulation. While this notion has been apparent for some time, its importance is becoming clear enough for articulation.[10] For instance, Amazon's reviewers provide lists of their favorite books, moving them into the coproduction of social capital as book buyers seek out list producers with book interests with which they agree.

A more recent phenomenon of this type relates to the use of Web 2.0 technologies for social networking, such as LinkedIn, Facebook, Second Life, Digg, and Twitter,[11] among many others. These sites all operate differently, but all produce the type of free notoriety and social followings that appeal to people in today's world. LinkedIn is a site primarily of professionals who track their business, personal, or family contacts through the software. Gone is the need to remember or store e-mails, phone numbers, or addresses. Of course, the user must supply them or have them coproduced by the subject person to whom they link. Your success as a LinkedIn member is the number of links you maintain, the number of people to whom you are related by one degree of separation, and the number of referrals you give or get, among several other criteria. The social capital in the site is free to a point. However, using LinkedIn to manage business relationships is a paid-for service. In either case, your ratings and, therefore, your *social strength* are known to anyone who links to you.

Second Life (SL) is an avatar-driven virtual world that mirrors real, or *first*, life through the Internet. SL is the epitome of the early web in which "no one knew if you were green" because your avatar is a being of your creation. Dressed, or not, humanoid, or not, the avatar does your business *"in world."* While some businesses create the same type of sleaze as real life, many are legitimate businesses—for example, the U.S. National Aeronautics and Space Administration (NASA), which is a model for how to do business in SL. Several years ago, NASA reduced all meeting travel budgets to zero, requiring that people find another way to conduct their work. The NASA SL site not only allows them to conduct meetings with all first-life accoutrements but also provides live shots of all NASA activities, such as space shots, images returning from Mars, and so on, so that their constituents can *be there.*

SL is characterized by a high degree of involvement for participants that is close to, if not the same as, that in first life. Further, organizations such as NASA improve their social capital through their SL presence. Individuals who participate in SL meetings soon become known to each other and take on the social activities they would in first life.

Facebook (FB) is a cross between LinkedIn and SL, in which you create a biography and link to "friends" and others to share photos, exchange e-mail, and conduct life. Many high-school and college students spend their Internet time (and phone and e-mail time) on FB. Similar to LinkedIn, your popularity is known by the number of friends. FB allows blogging, creation of messages shown for some time on others' "walls," and other methods of becoming known. In a slightly different wrinkle, you can also link to celebrities on Facebook and follow their activities, link to universities or businesses to get information about doing business and finding jobs, and so on.

Digg and Twitter are slightly different from the other sites discussed. Digg is a site on which you link news stories of the day or vote on others' story links to determine the most popular news items. A visit to the site offers the most "Dugg" sites, with links to 30 or so categories on variety of topics. Twitter is a means of sending messages in real time, tracking others' messages, and blogging to the world at large or to a specific group. Your "tweets," or messages, are posted in most recent order on a public page and read by others as the topic interests them. Once accessed, a tweet can lead to a profile and all tweets of an individual and all of their friends. When purposeful, both Digg and Twitter have individuals who are considered gurus of their subject areas and who are sought for their knowledge and links rather than for a social interaction.

These forms of social networking all provide the development of social capital of one type or another without monetary reward. However, all of these services require a critical mass of individuals seeking that social capital to be of value. If, for instance, Twitter's more inane entries—for example, "I'm bored"—were to become the norm, then it would rapidly deteriorate and fall into disuse. As it is used by groups, it provides a form of threaded discussion that can provide enormous value to its users.

Coproduction Benefits and Design

Coproduction can reduce and avoid costs for the product or service provider, increase switching costs for customers who embed the coproducing activities into their own organizational functioning and, frequently, increase customer satisfaction.

To determine if coproduction would benefit the process under consideration, review each step to determine if the role of the customer might be expanded or even if the customer could take over the step(s) as an optional activity. Consider different media for the coproduction activity, such as order processing, sales, service, and support. Define the quality needed for that step(s), how you would help customers maintain the quality level needed, and how the process would work assuming that coproduction is used. As needed, develop a return-on-investment (ROI) analysis to make a business case for changing the current method of doing the process step(s). If the ROI is favorable and quality issues can be defined, then recommend coproduction as part of the changes to the process.

Coproduction Summary

Coproduction is the transfer of work to someone who is not paid. Coproduction has many faces, from collaboration to work transfer to the development of social capital. Because coproduction produces benefits for both sides of the exchange, it is expected to grow in its economic importance, especially in relation to Internet-based activities.

Automation, Mechanization, or Both

Today, automation means plug-and-play hardware components operating via a standardized network, which is managed by virtualization software that chooses the available resources needed for the time needed, wherever they are available. Within this scenario, IT organizations need to develop the software architecture (application modules and software components), data architecture, and operations architecture with hardware, software, and network designs that all can be allocated via SLAs to their corresponding organizational components. From a nontechnical perspective, applications need to be linked to the organization mission in much the same way as the processes they support so that appropriate metrics and reports of status information fit organizational needs.

In the 1970s, IBM developed a technique called business systems planning (BSP) that sought to develop such comprehensive architectures. However, like all attempts that address current needs, the focus of BSP was on application process, and the company did not change in order to remain relevant in the nonmainframe world. Similarly, in the 1980s, James Martin and others popularized information engineering to focus on data architecture and management as the most stable component of organizations. The 1990s witnessed the maturation of object orientation as a set of methods for building agile applications with small components that encapsulated both data and process code for small, functional code objects. Now we are again witnessing the maturation of service-oriented architectures (SOA) and software as a service (SaaS), which build on all of these previous concepts to develop application architectures that leverage Internet service delivery of functions (e.g., Google maps) that are being incorporated into organizational applications (e.g., truck-route planning).

In addition, parallel developments to manage IT operations as a collection of integrated services are taking place in the movement toward IT service management (ITSM). The main services in ITSM relate to incident, problem, change, and release processing to support IT and development areas, and configuration, availability, capacity, continuity, service level, and finance in the infrastructure and operations areas.

Against this backdrop of constant change in the IT field, developing automated support for business processes previously thought incapable of being automated has become an enormous growth area. The problem is how to get from manual, partially automated, or poorly automated process support to a more productive, efficient, and effective state of automation.

To determine opportunities for automation, follow this basic process:

1. Determine automation feasibility:
   a. Is the process one that is strategically important for the organization?
   b. Is desired technology mature enough for the proposed use?
   c. Is the process one that has traits facilitated by process automation?
   d. Are available resources sufficient?
2. Determine the method of procurement:
   a. Make or buy?
   b. Insource or outsource?
3. Regardless of procurement strategy, perform an RFP or bid process, and perform an analysis of the responses.
4. Make a business case for the automation effort.

Automation Feasibility

Feasibility analysis determines the technical and organizational maturity of the area under study and determines the benefits of the automation effort to the organization. Several areas are evaluated, including strategic importance of the business process, technology maturity, requirements facilitated by automation, and resource sufficiency.

Strategic Importance

To determine strategic importance of potential automation (or reautomation or adding mechanical devices of some type) to a process, stakeholder benefits across the organization are analyzed. The mantra "better, faster, cheaper, more" often drives automation efforts without regard to the strategic importance of the effort to the organization. Defining the benefits and their importance to the organization will often guide other decisions about the automation effort, such as whether to outsource development.

The outcomes to be derived from automation should be enumerated for each stakeholder organization and rated against the strategic goals of the departments within the process scope as well as against the organizations strategy. To rate the benefits, different methods might be used. For instance, a simple 0-1-2 system can be used, with 0 indicating no match to a strategic goal, 1 indicating support for a strategic goal, and 2 indicating meeting of strategic goal. If all projected automation outcomes have zero benefits for meeting or supporting strategic goals, then the automation probably should not be conducted. If the automation is mostly *supporting* of strategic goals, then purchased software or outsourced development and operation should be evaluated for the cheapest method of conduct. If the automation benefits are *required to meet* strategic goals, then either customized, purchased software or fully customized development should be considered.

Thus support and attainment of strategic goals should motivate technology deployment in support of processes or manufacturing; methods and costs would differ depending on the outcomes.

Technology Maturity

Regardless of whether an automation team evaluates some type of commercial product or custom hardware and software, the determination of maturity includes, at a minimum, software functionality, software quality, future software viability, and vendor quality. *Software functionality analysis* requires a list of required features and functions for the software that is matched against the software's completeness in providing the features and functions. The list items might be prioritized or given a weighting factor. Either some numeric ranking of the software product compared to other software products or an absolute minimum acceptable ranking number indicates product maturity.

Software quality evaluation determines the acceptability of the number and type of errors over time and the length of time it takes the software vendor to fix errors. Online resources such as the archives of the U.S. Computer Emergency Readiness Team,[12] which reports bugs, or evaluation of the frequency of software upgrades can be used to determine if serious security breaches are an issue.

Future software viability is more qualitative than the other analyses. This analysis predicts the future of similar products and their expected configuration and functionality for some period into the future. A *technology roadmap* is a detailed planning method that takes as its starting point some future technology and deconstructs the target technology to determine its components' development needs. If specific product features are not fully implemented, then a road map might be created with the vendor to map changes needed for a product to be fully functional.

Process Automation Traits

Three process characteristics are facilitated by process automation:

- high transaction volume
- complexity of processing
- need for transaction tracking for either compliance or audit needs

These traits individually and collectively support business process automation. *High transaction volume* is a relative measure, usually expressed in an absolute number of transactions, such as 30,000 transactions per second. The implication is that normal processing is untouched by humans or is as close to it as possible. Exceptions requiring human processing need to be kept to a minimum or automated to speed processing and maintain volume per person. For instance, a help desk responds to 30,000 transactions per month, or roughly 1,000 transactions per day. If each transaction averages 15 minutes to resolve, then that is a total of 15,000 minutes, or 250 hours, or equivalent to 32 full-time workers. If the organization is expected to decrease volume or staff, then automation is a logical response to both requirements. Even a drop to an average of 10 minutes per transaction reduces the number of needed staff to about 20. At $60,000 per year per person, this is a savings of about $720,000 per year.

Complex processing is usually evidenced by multiple, intellectually difficult steps conducted by many individuals accessing one or more applications or databases, possibly from different geographic locations. There are two types of complexity—numeric and process. *Numeric complexity* relates to number of steps or transactions, such as 10,000 transactions per second. *Process complexity* relates to the intellectual difficulty or number of resources or actions (e.g., people, applications, databases, machines, number of handoffs, etc.) involved in the process. Any interruptible process, or any process with hand-offs between one or more resources, is prone to forgotten and lost transactions due to the volume of transactions being conducted. When automated, the process management software can track the handoffs, notify each person of the arrival of a transaction for their work, remind or escalate the notification after specified times, and ensure that the process is completed according to a specified time.

Audit and compliance requirements are those that require signatures to sign off acceptance or approval for certain types of transactions. For example, on-boarding, the adding of new staff to provide computer access, is a process that requires auditability. Typically, there is a set of software and services to which everyone with a PC is allowed access. The software-service set can be approved by a manager for a new employee. This is the first signature. Then, for any nonstandard data that require access by the person's job, the process owner of the data is required to sign approval for access. This can involve many different signatures or none at all. All signatures must be produced upon request during any audits as evidence of the company's practice of the on-boarding process. When automated, such a process tracks all of the required signatures, provides escalation, as needed, when they are not forthcoming, and stores all electronic signatures for easy audit retrieval.

These three sets of requirements thus identify a process that could be improved and managed in a cost-beneficial manner with process automation. If none of these characteristics are in the area under consideration, then process automation is likely to cost more per transaction than other forms of management.

Resource Sufficiency

Resource evaluation of internal organizational resource adequacy should support the operational use of the automated environment being evaluated. Resources evaluated include time, money, personnel skills, and the operational hardware, software, and telecommunications environment. If multiple products or automation strategies are being compared, then an assessment of needs for each scenario under evaluation is created, with numeric or priority ranking of each of the items evaluated to develop an overall "score" for each automation product or strategy.

Once these analyses are complete, the products or automation strategies are compared across all four dimensions in order to develop a single ranking. Frequently, the "best" or most favorable outcome might also cause the most disruption to the organization, leading to a recommendation of multiple best-of-breed products or automation strategies that highlight the trade-offs between minimizing the radicalness of change versus maximizing the return to the business.

Once the three assessments are complete and an overall automation strategy is developed, a feasibility report is generated. At this point, the report documents the evaluations and conclusions on maturity and organizational benefits. The next step in the evaluation process is to determine the best method for acquiring the application capability. For that analysis, procurement alternatives are evaluated.

Software and Vendor Evaluation

Evaluations all follow essentially the same process, whether for an outsourcing contract, a software product, or any other type of product or service. The RFP process is summarized in the following list, with each step elaborated in the following sections. The RFP process includes the following tasks:

1. Define the business requirements.
2. Define the RFP response format in document and spreadsheet templates.
3. Identify the vendors to receive the RFP.
4. Send the RFP, providing specific directions for using the response template and with an absolute deadline date.
5. Receive RFPs up to the deadline.
6. Read and evaluate all RFPs, narrowing the vendors for final comparison to between three and seven.
7. Perform a detailed evaluation using spreadsheets to provide an easily read format.

8. Develop conclusions and a recommendation report.

9. Enter negotiation with the vendor, and procure the product.

10. Install, test, and implement the product.

Define Requirements

Specific requirements, grouped by "must have" and "nice to have," should be developed and documented. The grouping of requirements should be readily understandable and use straightforward language. The following is one method of grouping:

- Product or service "life cycle" for both functionally and non-functional requirements:

  These requirements should be grouped in some logical order for the specific product or service. One possible grouping is by functional and nonfunctional requirements. Functional requirements might be grouped by the product or service, including, for instance, business life cycle; start-up; daily operations; reporting; shutdown; and data import, export, integration, metrics, and auditability. Non-functional requirements might include security, privacy, response time, availability, reliability, recoverability, and so on.

- Vendor requirements should all be defined to fit the context:
  - Financial stability might be evaluated by comparing financial ratings, age, or stability of executives.
  - Product commitment might compare frequency of upgrades, frequency of bug fixes, or speed of response for bug fixes.
  - Installation, start-up, and service support should all be evaluated.
  - Training provided as part of the acquisition price and as added service should be compared.
  - User group activity and requests for changes add to product requirements.

- Price considerations and responsiveness should be evaluated. Price should be defined to best fit the situation. Some components might include the following:

- ○ Costs (e.g., cost of four locations with 100 users per location) should be compared.
- ○ Product price plus training, support, annual fees, upgrade fees, or other costs as needed should be compared.
- • Technology-delivery methodology and details should be compared:

  Define all allowable variations for in-house or outsourced, open source or not, SOA/SaaS or not, and so on, for all of the following:

  - ○ hardware
  - ○ software
  - ○ core memory set (minimum memory)
  - ○ database
  - ○ security and privacy

- • Provide information on the format and content of vendor RFP response with information as specific as possible. Include a blank formatted template for the report and require its completion.

  Request responses in both paper and digital formats (".doc" or ".xls" only) for ease of importing comparison information.

Requirements are documented according to the policies and practices of the organization as if the application were being developed in-house. The goal is to provide a comprehensive set of requirements described in sufficient detail for a vendor to know whether their product meets the criteria. Requirements should be formatted for ease of understanding and use. For instance, bullet points or diagrams are preferable to text paragraphs, as they are more easily understood.

In addition to the requirements, the weight of each requirement or requirement category should be determined. This need not be done before the RFP is sent to vendors, but this step should be complete before RFP responses are received so as not to prejudice the vendor comparison.

The importance of performing this requirements-definition step first cannot be overemphasized. If a company does not predefine their needs before sending RFPs, then the evaluation process ends with an inability to compare vendor responses. By providing a specific format for the responses, they are automatically comparable and focus only on the items of importance in the decision process. Providing the response format can shorten the evaluation process by as much as several weeks.

Research the Available Technology

As a parallel activity to the definition of requirements, to the extent possible, research is completed in order to identify all vendors and products that can provide the needed capabilities. This is an exercise in defining the size of the market. In general, the larger the market, the more price flexibility there will be in the negotiations.

While collecting the data, you also can define requirements that relate to some of the offering requirements. Especially when evaluating something that is new to the company, you may not be able to surface organizational requirements without performing some of this research. The research serves an educational purpose for the staff performing the analyses and should provide sufficient information to reduce the feasible set of alternative vendors and products to a manageable few.

Typically, there might be 30 or more vendors offering a specific product. The goal in the research activity is to ensure complete definition of requirements and to determine the companies, usually less than 10, that will receive the RFP.

Send RFP to Vendors

The goal of this step is to provide a completely equitable process such that all vendors are treated exactly the same. This is both the ethical method of procurement and also the one least likely to end in accusations of any type. Equity implies all RFPs are sent on the same day, in the same manner, and have the same information, contact person, format for further information, and deadlines.

Questions may come from vendors. To keep the process equitable, all questions and responses should be made available to every vendor. This is sometimes accommodated through a face-to-face meeting with all vendors about halfway through the response period or through e-mail lists to which everyone subscribes. There should be a fixed period for questions to avoid being inundated for the response duration.

Receive RFPs

RFPs are received up to the deadline, which is usually stated as something like "noon on Monday, January 10." No exceptions to the end date are allowed unless the extension is applied to all vendors. In addition, early submission RFPs should not be reviewed until the deadline in order to avoid having one become a favorite.

Narrow the Field of Alternatives

All other things being equal, the goal of this step is to narrow the field of vendors to between three and seven to allow meaningful analysis and comparison. Narrowing can be based on a few criteria or on an overall analysis of all RFPs, with reduction of numbers based on a gross analysis.

Narrowing of vendor alternatives can be based on a few criteria, such as the extent to which the RFP requirements are addressed, product cost, infrastructure compatibility, or some other similar requirement. RFPs should be read to determine which, if any, clearly failed some test. For example, check to determine whether any did not follow the response template, omitted answers on the template, or did not respond to enough requirements.

Narrowing of vendor alternatives by summary analysis of all criteria, while most equitable, is also more time-consuming. However, analysis of response categories for management-reporting purposes is useful. All RFPs are ranked on each gross category (e.g., as a sum of all subcategory rankings), and an overall ranking is computed. A cutoff is applied to these average rankings to determine the vendor set for detailed analysis. As stated previously, the ideal is to reduce the set of responses to between three and seven, with three as the preferred number.

Perform Detailed Evaluation

Every requirement is evaluated for the extent to which it is met by the vendor. Methods of assigning numbers might be simple ranking, which is preferred, or assignment of a percentage. Number assignments may relate across the vendors or not (i.e., all ranks for a single item might sum to 100% across all vendors). In general, the simplest method is the easiest to explain and defend.

When products have similar implementations of a characteristic, they are assigned the average of the ranks that would be assigned. Items ranked second and third are determined to be equivalent. Therefore, on a scale of 1 to 5, both would receive a 2.5 rating, or (2+3) ÷ 2.

Figure 8.1 shows a simple analysis of three vendors for a database product. Simple ranking is used with assignment of 1, 2, or 3, depending on the extent to which a feature is fully automated. In this example, 1 is the lowest rank overall; the highest rank sum identifies the preferred product. Thus in the example, Vendor 1 would be the preferred vendor.

While ranking is ongoing, notes should be made regarding the criteria that resulted in one rank or another. This an important task in the review process, as it enables defense of the decisions made. The following are examples of the analysis criteria for each requirement:

- meets needs (must be specific)
- is compatible with technology infrastructure

Requirements	Vendor 1	Vendor 2	Vendor 3
10,000 records per relation	3.0	1.5	1.5
1,000 fields	1.5	3.0	1.5
Up to 16 relations open at once	3.0	1.5	1.5
Security at field level	3.0	1.5	1.5
Classes of users	2.0	2.0	2.0
User views	3.0	1.0	2.0
Cascading deletes	3.0	1.5	1.5
Entity/foreign key integrity	2.0	2.0	2.0
Company stability	2.0	2.0	2.0
Multiuser access/ update	2.0	2.0	2.0
Customer support	3.0	1.5	1.5
Cost	1.0	2.0	3.0
Total score	28.5	21.5	22.0

Figure 8.1. Summary RFP evaluation example.

- allows flexibility for change, updating, and customizing
- is easy to use as indicated
- provides for documentation adequacy (e.g., paper or online help; context-related or not)
- gives vendor support, rights, and viability
- identifies costs—acquisition, training, conversion, other, billing or payment methods
- has a delivery format that specifies ownership

Develop Conclusions and Report

Before any final report is produced, the results of the evaluation should be presented to the sponsor and any interested stakeholders for their own analysis and comments. At this point, politics and organizational constraints can surface a need to change the importance of some rank or weight that may alter the outcome of the analysis. When this happens, the report should reflect the change in a nonjudgmental way but also identify that without this constraint, the results of the process might differ.

For example, in Figure 8.1, Vendor 1's product was the most expensive, resulting in the lowest rank in that category. If the client decides that technical requirements can be compromised somewhat in the interest of keeping costs low, then Vendor 3's product might be selected. The report would reflect the desire that cost dictates the selection in a suboptimal way, as follows:

Cost is the most important selection factor; therefore, the recommendation is Vendor 3's product, which meets most product requirements. However, should cost restrictions be relaxed, Vendor's 1's product is superior in most categories and is recommended.

In general, the final report should provide sections relating to each category of requirements, with brief discussion of the highlights of the analysis, and should include the spreadsheet product comparison as an appendix. The report sections, with brief contents, include the following:

- *Executive summary.* The first sentence introduces the project goal and motivation. The second sentence identifies the recommended product. There might be another sentence on the major products evaluated, but only if the list is small.
- *Background.* This section provides a summary of the project motivation, sponsor, and RPF process
- *Evaluation.* This section contains one subsection per requirement category or evaluation subsection. Financial analysis should include some form of ROI or other meaningful financial analysis. ROI is derived by matching the total cost of the expected automation effort to the total returns from the automation effort over time to find the point at which the returns outweigh the cost.
- *Recommendation and justification.* This section summarizes the recommendations.
- *Next steps.* This section identifies responsibilities and costs for items needed to effect the recommended changes, such as infrastructure, negotiations, organizational changes, or policies and procedures.
- *Summary.* This is a restatement of one sentence per report section with recommendation clearly stated.

The report is presented, along with any supporting documentation, to the client stakeholders. Upon their decision, an automation project would be initiated.

Environmental Process Greening

There is no science of process or IT greening as of yet. As the world becomes more mature in thinking seriously about all business having a zero-carbon footprint (i.e., produces no adverse environmental impact), some areas of opportunity have become clear. While relevant to whole companies as much as to individual processes or their automated activities, environmental greening is a topic that should not be ignored. The areas of interest relate to energy use, recycling, and telecommuting. Each of these is discussed in this section.

Energy Greening

Energy greening includes increasing efficiency of heating, air conditioning, and computing equipment. By reducing the amount of energy used by each individual piece of electrical equipment, efficiencies can be gained. In IT, adoption of blade servers, grid servers, virtualization, or cloud computing can reduce the electrical needs by as much as 75%. In addition, the layout of a data center affects its energy efficiency. Plus, buildings can adopt smart-mote managed building automation for optimal heating, air conditioning, and even water use.

Use of alternative energies such as wind or solar energy should be evaluated as cheap sources of complete or partial power management for ongoing operations.

Greening Through Recycling

Recycling of electrical equipment to reclaim silver, dangerous chemicals, and other metals is important for environmental improvement. Also, paper recycling can be evaluated for its efficiency and, to the extent that paper is generated by a process, it should be recycled.

Greening Through Telecommuting

Telecommuting began about 20 years ago, with mostly small-business owners working out of their homes and using the Internet to stay connected to their customers and other key parties. Now, most *corporations* have telecommuting programs and *hotelling* of office space—that is, offices are assigned as needed, with few permanent space allocations. The number of telecommuters has steadily increased as a percentage of the working population in the United States and now accounts for over 20% of the U.S. workforce. As economic woes and high energy prices continue, this growth is expected to continue. In addition to being more energy efficient, companies can save about $10,000 per teleworker by requiring less office space and the accompanying infrastructure.[13]

Summary

Outsourcing is the movement of a function or related automated support to another company. Outsourcers can be located anywhere—the same building, the same country, another country, or even another continent. Outsourcing arrangements require an RFP process, with a bid selected for contract negotiation using a process similar to that for software selection. Outsourcing contracts require definitions of the work and its characteristics, including project management, growth, work coordination processes and contacts, service-level agreements, reporting, benchmarking, innovativeness, review, and noncompliance. Major problems experienced by outsourcing clients include outsourcing of core competitive capabilities, misestimation of turnover and coordination required, and differences in language skills of outsourcer staff.

Outsourcing relationships have four types of exchanges—product or service, information, financial information, and social trust building. Explicit recognition of each exchange is important for outsourcing success.

Outsourcing can save money and improve process support when conducted for noncore activities. SLAs should clearly articulate all operational aspects of the relationship. Outsourcing does not eliminate processes—it moves responsibility to another organization or individual, hopefully at a lower cost.

Coproduction is an alternative for process improvement that moves responsibility for work out to the customer or vendor, with no payment for the service. Coproduction has three forms: collaboration, off-loading of work, and the building of social capital. The collaborative form of coproduction engages otherwise passive receivers of a service to become partners in the effort. Off-loading of work is a transfer of process cost to the customer or organization that does the activity. Coproduction for building of social capital accrues from participation in social networking, which allows sharing of information of some type with the world at large. To the extent that one's sharing is sought by others, social capital accrues.

Automation is the movement of process steps to computerized or otherwise mechanized support. A feasibility analysis is conducted to determine automation, including determination of strategic importance of the effort, technology and organizational maturity, and feasible process traits.

The process traits most amenable to process automation are a high transaction volume, complex processing requirements, and the need for transaction tracking. Vendor selection for automated process improvement software follows a request-for-proposal (RFP) process where requirements are provided to vendors who submit bids, which are then evaluated through a rational process.

Environmental process greening has three components, each of which should be evaluated for the process being improved. Energy greening is an improvement in the electrical or operational efficiency of infrastructure for buildings, computers, manufacturing facilities, and related equipment. Recycling greening is a process change in which items that were previously discarded in general trash are separated out for recycling. Telecommuting is a form of process greening in that fewer organizational resources are needed to accommodate workers who now work at home.

PART III

End Game

Once the analytical work is complete, the rest of the process improvement project is concerned with formalizing recommendations, developing a cost-benefit analysis, error-proofing, developing metrics, and, finally, documenting the case for change in a final project report. The first chapter in this part discusses process redesign through error-proofing. A major task in this work is the compilation and reconciliation of all recommendations from all of the analyses. The last task discussed in this chapter is the validation and verification of the changed process, that is, its approval by key stakeholders, including the project sponsor. Once this is done, project success is assured, and the remaining tasks again enter the realm of generic good project management. The last chapter describes metrics development, with dashboards for transparent reporting of process operations and the development of the final report.

CHAPTER 9

Process Redesign

Introduction

Developing a good redesign is something of an artistic endeavor. There is no predesignated outcome and no cookbook for getting there. Therefore, the techniques in this chapter are mostly based on the experience and practice of the author in applying a process with the confidence that the process is likely to end in success. The process for developing the redesign is to evaluate all recommended changes to this point in the project, first rationalizing them into a smaller set, and then analyzing which sets are beneficial in terms of cost to the organization.

Many of the techniques used in other aspects of the analysis are applied to making sense of the recommendations, evaluating their worth, and selecting those most likely to result in a coherent, useful process. Compliance is reviewed to ensure that all required aspects of process management would be accommodated in the redesign. The role of innovation is explored from the perspective of making sure the redesigned process is not just rearranging the process using existing organizational infrastructure. Specific application of new techniques and technologies is evaluated to ensure that the process redesign can last for 3 to 7 years, with minor continuing improvement. All stakeholders review the process in a formal walk-through, and a case for change analyzing the financial aspects of the differences is developed.

Compliance Management

Compliance means obedience or conformity. Therefore, *organizational compliance* is actions that are made to comply with rules set by others. Requirements for audit or compliance are considered in order to ensure that the redesigned process includes needed controls. Virtually every company has compliance requirements for some legislative entity, whether federal, state, or local (see Figure 9.1). In the United States, all companies are governed by, for instance, the U.S. Patriot Act of 2001, the Health Insurance Portability and Accountability Act of 1996, the Fair Credit Reporting Act of 1970, and the U.S. Data Protection Act of 1998, to name a few. Public organizations have far more compliance requirements than private organizations—for instance, the Sarbanes-Oxley Act of 2002 (SOX), the Securities Exchange Act of 1934, the Fair Labor Standards Act of 1938, and so on. Further, companies doing business in other countries are bound by additional laws. Multinational companies, such as Intel, might be bound by hundreds of different legal entities (municipalities, counties, states, and countries), each with different compliance requirements.

Because legislated action drives many of the activities within organizations, and because much of that activity is only loosely defined, it is important to be clear about compliance issues relating to any process undergoing improvement. SOX compliance, for instance, has cost U.S. companies billions of dollars, yet the law itself offers little guidance regarding what is required. Section 404, Management Assessment of Internal Controls, is the section of SOX relating to reporting and control of a company's activities. Part of this section reads as follows:

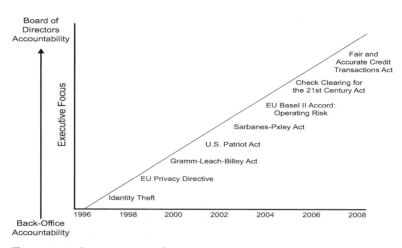

Figure 9.1. Corporate compliance requirements.

(a) Rules required.—The Commission shall prescribe rules requiring each annual report required by section 13(a) or 15(d) of the
Securities Exchange Act of 1934 (15 U.S.C. 78m or 78o(d) to
contain an internal control report, which shall—
   (1) state the responsibility of management for establishing and
   maintaining an adequate internal control structure and procedures for financial reporting; and
   (2) contain an assessment, as of the end of the most recent fiscal
   year of the issuer, of the effectiveness of the internal control
   structure and procedures of the issuer for financial reporting.

(b) Internal control evaluation and reporting.—With respect to
the internal control assessment required by subsection (a), each
registered public accounting firm that prepares or issues the
audit report for the issuer shall attest to, and report on, the
assessment made by the management of the issuer. An attestation made under this subsection shall be made in accordance
with the standards for attestation engagements issued or
adopted by the Board. Any such attestation shall not be the
subject of a separate engagement.[1]

What this says, in simple English, is that a public company must maintain, and prove that it maintains, controls and procedures for financial
reporting that are audited annually. The problem with this guideline is
that adequacy of controls and procedures are left to individual companies
to decide for themselves. Many companies, such as those in financial services, have had such requirements as part of their operating procedures
for years. However, manufacturing, retail, and other less regulated industries struggle with complying with SOX because no good definition of
"control and procedure adequacy" has been available.

SOX audits, at a minimum, look for the following four items:

1. Policies and procedures that state what information is covered by the
   policy or procedure
2. Documents that state how information is created, maintained, managed, and audited
3. Staff members who all must know and follow the policies and procedures governing their work, and dated proof of their compliance

4. Application software that relates to financial reporting and is able to trace from the general ledger back to transactions and from transactions to the general ledger

5. Application software that relates to access-rights management and is able to produce reports showing who has access to financial data, what type of access rights they have, how access right violations are tracked and managed, and how reporting is verified and validated as correct

Even with these more specific guidelines on how to comply with SOX, there is significant leeway in the interpretation of implementation guidelines. The purpose of this section, then, is to discuss general requirements for compliance that should be built into any process-change initiative. These general requirements are as follows:

1. Policies and procedures for financial transaction processing, which should contain information on the following five issues:
   a. *Access.* This issue addresses how accessibility is managed, including who has access, the allowable purposes, detection and management of transgressions, and deterrence practices.
   b. *Controls.* These issues address controls for all aspects of processing—for example, controls to manage transactions and processing for data accuracy, completeness, security, and privacy.
   c. *Change management.* These issues relate to change processes, actual conduct of changes, separation of duties, and proof of all aspects of change management.
   d. *Auditability.* These issues relate to transparency of transactions with capabilities to audit from transaction to general ledger and from general ledger to transaction.
   e. *Noncompliance penalties.* These issues deal with prior noncompliances and remediation of them.
   f. *Emergency issues.* These issues relate to management of emergency or extraordinary situations, including emergency access, change, and management approval.

2. Change management to data, transactions, documents, applications, and operational environments

3. Defined consequences for unauthorized changes of any kind

4. Appropriate authorization levels for receipts and expenditures
5. Both prevention and detection of unauthorized acquisition, access, change, or use of company financial information or assets
6. Measurements, monitoring, and management, all with evidence of the actions, on all aspects of accessibility regarding the items in this list

Therefore, any process dealing with any aspect of financial transaction processing should incorporate the previously listed areas in a process improvement project. There are many other compliance issues, such as health care information, payment card information, and so on, that might also dictate rules for the company process under review. All compliance must be carefully researched and accommodated in the resulting process design. All compliance areas should be reviewed by legal and audit organizations prior to the process being implemented.

Innovation in Process Redesign

Innovation means to introduce something new and different to a setting. The goal in process redesign is innovation that "thinks outside the box" to obtain a lean, clean, productive, and livable process. Livability may come as a surprise but is justified by a quote from Steve Jobs, Apple's CEO, who said, "Design is not just what it looks like and feels like. Design is how it works."[2] This notion is validated by a significant body of literature on the Technology Acceptance Model, which posits that usefulness and ease of use are the key criteria in technology-product adoption by individuals.[3] Thus a design goal is to be creative but useful, innovative, and simple. New techniques and technologies are evaluated to ensure that the resulting process redesign can last for 3 to 7 years.

Innovative practices can come from suggestions made by job incumbents through the interview process, through technological innovation, or through other means. The key outcomes sought include all of the outcomes we have addressed through the application of techniques in the last three chapters, including the following:

1. Improved quality
2. New market identification and development

3. Reduced labor
4. Production process improvement
5. Reduced raw materials
6. Reduced environmental impact
7. Reduced energy consumption
8. Regulatory conformance[4]

Thus innovation seeks to ensure that fresh thinking and ideas have been applied to problem-area improvements.

Process Redesign

The next step is to redesign the process. To reach this point in process improvement, we discussed the steps to map the current process and then lean out waste steps, clean the remaining steps, green all remaining steps to the extent possible, and develop a "blue sky," ideal process. Constraints from management on resources, organization change, or other aspects of the process usually prevent usage of the ideal process. However, the ideal also allows for development of ideas that might not have otherwise come up when only thinking in terms of the current process.

The process of redesign is deceptively simple, as summarized here:

1. Analyze all issues.
2. Brainstorm solutions:
   a. Identify
   b. Evaluate
   c. Choose
3. Compile final recommendations, and obtain approval.
4. Develop proposed process maps.

There is no one way of performing process redesign. Key activities that should be included in any method are review and rationalization of recommendations from all analyses. Often, recommendations are at odds and cannot be reconciled. These recommendations should be carried forward for cost analysis and selection of a preferred alternative by the project client and stakeholders (the validation group). Redesign, then, is the development of a proposed process (with possible alternatives) that includes recommendations from the prior steps. Recommendations that cannot be incorporated into the proposed process should also be identified for discussion with the validation group. An example of redesign is provided in the final report in appendix A of this book, which follows chapter 10.

Process Validation

In chapter 4, we introduced the technique of walk-throughs as a method for gaining both validation and verification at the same time. The technique is again applied to the redesigned process to ensure that it meets all needs, contains minimal non-value-adding activities, automates the process to the extent reasonable, and improves cost, labor, and environmental impacts. The walk-through for process redesign is, again, the culmination of numerous individual walk-throughs of the redesigned process with subject matter experts, those who participated in interviews, those who will manage the revised process, and some of those who will work under the revised process.

Case-for-Change Financial Analysis

A *case for change* is a document or part of a document that outlines the business justification for changing the process (or any other organizational feature, function, or activity). There is no set method for developing or documenting a case for change, but it usually contains some combination of the following tasks:

1. Perform process analysis.
2. Design the ideal or desired process.
3. Perform gap analysis (desired vs. current states).
4. Define the steps (and costs) to obtain the ideal state:
   a. Develop recommendations.
   b. Review with client.
5. Revise, as needed, to fit constraints.
6. Develop final report.

Process analysis is what we have discussed up to this point. In the remainder of this chapter, we will define the ideal or desired process from all of the recommendations gathered and perform a gap analysis, defining the steps and costs required to obtain to the desired state. Then, a final report is produced.

Proposed Changes

The first step in developing a case for change is to define the recommended changes. In the case of a process redesign, the goal is to "paint a memorable and positive picture of how things will be different once the change is implemented."[5] For each recommendation, summarize the problems being solved through the change, what the outcomes will be if the change is not approved, and why the change is needed. Other arguments might include how competitors perform the same process, how this company compares to best practice in the change area, and how this comparison will be altered as a result of the redesigned process.

Once the rationale for change is presented, discuss the changed process in detail with before- and after-process descriptions. Relate the proposed changes to the organization's mission, with benefits of the change defined and monetized (i.e., have the assigned dollar value for either reduced or avoided costs).

Cost Analysis

This section presents basic financial analyses that support the case for change. Two types of analysis are typical: return on investment (ROI) and net present value (NPV). The outcomes are similar in that if the results of the analyses are favorable then they support going forward with the project. If the results of the analyses are not favorable, then the project probably would not get to this point.

Preparation for developing these two analyses is not trivial and should be done with utmost care, as any incorrect projections can skew results in any direction. First, the expected reduction in costs or expenses and any foregone costs should be computed. To develop this analysis, the cost of the current process should be developed. Then, the cost of the proposed process should be developed. Expenses may accrue every year and should be computed for a 5-year period, although the duration is subject to organizational convention. The formula for the expense reduction is shown in Figure 9.2.

Next, any increase in revenues generated from the revised process should be computed over a 5-year period. To compute the cost of each process, the following factors are considered: salary expense, benefits expense, overhead allocation, plant and equipment, computing expense, telecom expense, raw materials expense, and any other components. These costs are only for performing the process, not for changing from the present method to the new process, which requires its own analysis.

Next, return on investment (ROI) measures of the incremental gain in dollars for each dollar spent—that is, a ratio of investment return relative to the investment cost—should be computed as shown in Figure 9.3.

ROI requires estimates of the change in revenue, monetized value of increases in customer goodwill, and so on that will accrue from the proposed process. Returns might be zero if the cost of the new process saves significant money, but a negative return is unlikely to be approved unless some other outcome provides positive benefits.

The last financial analysis that is performed is an NPV analysis, which takes into account the time value of money in discounting future cash flows. The purpose of NPV is to make all comparisons of alternative projects in constant, current monetary terms. The formula for NPV is shown in Figure 9.4.

All of the numbers generated for the analysis should be shown in a spreadsheet for complete financial transparency. Figure 9.5 shows a sample spreadsheet without any numbers. The spreadsheet will be completed for the SCI call center case in appendix A following chapter 10.

Expense reduction = Cost of current process − Cost of future process

Figure 9.2. Expense reduction formula.

$$ROI = \frac{\text{Gain from investment} - \text{Cost of investment}}{\text{Cost of investment}}$$

Figure 9.3. Formula for return on investment.

$$NPV= \sum_{t=1}^{T} \frac{C_t}{(1+r)^t} - C_0$$

Figure 9.4. Net present value formula.

	Year 0	Year 1	Year 2	Year 3	Year 4
Expense reduction					
Revenue generation					
Proposed process investment					
Net impact					
Net present value					

Figure 9.5. Proposed format for financial analysis.

Failure Mode and Effect Analysis

Failure mode and effect analysis (FMEA) is a technique to error-proof processes. FMEA's goal is to anticipate all possible errors and prevent their occurrence as part of the process design. In essence, FMEA assesses what might go wrong in each step of a process and, after prioritizing the issues, mitigates those most likely to seriously damage the company. While FMEA sounds daunting, we all practice it to some extent in everyday life. If you know and take shortcuts to work when there is a traffic jam, or if you take actions to avoid some inconvenience during the day, such as planning errands to avoid high-traffic hours, then you are practicing FMEA.

Failure analysis can take place at many stages and can focus on many alternative aspects of a product or process, including those listed here:

- System focuses on global system functions.
- Design focuses on components and subsystems.
- Process focuses on manufacturing and assembly processes.

- Service focuses on service functions.
- Software focuses on software functions.

In addition, FMEA can be useful in many stages of a single product's life cycle, such as the following:

- A new product or process is being designed.
- A change is made to the operating conditions under which the product or process functions—for example, an equipment upgrade is made.
- A change is made to either the product or process design, which are highly interrelated—that is, when the product design is changed, the process is impacted and vice versa.
- New regulations require changes for compliance.
- Customer feedback indicates problems in the product or process.

As with most activities that seek to improve a product, care must be taken not to overdesign. Product quality and reliability are both important. Overdesign might improve quality but decrease reliability. Therefore, FMEA provides a method for surfacing ideal failure-proofing that may be balanced against the practical needs of the product or process. Automated tools are essential for all but the simplest processes, as FMEA generates an enormous amount of information.

The steps in performing basic FMEA are deceptively simple:

1. Map the process.
2. Convene an interdisciplinary team that is representative of all process areas to be considered.
3. Create the FMEA evaluation form:
   a. List each process step and the physical components used in each process step such as computer applications, robots, electrical components, geographic region of use, and so on.
   b. For each list entry, list *every* possible cause of failure mode (error). A failure mode is defined as the manner in which a component, subsystem, system, process, and so on could *potentially* fail to meet its design intent. Failures are not deviations from a standard—they

are the root causes behind a deviation from a standard. A failure mode might be, for instance, product corrosion, an electrical short, or failure to identify data-entry errors. Methods such as root-cause analysis (RCA) might be used to find all potential errors.

4. For each failure mode, identify the effects of each. The effect is the outcome for a customer, such as an experience or perception. Customers can be internal or external to the organization. For instance, call-center representatives are customers of the organization's IT department.

5. For each possible failure, assign numbers from 0 (low) to 10 for its severity, probability of occurrence, and detectability.

   Severity is a measure of error criticality of the eventual, final product or process: The more the impact a measure has on the final product, the higher the severity rating. One rating system adapted from the U.S. government is as follows:

   a. *Level I.* Death, loss of critical proprietary or private information, complete systems disruption, severe environmental damage, or some completely undesirable event (e.g., weather or other incident requiring evacuation or loss of site or data center)

   b. *Level II.* Severe injury, loss of proprietary or private information, severe illness related to technology use, or major damage to systems or the environment (e.g., system outage lasting 1 week)

   c. *Level III.* Minor injury, minor occupational illness, or minor system or environmental damage, acceptable outcome with management review (e.g., system outage lasting less than half a day)

   d. *Level IV.* Less than minor injury, occupational illness, or less than minor system or environmental damage (e.g., loss of disk storage or partial network outage)[6]

   The probability of occurrence is a measure of likelihood or frequency of the failure:

   a. *Frequent.* Possibility of repeated incidents

   b. *Probable.* Possibility of isolated incidents

   c. *Occasional.* Possibility of occurring sometime

   d. *Remote.* Not likely to occur

   e. *Improbable.* Practically impossible

Detectability requires an understanding of current means of prevention, and the detectability rating is of the ability of the current means of prevention to identify the failure. Examples of detectability ratings include the following:

a. 100%: Possible to identify all occurrences
b. 75%: Likely identification of occurrences or errors can be anticipated if monitored
c. 50%: Some possibility of identifying occurrences or can identify it as it occurs
d. 25%: Low probability of identifying occurrences until after the error has occurred
e. 0%: No ability to identify occurrences until a user or customer notices the problem

6. Compute the *risk priority number* (RPN). The higher the RPN, the higher the priority for fixing the error:

$$RPN = severity \times occurrence\ probability \times detectability$$

7. Based on RPN prioritization, develop a remediation plan.
8. Implement the actions, including measures that will provide evidence of the success of the changes (this can take months).
9. Review results, update the FMEA table, and reassess RPNs. This should be done after at least 3 months of use of the revised actions to allow the sample of control measures to sufficiently report on the success of the changes.

The FMEA process appears simple because each step has understandable actions that may be taken. It is complex because each step takes a significant amount of work to uncover all failure modes, to research and define every possible failure, and to research and define all current means of detection and prevention. This is the case especially when the detection means, for instance, are embedded in software that runs a piece of equipment for which no documentation is available. As a result of the complexity relating to the identification of all possible failures and all current means of detection, FMEA exercises frequently focus on a step of a process or a known problem area rather than on a whole process.

Figure 9.6 shows a partial FMEA diagram for a call center. The termination code problem related to incorrect termination codes entered by

Step	Function	Failure Mode	Effect of Failure	Severity Rating	Potential Cause of Failure	Occurrence Rating	Possible Means of Detection	Detection Rating	Risk Priority Number (RPN)	Preventative Actions to be Taken
Logon	Logon to PC	Logon fails	CSR cannot work	2	New emp	2	Logon fails	2	8	Reboot delays usually no more than 1/2 hour
Logon	Logon to Davox	Logon fails	CSR cannot work	2	New emp	2	Logon fails	2	8	Reboot, check employee added to Davox, no others; delays usually no more than 1/2 hour
Logon	Logon to campaign	Logon fails	CSR cannot work	2	New emp	2	Logon fails	2	8	Reboot, check employee added to Davox, no others; delays usually no more than 1/2 hour
Logon	Logon to campaign	Logon fails	CSR does not get paid	10	SW Bug	6	CSR Paycheck	10	600	Custom software
Payment	CC Number verification	Number not legal	System hangs; Customer has to provide information again	8	SW Bug	8	None	8	512	Custom software
Payment	CC Transaction authorization	Wrong length number	System hangs; Customer has to provide information again	8	SW Bug	8	CSR verify	8	512	SW validation
Payment	CC Transaction authorization	Non-numeric	System hangs; Customer has to provide information again	8	SW Bug	8	CSR visual verify	8	512	SW validation
Payment	CC Transaction authorization	Empty	Request for entry	6	Op Err	4	CSR training	0	0	No error; software does check this
Payment	CC Transaction authorization	Dashes in wrong place	System hangs; Customer has to provide information again	8	Op Err	6	CSR training	8	384	SW validation
Term Code	Termination code process	Illegal code entered	System error message	6	Op Err	0	CSR training, SW	0	0	No error; software does check this
Term Code	Termination code process	Legal code, does not match trans	Recall customer, wrong accounting, wrong activity counts	8	Op Err	8	CSR training	10	640	Custom software needs to link term code entry to transaction type

Figure 9.6. Call center partial FMEA.

call-center representatives for collections transactions. Since the error was undetectable in its present form, a fix required custom software to link a termination code to a payment type based on the screens visited for the transaction. The impact of the problem was indirect. Customers who made payment or promised to pay were legally entitled not to be called again for the same charges. If those same customers were called more than once, then they complained back to the client organizations that, in turn, complained back to the call center. With an RPN rating over 600, this problem had the highest priority for correction and was forwarded to the CIO for implementation.

As with every technique, FMEA can be customized for specific industries and can include much more information than provided in the example. For instance, life-sustaining industries, such as health care, recommend FMEA forms that include columns to show analysis for the following:

- a hazard rating
- whether or not there is a single point of failure
- different options beyond detection to accept, control, or eliminate the failure
- definition of outcome measures for the failure
- responsible person and management approval

With these additions to the basic FMEA template, the FMEA analysis becomes evidence of many other related actions in event of an audit.

FMEA fits in any process management program from a one-time use to continuous improvement. Part of risk management discipline is for managers to decide the following:

1. High or severe risks to prevent
2. Medium risks to manage
3. Low risks to ignore

FMEA provides a sound foundation for those decisions. Risks to prevent and manage both require detection and remedy if an event were to occur. Risks to prevent also require mitigation, that is, system or process redesign, to reduce their probability. Every risk should have some means of detection to ensure that action is taken based on management needs at the time. Figure 9.7 shows a general mapping of severity and frequency, grouping them as high, medium, and low risk.

FMEA has been compared to RCA as a method for identifying causes for errors. While there are similarities—both are based on an interdisciplinary team, a process map, systemic analysis, and outcome of areas and their priorities for remediation—the differences are significant. RCA is usually post hoc, analyzing some critical incident to prevent its future occurrence. FMEA seeks to prevent errors by anticipating what *might* go wrong and by determining how best to manage the situation. In an ideal world, FMEA would obviate the need for RCA by having anticipated and prevented all failures. However good this state might be as a goal, it is unrealistic. For instance, how many organizations double-check the electrical company's computations of their electricity needs? Even the company used as an example in the RCA discussion had not thought it necessary to do that until they experienced a critical incident.

Advantages and Disadvantages of FMEA

FMEA is a powerful technique that can identify and prioritize problem prevention and detection measures. The advantages and disadvantages of this method are summarized in Figure 9.8.

Statistical Process Management Revisited

Recall that statistical process control (SPC) is the analysis of large quantities of measures, primarily taken from manufacturing machines, to determine if the measures are within tolerance limits of required quality. SPC is used mostly in automated workflow and manufacturing environments that have defined standards of quality. Periodic measures of the work are

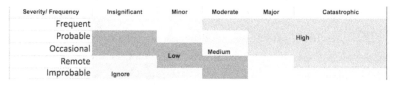

Figure 9.7. Risk assessment.

Advantages	Disadvantages
Problem finding and diagnosis are based on fact and expertise.	It is time-consuming.
It can identify potential solutions to problems.	It may require special training for participants.
It prioritizes problem areas for further action.	It may focus on symptoms rather than causes.
	It may overdesign a process.
	Participant bias may prevent problems from surfacing.
	It can be costly.

Figure 9.8. Advantages and disadvantages of FMEA.

taken, stored, and mapped for further analysis. In this section, we discuss rudiments of SPC setup and how it is used to develop process metrics.

To develop SPC controls requires several considerations. SPC works best on high-volume processes that are at least semiautomatic and that need real-time control. In this way, you are controlling what the machine does, not operator actions such as setup. For instance, integrated chips, nanotechnology, biotechnology, plastics, chemicals, telecom, pharmaceuticals, aerospace, and automobile manufacturing are all examples of technologies that benefit from SPC. Similarly, automated workflow, insurance, credit, payment, financial instrument purchase, and so on are service industries that use a form of SPC.

If you are setting up the workflow or production line as well as the SPC process, then determine the tasks that are needed to meet the goal, that is, create a detailed process map. On the process map, indicate specific tasks carried out by a machine and the tasks performed by humans. For each automated task, describe any setup required. Conduct an FMEA exercise to identify all possible causes of errors in the process and product. The characteristics that are most amenable to SPC are those in which the controls are capable of accurate and objective measurement. Thus the FMEA might find many possible causes of errors, but only a fraction will fit the SPC criteria.

For each cause selected, define precisely what data are needed to determine if the task is being performed correctly. This should be specified for both human and automated tasks. Then, determine how the data can be collected. For instance, automated machines have the capability of taking built-in measurements. The software might come with the needed measures, or it might be programmable for customizing measures. If embedded measurement software is not feasible, optical readers or add-on hardware with embedded software might be required. If metrics cannot be automated, then SPC may not be feasible.

Determine the extent to which the variability of processes needs to be considered in taking measurements. That is, if there are several places within a given process task that could provide readings, then you need to do enough analysis to identify the one point that provides the most accurate reading of desired behavior.

While SPC reports will eventually be automated, to determine the applicability of SPC to a specific measure, one or more manual reports should be created. SPC requires normally distributed data. The following manual process can be followed to develop SPC reports to determine whether the data are normally distributed. This process is followed for each characteristic to be measured:

1. Take a sample of 100 readings on the characteristic to be measured.
2. Use the sample to develop an initial SPC chart. Manually, turn an 8 ½ × 11-inch sheet of paper on its side. On the left side, in the middle, write the desired outcome measure for the characteristic. For instance, for the distance between holes on three-hole punched paper, say the distance is 2 ¼ inches. The central measure is 2 ¼ inches; draw a line across the center of the page and write "2 ¼ inches" on the left side of the line.

   For each line above and below the centerline, create a series of increments. Increments should allow 150% variation in the measure so that the upper limit (10th line up from the centerline) would be 3 3/8 inches and the lower limit (10th line down from the center-line) would be 1 1/8 inches. The amount of total variation, 150%, is divided into 10 to 15 increments so that accurate depictions of actual measures can be obtained. If we choose increments of 10, each increment will be 0.1125 inches different from the one below or above the centerline.

3. Determine the allowable margin of error for the punch distances— in this case, 0.1 inch.

4. Draw light lines to show the tolerance limits.

5. Manually plot the numbers from the sample on the diagram using the x-axis for time of sample taken and the y-axis as the measure of the sample item.

6. Next, analyze the diagram. If any of the following conditions apply, then SPC may not be useful because the process is not stable enough:

   a. More than 10 consecutive data points on the same side of the mean (center) line

   b. More than 10 consecutive data points heading in the same direction, either increasing or decreasing

   c. Single data points that are clear outliers that cannot be explained

   d. Any distinctly nonrandom recurring cyclic or wavelike patterns in the line

7. Calculate a "capability factor" as the maximum reading minus the minimum reading (this is the process spread), divided by the total tolerance spread. If this capability factor is less than 1.0, either the process needs redesign, or it is not amenable to SPC. If the capability factor is greater than 1.3, then SPC should be capable of reducing the nonconforming characteristic. If the value is between 1.0 and 1.3, then variation may be able to be reduced but cannot be guaranteed.

8. The last evaluation is to determine normality of distribution for the data (see Figure 9.9).

   a. Draw a vertical line down the right side of the sheet, and to its right, write the number of data points contained within each line.

   b. Take another piece of paper and draw a horizontal histogram, plotting the number of points per line.

   c. Analyze the final diagram and, if approximately normal, this step is amenable to SPC monitoring.

These actions and decisions are taken for every step of a process and for every characteristic to be measured for which SPC is considered. It is obviously time-consuming and costly, but SPC is wasted on nonnormally distributed, or clearly uncontrolled, process steps. It is important

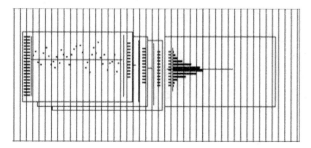

Figure 9.9. Manual SPC chart showing data distribution.

to qualify every use of SPC as having the potential to meet the goal of assignable variance reduction.

Once SPC is up and running, the next hurdle is interpreting the control charts that are generated. Control charts vary depending on whether or not the characteristic being measured is continuous or categorical. Figure 9.10 shows the relationships between the variable type, sample, and report type generated. Each report type is briefly described in Figure 9.11.

These charts are not used in isolation. Sample charts of variance or x-bar (sample average) charts might be used with c-charts (count) and u-charts (unit deficit count) to determine the need to explore specific samples for defects. The x-bar chart would identify the samples needing more information. The c-chart would be used to identify the total defects in the sample. The u-chart would evaluate defects per unit. The company might have a rule that for any sample ±3σ, with total defects over 100 in the sample and with average number of defects per item over 15, reject the sample. This type of rule requires all three charts to determine which samples are rejects.

In general, conditions needing further follow-up on any single diagram include the following:[7]

- any points outside the ±3σ control limits
- 4 of 5 successive points ±2σ on the same side of the centerline
- 6 successive points that increase or decrease
- 8 successive points on the same side of the centerline
- 7 successive points that are ±1σ and on the same side of the centerline
- 14 points on the same side of the centerline

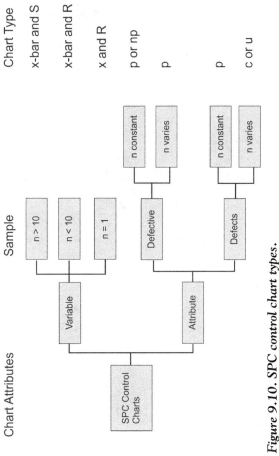

Figure 9.10. SPC control chart types.

Chart type	Interpretation of contents
X-bar (sample average) charts plot the mean value for groups of measurements.	Group mean plots identify batches for evaluation when anytwo dots are above the upper control limit (+3σ) or below the lower control limit (−3σ).
The s-chart monitors within group variation.	This diagram help make sense of variations in the X-bar chart above by evaluating within-group variation.
The R-chart monitors the range of variation within small samples.	Shows difference between high and low subgroup ratings for small samples >1 and < 10 measures. Because this chart is showing a range, the control limits are likely less than 3σ.
The x-chart plots the individual measurements.	The interpretation is the same as X-bar, keeping in mind that each reject is a single item.
For n = 1, the r-chart monitors the difference between the current and previous measurement.	The change in direction of large quantities would be the cause for further investigation with this diagram.
The np-chart monitors the number of defective items in samples of constant size.	Defective items can have any number of defects.
The p-chart is used to monitor the percentage of defective items in samples of either constant or varying size.	The meaning is similar to np-chart, differing in that percentages have different accepted tolerances.
The c-chart monitors the count of total defects in a sample of constant size.	This chart indicates total defect count, regardless of the defect location.
The u-chart is used to count defects per unit.	This chart indicates a count of defects in a single unit (e.g., a car).

Figure 9.11. SPC charts and contents.

Advantages and Disadvantages of SPC

Control charts are very useful summaries of processing, over time, when voluminous data are collected. The advantages and disadvantages of SPC are listed in Figure 9.12.

Force Field Analysis

Any change effort, no matter how small, is subject to resistance. *Force field analysis* (FFA) offers a method for diagnosing situations by looking

Advantages	Disadvantages
It improves overall product quality.	Poor measures result in poor control—garbage in, garbage out.
It simplifies error finding.	It requires sound understanding of statistics and sampling.
It simplifies tasks for control engineers who are trying to use quality data for process control.	A single process may require multiple measures and monitoring of many variables; very complex.
It summarizes complex information in such a way to show variation and patterns in variation.	It is time-consuming.
Error and problem diagnosis is based on fact.	It is costly.
It has reduced learning cycles for setup and control.	It is useful only for normally distributed data with assignable variance.
It has evolutionary operational improvement.	

Figure 9.12. SPC advantages and disadvantages.

at forces for and against a decision or change. FFA is a group brainstorming process that focuses attention on those factors that force or otherwise support a decision and factors that oppose, restrain, or resist a decision. No special skills are required for FFA groups, but the group should be fully cognizant of the decision or change under review and its potential ramifications. To perform FFA, the following steps are conducted:

1. Draw two columns, with one header running across both.
2. Write the planned change in the header area.
3. Label one column "driving forces" and the other one "restraining forces."
4. List the forces in the two columns.
5. Rate the relative importance of each item in both for and against columns.
6. Once you think the list is complete, review each force to evaluate if it has equal pro-con entries. Forces seek equilibrium—often for every positive force there is also an opposing negative force. This step is performed to determine if there are counterweighting forces:

   a. For each positive force, seek to match it to a negative force.
   b. Conversely, for each negative force, seek to match it to a positive force.
7. Once the list is complete, focus on each restraining force, developing a plan for managing the issues and people:
   a. Define how it can be removed, reduced, or managed. Encourage creative but realistic thinking. Both direct and indirect actions should be considered. A direct action would directly confront the negative force in some way, while an indirect one would be to conduct an activity that should reduce the negative force without direct confrontation.
   b. For each pair of counterweighted forces, analyze just that pair and determine all of the factors that would cause someone to fall into one group or the other. How can the factors that move someone into the positive-forces column be leveraged to optimize the positive force?
   c. When an opposing force is an individual, discuss the source of negative affect and how it can be reduced, co-opted, or removed from the situation.
8. Next, focus on remaining positive forces. For each, identify individuals who exemplify each characteristic or factor. Discuss how they might be leveraged to increase acceptance of the changes.

FFA assumes that for any given situation, management of the supporting and restraining forces will influence any change that is planned. Supporting influences might include financial pressure, government regulation, incentive earnings, competitive forces, and so on. Conversely, restraining forces are any resistances that might keep the change from being successful. Examples of restraining influences might be apathy, hostility, poor maintenance of equipment, loss of political power, perceived loss of face, and so on.

Consider the dilemma of the new manager who takes over a work group in which productivity is high but whose predecessor continually pressured his subordinates to be even more productive. The former manager decreased work satisfaction to achieve increases in output in the short run. By doing this, however, restraining forces against productivity developed, such as increased hostility and antagonism, and at the time of the former manager's departure, the restraining forces were beginning to manifest themselves in turnover, absenteeism, and other actions, which subsequently lowered productivity shortly after the new manager arrived. The new manager faced a new equilibrium at a significantly lower productivity.

The FFA in Figure 9.13 summarizes the situation. In the supporting column, the positive outcomes of the situation are increased sales and increased staff efficiency. Those two positive aspects of the situation are countered by pressure on subordinates, hostility, absenteeism, and turnover. There are no matching positive effects for the negative ones. The situation is fairly clear that the restraining forces will need action to improve the situation. The problem is how to reduce the restraining forces without sacrificing or reducing the positive ones.

Notice that these restraining forces are symptoms that, if treated alone, will not fix the underlying problem of anger at management. Thus the first step is fact-finding to determine the root cause of these symptoms.

One method of restraint reduction could be to undo the outcomes of the prior manager; however, that has negative outcomes for the managerial perception of the new manager, that is, he would be perceived as blaming the prior manager for the situation. Another approach is to indirectly address the restraining forces in order to reduce their effects. This can be done without mentioning the prior manager in any way and would be preferred over a blaming scenario.

One indirect approach is to take time away from the usual production operation and engage in problem solving, training, and development. In the short run, output will tend to be lowered still further. However, if commitment to objectives and technical know-how of the group are

Productivity driving	Productivity restraining
Increased sales—1	Pressure on subordinates—3
Staff efficiency—1	Hostility—5
	Absenteeism—3
	Turnover—2

Figure 9.13. FFA analysis of productivity dilemma.

increased in the long run, then they may become new driving forces, and these, along with the elimination of the hostility and the apathy that were restraining productivity, will now tend to move the balance toward a higher level of output. By understanding the forces and their interrelationships, the new manager was able to turn the situation around. This example not only shows that FFA provides a useful framework for diagnosing interrelationships, such as those for productivity, but also allows its users to analyze how short-term decreases in productivity, with good management of restraining forces, can lead to improvement of all relationships in the long term.

Thus using FFA as a framework for analyzing forces for and against a course of action, positive changes might be derived from raising supporting forces, reducing restraining forces, or both. In the example given, by reducing restraining forces and removing the pressure for productivity, equilibrium between productivity and work satisfaction was achieved again without overtly addressing any of the issues.

Advantages and Disadvantages of FFA

FFA is a technique for analyzing the forces present in any situation; it is particularly useful in analyzing resistance to proposed changes. The advantages and disadvantages of this method are summarized in Figure 9.14.

Advantages	Disadvantages
It directly confronts organizational issues to deal with change resistance.	Problem finding and diagnosis can be conjecture or opinion.
It can identify potential solutions to problems.	It may not identify all forces.
It is inexpensive.	It may surface issues the organization does not want to address.
It does not require extensive time.	

Figure 9.14. Advantages and disadvantages of force field analysis.

Summary

Before redesigning a process, compliance requirements should be checked. Every organization is bound by one or more legal requirements; multinational organizations must comply with the laws in every country in which they operate. The complexities of compliance management require organizations to be able to prove that they comply, usually by providing written documentation of policies and procedures and some type of transaction evidence that shows the procedures in action and the methods of policy evaluation, including detection and prevention of unauthorized activities.

Process validation for the recommended changes and their rationales should also be performed. Walk-throughs with stakeholders, subject-matter experts, and other affected parties should be held to accomplish validation.

Next, the case for change is developed. This is a documenting of all of the problems, all of the recommended solutions, and a financial analysis of the costs and benefits. In addition, identification of the affected parties, the need for organization changes, and a plan for completing the recommended changes should be part of the report.

FMEA is a technique for error-proofing processes. It can be used to analyze any item that is subject to failures and is useful at different stages of a product's life. The key activities of FMEA are to define all possible product breakpoints, breaks, and all possible points of failures. Then, the severity of each failure, the probability of its occurrence, and the likelihood of the failure's detection are defined. The RPN is computed by multiplying scores assigned for severity, probability, and detectability. Sorting the RPN from high to low provides simple prioritization for implementing failure prevention plans.

SPC is the analysis of large quantities of measures taken, primarily from manufacturing machines, to determine if the measures are within tolerance limits of required quality. SPC requires normally distributed occurrence of variations and works best on high-volume processes that are semiautomatic or fully automatic, needing real-time control. Depending on whether the variable measured is continuous or categorical, and depending on the sample sizes being evaluated, different SPC charts are created. While the content of charts differs—for example, depicting variance between samples, variance within samples, percentage variation, range of variation, and so on—they are all interpreted somewhat similarly in that any points outside control limits are deemed as requiring further investigation as to the cause of variance. Other rules include any 8 successive points on the same side of the centerline, any 6 successive points that increase or decrease, 2 of any 3 points in the $\pm 3\sigma$ zone, 4 out of 5 points in the $\pm 2\sigma$ zone, and so on. Control charts and SPC improve overall product quality by providing real-time feedback and management capabilities. SPC simplifies error finding, simplifies tasks for control engineers, and summarizes complex information in order to simplify interpretation. SPC is time-consuming, costly, and, if measures are poor, is unlikely to result in improved control.

FMEA identifies prioritized means to meet goals but does not address how to prove that changes were successful. In applying SPC tenets, as the FMEA exercise is conducted, it is a good practice to identify variables for measurement. Chance, chronic, or common variance is variation that is inherent to a process and cannot be eliminated without changing the entire process. Assignable or sporadic variance is caused by something other than nature and therefore can be reduced or eliminated by finding and eliminating its cause. Continuous variables are measured on a continuous scale and can be identified with a high degree of accuracy. Attribute variables identify discrete, binary characteristics that are either present or absent. Continuous measures are preferred over attribute measures wherever possible because they provide more information about the nature of the variation.

FFA is used to diagnose acceptance or rejection of changes through definition of forces supporting and resisting a decision or change. By analyzing the FFA entries, managerial actions can be defined to minimize impedance from resisting forces and maximize outcomes from supporting forces. FFA is an inexpensive, simple technique to master. Care must be taken in its use to ensure that all forces are identified.

CHAPTER 10

Measures and Final Report

Introduction

Measurement of any work process or practice is . . . imperative . . . Whether we are talking about a benchmarking project or just tending to day-to-day management, without numbers we don't really know what we are doing . . . Without metrics, managers are only caretakers.

—Jac Fitz-Enz, *Benchmarking Staff Performance*

Measurement provides the feedback necessary to manage a process, product, or business. Further, metrics provide a discipline for developing objective and meaningful decision criteria from information based on fact. In most organizations, thousands of measures are taken about every facet of business life, but few measures have meaning without understanding their context. Part of the challenge of designing measures is to also design how they will be reported and presented to the intended audience. This chapter begins with the balanced scorecard as a framework for discussing measures and metrics. Then we revisit benchmarking and discuss the importance of different types of benchmarks for comparison of organizational success. Next, presentation is discussed with respect to developing customer-oriented metrics and dashboards to present them. The ongoing use of metrics for continuous improvement is then defined.

Every project ends with some documentation of its methods, analysis, findings, and recommendations. This section summarizes the contents of a business case that constitutes the final project report for a process improvement project. In that section, the future of project management and the role of process management in moving white-collar work to a service orientation are discussed. We conclude with a brief discussion of processes in the context of information technology (IT) service management.

Balanced Scorecard

The balanced scorecard concept of measuring organizational success grew out of W. Edwards Deming's quality work in Japan in the 1950s. Robert Kaplan and Richard Nolan published the first of many papers and books on the balanced scorecard to encourage companies to systematically measure and manage by the numbers. A *balanced scorecard* is a series of measures on different dimensions to achieve a holistic view of the organization. Kaplan and Nolan[1] recommend that four dimensions be measured: financial performance, customer satisfaction, learning and innovation, and internal processes (see Figure 10.1). Others recommend different dimensions, such as "employee," and as many as eight dimensions have been recommended.[2] The point of a scorecard is to develop a view of the whole organization's health for use in charting the organization's future.

The scorecard concept shifts managerial focus from management by *objectives* (MBO), that is, what you are expected to do, to management by *results*, that is, what you have actually done. This shift is an important

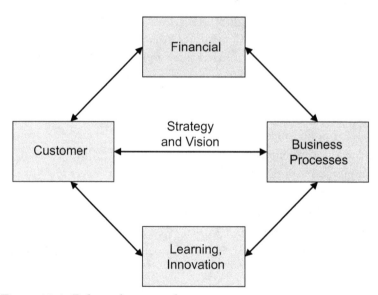

Figure 10.1. Balanced scorecard components.

Source: Adapted from Kaplan and Nolan (1992).

one, since in MBO, you might meet all objectives but have few results. Human resources research on salaries, motivation, and other factors concludes that people do what they are paid for. Therefore, the shift from managing objectives to managing results signals to all that positive outcomes are required.

Figure 10.1 depicts the four areas of traditional scorecard reporting. In general, the organization annually holds objective-setting sessions to develop its direction and ensure that the tactics match the strategic mission of the organization. Initiatives are identified that are expected to meet the objectives. For each initiative, targets for performance are defined, and for each target, measures are defined. Targets and measures become the focus of activity, since for many, meeting the targets determines salary in the organization. Poor performance might mean job termination.

To define a balanced scorecard, each component is defined starting at the highest level of abstraction down to measures such as those shown in Figure 10.2. Perspective and objectives are strategic, initiatives are tactical, and targets and measures are operational. Each perspective leads to definition of objectives for that level, which are achieved by one or more

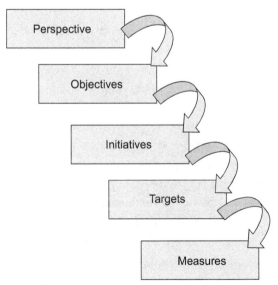

Figure 10.2. Balanced scorecard component perspectives.

Source: Adapted from Kaplan and Nolan (1992).

initiatives. Each initiative has targets for completion and success, which are reported on by measures.

Each perspective has objectives for meeting the overall strategy for the organization. For finance, an objective might be to decrease expenses by 5%. Notice that the objective is specific, quantitative, and simply stated. But objectives are unlikely to be met without tying them to specific initiatives. For instance, reducing head count by 2% might lead to a 4% reduction in expenses, while reducing travel expense by 3% might reduce expenses another 1 to 2%. The initiative to "reduce travel expense" might lead to a new policy—for example, "No travel will be booked for first-class or business-class tickets for travel under 10 hours of flight time." Another policy might be "No expenses will be reimbursed without a receipt." Measures of those initiatives, plus measures of overall expense categories, are needed for verifying that initiatives or objectives are met.

Objectives relating to internal processes and practices might relate to a production line in manufacturing or processes in service organizations. Key questions relating to scorecard perspectives include the following:

1. *Financial.* How do our shareholders perceive us?
2. *Customers.* How do we become the most valued supplier to our clients?
3. *Internal processes.* What processes must we excel at to achieve financial and customer objectives?
4. *Innovation and improvement.* How do we improve processes and systems to create value? How do we continue to learn and grow?

The balanced scorecard provides a vehicle for executives to communicate their vision and strategy to everyone in the organization. By defining performance targets, it also provides a means for linking strategic goals to individual performance. By measuring and monitoring performance, feedback to the executive group is provided. The executive group can then adjust its strategy, objectives, and initiatives based on the success of its ongoing efforts. Over 65% of companies in the United States and Europe use some kind of balanced scorecard approach, and it is touted for use in managing production, IT, and other functional areas of a business. Further, with the passing of the Government Performance and Results Act of 1993, all U.S. government agencies were required to adopt a balanced scorecard for reporting their activities. The scorecard has subsequently been widely adopted throughout municipal, county, and state governments.

Advantages and Disadvantages of Balanced Scorecards

Balanced scorecards have far more return for organizations than cost. Nonetheless, there are both advantages and disadvantages, which are summarized in Figure 10.3.

Strategic and Customer-Oriented Metrics

Measures, such as those taken with statistical process control (SPC) are embedded in equipment and are "ground-floor-level" measures that determine success or failure of a single item or batch. However, metrics are meant to be presented to management, which has neither time nor tolerance for details that require much effort to understand. Further, the higher the managerial level, the less detail they want in initial reports. However, most managers also want the luxury of drill-down to the nth detail should they want it. Therefore, more customer-oriented means of reporting metrics are needed to provide for customer and executive audiences. *Strategic and customer-oriented metrics* are metrics that report at a level of meaning to the user, who is either executive or customer. Recall that Six Sigma describes the *voice of the customer* as the "stated and unstated needs or requirements of the customer"[3] that provide input

Advantages	Disadvantages
It can present an overview of all critical organizational activities.	It can lead to reluctance to change within the organization.
It can improve decision making.	It requires organizations to be systematic in tying objectives to initiatives.
It can more closely tie operations to strategies.	Measures may focus on the wrong things.
	It may surface areas the organization does not want to confront.

Figure 10.3. Balanced scorecard advantages and disadvantages.

to techniques for process and product design such as quality function deployment. Metrics are also called the *voice of the customer* in that the customer should define their version of process success, and that definition is used to define metrics for reporting.

Typically, measures such as SPC are taken and dealt with at the level of the organization in which they are taken. For reporting up the organization, details are summarized or otherwise massaged to develop a more strategic view of the business area as defined by stakeholder managers.

An example is IT operations. Most, if not all, organizations take measures of their available time (uptime) for each piece of computing equipment. From these statistics, they arrive at a measure of uptime for each type of equipment, such as central processing unit (CPU) cycles, print time, or telecom connections. Sometimes this type of number actually leaks out of the IT organization even though it is essentially meaningless to its users. These metrics are useful for predicting and preventing equipment failures, for determining problem areas for further evaluation, and as components of more summarized metrics.

To develop customer-oriented metrics, one must first ask, "How does the customer view this operation?" In IT operations, *service-level agreements* (SLAs) might help to understand the customers' view. SLAs describe what services are available, how much they cost, and their expected availability. SLAs also define penalties for not meeting the agreements; in outsourcing or charge-back organizations, this means foregoing payment for some period. SLAs have two sets of definitions: customer and technical. Technical SLAs are defined in terms of CPU cycles, telecom links, or equipment uptime. Customer SLAs are defined at the *service* level, for instance, "communication services consisting of voice, voicemail, and e-mail services will be available at all corporate sites and via VPN 24-hours/day 7 days/week with <.01% lost time." The software and hardware are not defined in terms of technology, but in service terms—for instance, "Customer order processing via the Internet will be available 24-hours/day 7 days/week with 100% completed order accuracy." Since the definition of the service is in terms of overall availability, the metrics reported to customers should be at the same level and for the same criteria. This usually means a 180-degree shift in how the IT operations group reports on its work. Technical SLAs match customer services to the IT services (people, process, resources, and technology) that provide the service. Reporting of availability for any given service, then, is the combined uptime of all technologies and actions used in service performance. If tapes (T), CPUs (C), disks (D), telecom links (L), and printers (P) all are involved in providing e-mail, then the uptime for the service is computed with the following formula:

$$\text{service availability} = \text{avail} (T \times C \times D \times L \times P)$$

If each service has 99.99% availability, the service availability is 0.9994, which, in a 31-day month, means approximately 27 minutes of downtime. If this time were in the middle of the night, during which time the company does little of its work, then this may not have bad consequences, but if the company is an airline, for instance, then this could translate to $50+ million of lost revenue. In the example in Figure 10.4, the uptime for different services is dependent on the number of resources used in providing the service. The numbers at the right, but in downtime and uptime, provide a means for discussion about the quality of computing service, whereas the old numbers are not able to be interpreted in customer terms in any case because they are aggregates. The customer-oriented numbers also provide a basis for developing costs and estimates of impact about technology upgrades and redundant processing. Thus the first step in developing a dashboard is to define all metrics in terms of the customer they serve and technologies involved in providing each service.

Another method frequently used requires the development of key performance indicators (KPIs) to determine what best to measure.

Before		After	
	Up-Time	Downtime in Days	Up-Time in Days
CPU	99.92%	E-mail	3.81	26.19
Tape	99.12%	Order Entry	4.04	25.96
Disk	99.95%	Internet	2.43	27.57
Print	95%	Accounting	4.04	25.96
Telecom	92%			

Figure 10.4. Example of customer-oriented metrics.

Performance metrics measure *what* you are doing by assessing overall performance in the target area. They are external in nature and are most closely tied to outputs, customer requirements, and business needs for the process. Each KPI would have measures developed and taken during the course of process execution.

Diagnostic metrics are measures that ascertain *why* a process is performing the way it is. Diagnostics tend to be internally focused and are usually associated with internal process steps and inputs received from suppliers. Further, diagnostic measures are not regularly taken but are used when a process has moved outside the normal range and is being diagnosed to determine the reason.

To create measures, follow these steps:

1. Identify customers and outputs of the process. Customers may include end users of products or services, process managers of downstream processes, and process users. Refer to the process map, as needed, for this information.

2. Determine customer needs and requirements. Useful techniques include reviewing outputs with customers to gain their buy-in, establishing their needs and requirements, and having *them* define how best to measure their part of the process. Use the same process with suppliers to quantify measures of their product quality.

3. Define effective measures, including both performance and diagnostic metrics. Brainstorming, mind maps, and affinity diagrams are useful tools for defining measures.

4. Align metrics for each process with those for the higher level processes of which they are a part. This requires comparison of other related metrics.

   a. Create a table, where the rows of the table are labeled with the key measurement areas. Head columns with metric description, current performance level, short-term objective, long-term objective, competitive benchmark, the measure, and how the measure is to be taken.

   b. Complete the table for each measure created.

   c. Evaluate all measures for an area.

d. Revise or otherwise align measures, as needed, to ensure complete coverage of the area or process to be measured and to ensure as little overlap as possible between measures.

SMART is an acronym to describe a well-defined measure. SMART means Specific, Measurable, Actionable, Relevant, and Timely. Each SMART term is defined as follows:

- *Specific measures* are unambiguous, precise, simple, and targeted to the area being measured. For example, a good measure of customer satisfaction is direct feedback from customers on how they feel about your service or product. A poorer metric, because it is indirect, is a count of returned products or number of customer complaints.
- *Measurable* measures are composed of data that are accurate and complete.
- *Actionable* metrics provide clear performance direction so that reviewers know when corrective action is required.
- *Relevant* measures measure only things that are important enough to report to the customers.
- *Timely* metrics are those for which data are available as needed— for example, through an online dashboard.

Development of measures is not a one-time activity. Once measures go into production use, they are reevaluated as they are used to validate that they measure what was intended and that they do it in an actionable, useful way. Any metric that does not meet both criteria should be redesigned and the cycle of development reiterated.

Advantages and Disadvantages of Strategic and Customer-Oriented Metrics

Using the voice of the customer to report on organizational activities is important in presenting meaningful information. The advantages and disadvantages of customer-oriented metrics are detailed in Figure 10.5.

Advantages	Disadvantages
They improve the perceived quality of the good or service.	They increase accountability of the provider.
They provide a basis for costs and impacts of change on the service.	They require a new way of interpreting information about organizational operations.
They improve customer satisfaction and understanding.	They may lead to a reluctance to change on the part of information provider.
They provide a basis for discussion on improvements that might otherwise not be present.	

Figure 10.5. Strategic and customer-oriented metrics advantages and disadvantages.

Presenting Metrics: Dashboard

In addition to finding a method of presentation that is meaningful to the audience, executives need to monitor a whole organization, not just one or a few parts of it. Therefore, they need metrics for every part of the organization. A *dashboard* is a visual, usually real-time or online, series of performance reports that depict the health of organizational components. Sophisticated dashboards have *drill-down* capabilities such that when more information on a specific metric or business area is wanted, the user clicks on that part of the dashboard and a more detailed report is available. The best drill-down capabilities go from the voice of the customer to the lowest available level of detail. Dashboards can also provide business logic and rules underlying summary reports while providing detailed supporting data with a drill-down capability.

Because dashboards are programmed, they can embed intelligent functions, such as an escalation feature to raise awareness of a problem up the management hierarchy as it ages and has no resolution. Another type of intelligence might be to embed triggers for support processes when certain performance criteria are (or are not) met.

Dashboards can have different orientations and include the following:

- strategic impact performance maps with cause and effect
- geographical dashboards
- management reporting dashboards

- functional dashboards
- process performance dashboards

Dashboards can be linked to business strategy and how it is implemented. For instance, if the company uses the balanced scorecard at the strategic level, then the dashboard would present the perspectives of the organization and summarize each initiative's status. At the level of manager of an initiative, the dashboard might show how each organizational component is behaving relative to the initiative.

Dashboard design is a combination of knowledge and artistry, requiring deep understanding of the goals, uses, context, and content of the final product. Some characteristics of dashboards are generic, including the following:

- Provide all needed functionality.
- Allow drill-down.
- Use meaningful, tasteful colors. Colors should have typical meanings for the culture (e.g., in the United States, red may symbolize bad, dangerous, or a stopped condition; yellow symbolizes a slow, marginal, or cautious condition; and green symbolizes go, good, or a safe condition).
- Use appropriate graphics.
- Design with the notion that 27% of the population has some form of color-blindness and sees primarily blues and browns. Red, green, and yellow are all seen as shades of brown, so if these colors are used, then provide other cues, words, or shapes to indicate status.

All dashboard metrics should show both current value and acceptability range or target criteria. If the dashboard is to report on a balanced scorecard, then sections for each perspective contain information on that area's major initiatives. If the company has multiple geographic locations, then the dashboard should contain information by country.

Even with an understanding of these characteristics, dashboard design is a complex, iterative activity for choosing meaningful, tasteful graphics that also convey requisite meaning. An example of a good dashboard design is presented in Figure 10.6. The design elements that make this a

Figure 10.6. Sample sales dashboard.

good design are consistency of presentation, controlled use of color, and a combination of graphics with absolute numbers, with gauges to indicate trend, acceptability, and actual readings for most information categories. The small gray dots in the "past 12 months" number grouping show that market share is below its target and needs attention. Dashboards should provide a snapshot, with drill-down of details, for executives and managers to monitor their progress toward business goals. When properly designed, they can be useful and help drive business decisions. If they miss key items for measurement and monitoring, then they can also hide information and hinder organizational effectiveness.

Advantages and Disadvantages of the Dashboard

Using the voice of the customer to report on organizational activities is important for presenting meaningful information. The advantages and disadvantages of this dashboard are detailed in Figure 10.7.

Benchmarking Revisited

Recall that a *benchmark* is a point of reference against which other measures at different points in time are compared or measured. There are three main types of benchmarks: internal, external, and best practice. Baseline benchmarks, all of which are internal, include cycle time, financial, efficiency, effectiveness, and quality. Chapter 5 discussed both internal and best-practice benchmarks. Here, we elaborate on that discussion in describing external benchmarks.

External benchmarks include performance, process, and strategic types. *Performance benchmarks* are those that compare results for some activity. An example is a benchmark that evaluates sales per employee against other companies, both in and not in the same industry. A *process benchmark* measures how processes are performed, with an example being the claims-payment process of an insurance company. A process benchmark might measure, for instance, number of steps, number of specialties involved, time from claim to payment, technology used, and so on. *Strategic benchmarks* compare strategic decisions and outcomes at a more abstract level and include, for instance, decisions about target markets for a product or introduction date for a product type.

Advantages	Disadvantages
It provides an instant snapshot of business conditions.	If it is missing key information, then it may hinder organization management.
It improves executive knowledge and understanding.	If it is poorly designed, then it can obscure information and hinder understanding.
It provides feedback that allows strategy-initiative links to be adjusted as needed over time.	It can be costly to build.

Figure 10.7. Dashboard advantages and disadvantages.

Figure 10.8 shows three basic models for external benchmarking: one to one, group, and mediated. In using *one-to-one benchmarking*, a company selects possible partners based on some chosen characteristic such as size, revenues, or industry. The company approaches each possible partner and arranges a benchmarking agreement with each. The benchmarks of the multiple partners are shared only with the company with which they have an agreement. *Group benchmarking* is initiated by a single company that solicits other companies to partner and share benchmarks. *Mediated benchmarks* have data collected by a third party, such as a trade group or research institution, with the understanding that all collected and aggregated data become available to each participating company.

In all types of benchmarking, care must be taken not to discuss or include any information regulated for pricing, marketing, production, product information, customers, or fiduciary responsibility. Also, partner choices must consider potential conflicts of interest over the data gathered and avoid any potential for legal or ethical criticism.

An example of comparable processes might be waiting times for hospital admissions, hotel check-in, bank-teller transactions, school registration, concert ticket purchases, and so on.

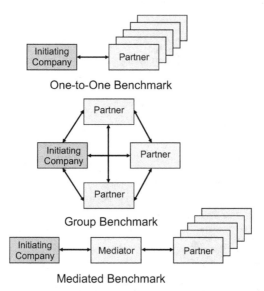

Figure 10.8. External benchmark types.

The motivation for benchmarking is to verify the status of a process, product, strategy, or other entity by comparison with other organizations. The major outcome of external benchmarks is a ranking or rating of the company relative to the benchmark partners. From this knowledge, gap analysis is conducted to determine where and how your organization might improve. Part of the selection of benchmark partners is to obtain best practice for your industry or world-class performance for some generic activity. In addition to determining how to improve the company's conduct of the target process, the best-practice or world-class comparisons help in setting targets for performance of the redesigned process. If the targets are not obtained as part of the baseline benchmark activity, then they should be obtained as the redesign is taking place to ensure the best possible process redesign. Further, target goals, best practices, and world-class benchmarks are used in monitoring improvement, which is discussed in the next section.

If the gap between benchmark performance and best practice is great, then intermediate goals are set with the eventual target defined with the length of time required or allotted to get there. For instance, if the company's performance is 25% of best practice, an analysis of cost to obtain best practice might be conducted. That analysis might determine that 50% of the cost will allow you to attain 75% of the target, but the last 25% would be 50% of the cost. From this analysis, you might decide that 75% of best practice is all the company can sustain at present; therefore, the target would become 75% of the best-practice measure, and to get there would take 5 years with a 20% improvement on current practice each year. These are still ambitious goals that would also require changing managerial job description expectations, bonuses, performance measures, and so on.

Advantages and Disadvantages of Benchmarking

Benchmarking is a useful and productive activity that can help poor-performing companies develop a plan for action based on how they rate against peer organizations. On the other hand, well-run organizations can suffer from benchmarking. The benchmark might show, for instance, that a company is better than its peers on 80% of measures but that they are also spending significantly more to maintain that position. When cost cutting occurs, these same managers might be criticized for "being better" and not at par with their competition, that is, executives might manage by comparison. As a way of saving money, executive management might reduce budgets and staff to specifically decrease the company's competitive position. This is a short-term solution to a long-term situation that can alter the course of a company's success. The advantages and disadvantages of benchmarking are detailed in Figure 10.9.

Monitoring and Improvement

The intent of SPC and benchmark reports on business practice in the short term is to run the business. In the long term, though, monitoring is useful for trend analysis and improvement. *Monitoring and improvement* describes the periodic assessment of processes for improvement. We differentiate this from continuous improvement, which assumes ongoing evaluation and improvement efforts. Every company needs periodic reevaluation of processes in order to debureaucratize, remove non-value-adding activities, and otherwise streamline and rationalize the process. Not every company needs, or can afford, continuous improvement. Continuous improvement implies an ongoing group to oversee, compile, interpret, and act on performance reports from around the organization. Periodic improvement implies an ad hoc group, convened for 4 to 6 weeks periodically—say, once a year. The ad hoc group reports on findings, identifying trends and recommending improvements or further evaluation of suspected trouble areas.

Advantages	Disadvantages
It provides a basis for improvement targets.	It requires trust of other organizations and that they provide truthful data.
It improves executive knowledge and understanding of industry position.	It can be costly.
	It may provoke management by comparison.
	Measures must be taken exactly the same way and have exactly the same meaning to be faithfully interpreted.

Figure 10.9. External benchmarking advantages and disadvantages.

Having an ad hoc group conduct periodic evaluation does not mean that ongoing monitoring is not done. Rather, ongoing monitoring is used to manage daily activities without specific attention on noticing trends or seeking improvements. Some trend might be so obvious that a change action will be required without an ad hoc group. The group simply ensures that someone is looking for areas for improvement on a regular basis. There is no one best way to monitor for improvements, just as there is no one best way to measure a single activity. Much like conducting an audit, the ad hoc group decides what information to attend to and what can be ignored.

The improvement team starts by reviewing the previous assessment and evaluating statistics generated from each process over the period since the last improvement assessment. They then create an initial evaluation to continue, or not, in evaluating a specific process. If they decide to continue, then the team either requests further information, conducts a process audit, or continues with its assessment. Benchmarking might be conducted as part of the assessment exercise, with the results factored into the analysis.

The outcome of the assessment or audit would consist of recommendations for each reviewed process relating to the state of the process, its conduct, cycle time, cost to the company, outcome quality, relationship to balanced scorecard activities, benchmark comparisons, and any needs for improvement.

A dashboard of assessment outcomes might be used to present information to executives in the case of continuous improvement activities. With an ad hoc group, a report or memo would summarize the findings and recommendations. Often, one of the team members becomes the person to lead a recommended improvement effort.

An ad hoc team performing assessments needs to include people who represent both the low-level technical aspects of processes being evaluated and the executive view of organizational strategy and how the process fits in that plan. Smart companies assign their most promotable people to assessment teams as a way to help them become knowledgeable of a cross-section of the organization and to meet and work with their likely future peers.

Advantages and Disadvantages of Monitoring and Improvement

Monitoring, at least periodically, is needed to keep a company from lagging behind its peers in innovation and use of new methods, technologies, and processes. It can be conducted as an ongoing activity, but it need not be. The advantages and disadvantages of monitoring and improvement are presented in Figure 10.10.

Business Case

The business case, or final report, is the last step of any consulting engagement or internal consulting project. The business case might take the form of a formal document, memo, or other type of report. It is addressed to the project sponsor, who uses the document as the basis for signing approval for project completion. The project activities, in general, include the following sections:

- project formation
- development of current process map
- analysis
- recommendations
- proposed process map
- benchmarks, measures, or both
- project summary
- signature page
- appendices

Notice that the document's sections omit key aspects of a case for change. Sections of a change case that may or may not be in a final report include

Advantages	Disadvantages
It provides opportunities for regular, periodic improvement.	It can lead to disruptive organizational life.
It provides opportunity to become world-class by comparison to the best performers.	It can overtake "getting product out the door" as the goal.

Figure 10.10. Monitoring and improvement advantages and disadvantages.

financial analysis, jobs and roles affected by proposed changes, and a project plan for the changes. The next sections discuss these various parts of the report.

Cover Page

The cover page for the final report should identify the name of the report—for example, "Final Report for the SCI Call Center Technology Analysis"—and the report date and list the names of participants charged with developing the project outcomes.

Executive Summary

Probably the most difficult section is the executive summary. Novices want to gain executive attention and believe that more information is better. While executives want to know what types of decisions are needed and if there is a credible business case, they prefer all of this information in the shortest possible summary.

The challenge of the executive summary is to tell a whole story in less than one page, preferably less than a half page. John Clayton's famous *Harvard Business Review* article[4] on executive summary contents recommends one sentence on each of the following topics:

- the need or problem that prompted the report
- the recommendations and their value
- substantiation for the recommendations as the right solution

The challenge, in addition to brevity, is to keep the summary "clear, clean and to the point."[5] This means removal of all adjectives and adverbs and a focus on the customer and product, not the project team or their efforts.

Therefore, the best executive summary is one that is a concise, clear description of project outcomes and their value, with any available supporting information showing that this solution is the best.

Often, a substantial project may develop a hundred or more recommendations that are not distillable in three sentences. In that case, choose the most critical changes and summarize them. In any case, the goal is an executive summary that is less than a half page. An example of an executive summary is presented in the appendix following this chapter.

Introduction

The final project report introduction should identify the major goal of the project, the sponsor, and a description of relevant information that the report reader needs in order to understand the project context.

Project Methodology Summary

The methodology section answers the questions who, what, when, where, why, and how as they relate to the conduct of the project. The "who" identifies the project participants from the subject organization and the roles they played. The "when" identifies key dates for the project to provide background for the sequence of events. The "what" information itemizes the major steps and activities of the project and should roughly follow the outline for the report. The "where" describes where the work was conducted. The "how" describes forms of information elicitation, any techniques used, the forms of analysis, and synthesizing exercises for developing recommendations, as appropriate. This section should be brief and is only to provide project context, not a history of all activities.

Current Process With Current Process Map

While often called an "as is" map, the formal term "current process map" should be used in the final report. The process map set should include an overview diagram that summarizes the whole process, or processes if more than one is analyzed. The map should be in a form that is easily accessible to all stakeholders, preferably on an Internet site. The map should also be included in the final report document as an appendix link or embedded document. The report provides a text description of the process and refers to the map for its details.

Analysis Results With Recommendations

The analysis should discuss each analytical technique, explaining in one to two sentences what the technique is and why it was chosen for this particular analysis. Then, each is discussed with embedded figures (if they fit, or reference icon links for separate documents, if not). Each analysis should have a discussion of the results, with the analytical outcome and accompanying recommendations. Every recommendation should be clearly tied back to one of the analytical techniques.

This tying of recommendations to analytic technique is important because, as a process expert, you are paid for your knowledge of and expertise in applying techniques and not for opinion or unsubstantiated thoughts. Therefore, no recommendations should ever be made that are not tied to analysis results of some type.

Often, problems with recommendations that do not directly relate to the project goal are found. In this case, they should be discussed with the project sponsor as to whether or not they belong in the report. The project sponsor's decision should be followed. If allowed in the report, then there should be a section of each affected analysis that discusses these recommendations as outcomes of the project that are beyond the project scope.

Recommendations Summary

This section is a simple summary list of all recommendations. The best way to create this list is to review each analysis section and list the recommendations from that section. In this way, recommendations that are not tied to some form of analysis are avoided.

Often, the project team may see an opportunity for follow-up projects that could be done by one or more members of the project team. These should be put in a subsection of the recommendations titled "new project recommendations." *New project recommendations* should list each recommendation, define how it was derived, discuss the work to be done, and describe what the expected outcome would be. Consulting companies use this as an opportunity to develop an ongoing relationship with the client organization, but care should be taken not to "sell" the next job.

The focus should be on the work to be done and the skills needed—not on who should conduct the work.

Proposed Process

The proposed process section includes a process map with explanation. The proposed process map should incorporate all recommended changes. In addition to discussing the process, any role changes should be discussed. To the extent known, people who will be changing roles or who are otherwise affected by the changed process should be identified. If known, any new job or role incumbents should also be identified.

Benchmarks and Measures

Every changed process should have, at a minimum, a baseline benchmark and three to five measures. The baseline benchmark provides the basis for proving that the changes have accomplished the goal. Other benchmarks (e.g., some type of external benchmark) may also be conducted to provide best practice or comparative information to define goals for the changed process.

Measures for the changed process need to accomplish two goals. First, the changes should have measures that prove they were successful. So for a call center, for instance, the software that requires customer service representatives (CSRs) to log on to a campaign would be considered successful if no campaign log-ons are missed. Therefore, some way to measure campaign log-ons for CSRs would be recommended.

Second, the measures must support ongoing management of the function in its new form. This means provision of three to five customer-facing metrics that provide a means for measuring business function success due to system or process availability and functioning. Customer metrics are usually summaries of several detailed metrics, providing for development of dashboards with drill-down capabilities.

Signatures

Every project needs an end, and the end is determined by a formal sign-off by the client. One method of obtaining this sign-off is by attaching a sign-off sheet to the final report. This accomplishes two things. First, the project is deemed successful and at an end; therefore, the staff on the project become available for other assignments. Second, it signals the user that they must take ownership for the changes and continue their operation without the project team.

Signatories to the final project report, at a minimum, should be the project sponsor (whoever is paying for the project) and the project manager. In some situations, it may be desirable to have a corporate signatory with budgetary approval levels appropriate to the project, or the entire project team, as potential signatories to the document.

Often, when improvements are done as consulting engagements, project sign-off marks a point for renegotiation of ongoing work by one or more members of the project team. Thus the signing marks a time at which "selling" of follow-up work could be done.

Appendices

Appendices may be attached to the final document or can be separate documents. When separate, they should have inserted icons that directly link to each document. Appendix documents for a process improvement project might include process maps, change requests, dictionaries of terms, data-center schematics, a case for change, analyses, work papers, or other supporting documents. Only relevant sections should be included. Dictionary, change, and supporting document sections are the most common and are briefly defined here.

Dictionary

Projects often address company functions that are not generally known in the organization or that have arcane names, such as those used in the military. When this is the case, a dictionary should be created. However, dictionaries should not be used when there are no unusual, arcane, or unknown terms.

Change Requests

Change requests document the resolution of requested changes that deviate from a project contract or statement of work. All changes should be documented in formal change reqests. These documents describe the change; provide an analysis of project impact, due dates, and responsible parties; include possible project activities to be omitted as a result of the change; and, if rejected, a reason for rejection. If there are no change requests throughout the duration of the project, then this section is omitted.

Supporting Documentation

During any project, documents are collected to provide background information to the team, identify problems and issues for follow-up, and record supporting information for the project. Ideally, as mentioned earlier in this book, these are best stored in an intranet repository and should be identified with links to each item in this section of the final report. To the extent that the documents are paper, they should be included in the sponsor's version and the team version of the final report, with a reference to the physical storage location in other documents.

As paper is difficult to maintain for any length of time once the project team disperses, physical artifacts require the appointment of an "owner," who should be identified in the final report. The *documentation owner* is responsible for preserving the project's documentation for some company-defined period of time. If there is no supporting documentation gathered throughout the duration of the project, then this section is omitted.

Conclusion

In this section, we discuss the future of process management and how it relates to servitizing organizations. Over the last 50 years, the U.S. economy has migrated toward a predominance of services jobs without changing companies' functioning to be servitized. Servitizing is described in this section and related to IT functions in the final section.

Future of Process Management

Over the last 50 years, process management has been a fad that has come and gone two or three times. Since the recognition of the transition to a service economy over the last 20 years, the importance of customer experience management, and the recognition that process management is required to best leverage information technology investments, it appears that process management is now here to stay.

Without standardizing processes, especially in large organizations, guaranteeing some modicum of consistency across service delivery is virtually impossible. By standardizing and measuring performance at the individual, group, and function levels, the desired level of consistency becomes possible. However, consistency does not guarantee customer-facing service necessities, such as a smile, cordiality, deference, and so on, without changing the reward system and without continuous training and management. Thus continuous management is the sustaining force for process management.

Automation has also altered how processes are evaluated in an organization. As digital-document technology has matured and dropped in price over the last 15 years, companies that are not as information intensive as early process-management adopters, such as financial services and insurance, are now finding it cost beneficial to automate process management. The jobs being supported by automated processes are mostly white-collar jobs that previously were thought not to be amenable to automation. This trend will continue for at least the next 5 to 10 years. Beyond that, we may experience a paradigm shift such that all jobs are designed to be as fully automated as possible from their beginning, rather than retrofitting the automation. By that time, we may be wearing our computers and managing all aspects of life and work via automated means.

Role of Process Management in Servitizing Organizations

Services are nonreturnable goods that are often fully supported by information technology to satisfy wants, needs, and aspirations of an organization's customers or users. Services tend to be voluntary, noncoercive, and built to produce a positive experience for both the user and provider. Services can be individually defined, such as creation of an architectural diagram, or embedded in a product, such as an emergency room in a hospital or help desk in an online course system. IT services range from intangible to partially tangible, from help desk support to PC provisioning. Services often involve coproduction, especially as made available through the Internet. Many services are information based, but some are based on relationships and social capital.

As early as 1940, researchers discussed the provision of services in conjunction with manufacturing activity. Early services, for instance, were repairs or returns of manufactured goods. As technology and business evolved, services developed in a wide range of venues and range from fully automated, as most Web 2.0 software products, to partially automated, such as delivery of food at a restaurant.

Many of the techniques applied throughout this book apply to both processes and services. For instance, all tenets of Six Sigma apply to services.[6] Service level agreements (SLAs) are contracts that describe the customer service provided. SLAs have an accompanying technical definition that describes the technology, people, and process that service delivery requires.

All services have one or more embedded processes with their input-process-output (I-P-O) characteristics. Therefore, process management is integral to, but distinguished from, service management.

The term *servitizing* means the change from product or process orientation to service orientation. A service is a self-contained system with customers and goals, in an environment with human, physical, and informational enablers and one or more I-P-O process systems. Unlike most other business offerings, a customer can participate in all of the service components.[7] Therefore, the best services have significant and representative customers who act as advisors on service design and provision. Focus groups are useful for this type of advisory role.

In addition to service components that require definition and harmonization, criteria used to differentiate service systems include capital intensity, extent of customization, service object, tangibility, level of customer involvement, and employee discretion.[8] The same service offered by two different companies is likely to be similarly defined in terms of the components (i.e., goals, I-P-O, etc.) but differ on the extent of customization, tangibility, customer involvement, and so on. As a result, companies seeking to move toward service orientation need to carefully define not only the service but also how the service will be delivered.

One service example is a car dealership that offers free loaner cars when a car is brought in for servicing. The dealer provides a free car wash after the car service is complete and provides a cookie or candy to the owner upon pickup. The loaner car is a service, the service on the car is a service, the free car wash is a service, and the cookie or candy is a service. In a service industry, such as car servicing, work is performed by an anonymous technician who the user must trust is skilled enough. As services are added, the perception of the technician's skill is enhanced. Thus there is a halo effect with additive services that carries to the "basket" of services. Measuring customer service satisfaction requires that one understand how many, and what, services are involved in providing "the service" and measuring each.

IT Service Management and Process Management

IT organizations have three main suborganizations for development and acquisition of applications, data and database management, and infrastructure management and IT delivery. Infrastructure and IT delivery has received little management consideration until the last 10 years, as trends in offshoring and outsourcing focused attention on the need to run IT like a business. It has long been known that 80% of an application's cost is realized in its years of maintenance. Yet only recently has cost management's focus turned to the actual running and supporting of IT delivery and its impact on the organization.

In the 1980s, the UK government embarked on an exercise to improve its operational functioning in the hope that it would improve the value of IT to the government. The outcome of the UK exercise was the first version of the IT Infrastructure Library (ITIL), a series of books that document best practices in the management of the IT operations function. Now in version 3.0, ITIL shows how organizational strategy and a need for improvement can both drive process and service improvement. The general field of IT management built on ITIL has come to be known as IT service management (ITSM). From an ITIL perspective, a *service* is "a means of delivering value to customers by facilitating outcomes customers want to achieve without the ownership of specific costs and risks."[9]

ITSM is the collective set of services needed to servitize an IT organization. ITSM is bigger than ITIL, which only addresses operational aspects of IT. In addition, there are audit, control, acquisition, development, quality assurance, data management, database management, and other aspects of IT management that are also classified as ITSM.

Skeptics scoff at ITSM as just another name for "good" management, but, in fact, the service aspect turns an IT organization 180 degrees from its prior management. A short example illustrates this difference. Non-servitized IT-operations organizations will have specialties for networks, operating systems, databases, software, mainframes, and servers. Each specialty operates in what is essentially isolation from the others, without regard to how they might need to cooperatively deliver IT capabilities. An example of this is Internet order entry. Metrics, if taken, will measure each specialty independently and will not aggregate them to develop meaning beyond the raw measures. When each area works individually and an outage occurs, finding the source of the outage and restoring normal operation will necessarily take a long time because there is no centralized source of information about the components involved, their relationships, and their interconnections. Accountability for "the service" of Internet order processing does not exist—therefore, the service does not exist.

In contrast, the service "Internet order processing" comprises the previously mentioned specialties, working together to ensure uptime according to an SLA. The measures of each isolated specialty are taken individually and then integrated to develop a measure of Internet-order entry availability. Only the aggregated measure is reported to the client organization, although the isolated measures are still used within the specialties to manage each area. All aspects of the Internet-order entry configuration—people, process, hardware, software, data, database, network, and so on—are defined as *configuration items* (CIs) in a *configuration management database* (CMDB). When an outage occurs, the CMDB is checked to determine all of the elements involved in supporting the service, which are systematically, simultaneously checked until the error is found and service is restored. The group of people, working in concert, can be informed and mobilized via automated software. The manager accountable for Internet order entry can be automatically notified about the outage so that there is instant managerial attention to the situation. The accountable manager can be an IT person or a user responsible for order processing. Outages are significantly reduced in average time to return to normal service; through service management, many outages can be recovered before the user community is aware of a problem.

Definition of a service has all of the characteristics defined and requires two definitions. The first, "easy" definition is the service as the customer sees it. These are documented in a *service catalog*. The second, "hard" definition is of the technology service components as delivered by the IT organization; this is essentially a definition of the capital intensity of the service. ITSM services are highly capital intensive, since they comprise hardware, software, data, and database artifacts, all of which can be quite costly. Complicating the technical definition are emerging technologies for virtual and cloud computing, which obscure the specific base technologies used in service delivery.[10] If the difficult technical service definition is formed, then it reaps many benefits to the organization, such as allowing computation of an actual, likely total cost of ownership (TCO), average cost per transaction, average cost per customer, and similar measures that are not possible without at least some level of servitizing.

Customer contact, extent of customization, and level of customer involvement can be defined during service design; that is, there is a wide range of discretion that can be used to provide each of these service aspects. ITSM service objects include the provision of generic IT services, such as organizational communications (e.g., phone, fax, e-mail, voicemail, etc.), as well as specific IT services, such as SAP (an enterprise resource management software application). Customer contact with a help desk for generic services, such as communication services, might be low, having 95% automated coproductive assistance. SAP, on the other hand, may require 50% automated and 50% human customer contact. In some services, such as PC provisioning, there may be levels of service—for instance, executive, professional, and clerical—such that executives are served within 2 hours but clerks wait 2 days.

Tangibility of service in IT is usually defined as the difference between manual and automated aspects of work. For instance, reports generated automatically and stored on a shared device for general access would be an intangible service, while reports printed and delivered by 10:00 a.m. would be a tangible method of delivery.

Finally, employee discretion would be defined through process design and governing policies to indicate levels of responsibility, escalation to increasingly higher levels of management, and so on. One goal of ITSM is to push decisions, accountability, and responsibility as low in the organization as possible. This, plus automated support and escalation, allows a help-desk representative to become the person who will coordinate needed resources to resolve outages and support customers.

ITSM is an important topic in a process management book because processes are at the heart of services. The characteristics of the service are embedded in the method of process delivery and become part of the method of service delivery. The ability to define, analyze, improve, and measure processes is the first step in being able to define services.

Summary

Measures determine whether a company is meeting its goals, whether redesigned processes are performing better than the prior method, and why problems are occurring. But measures alone are not sufficient for helping managers and executives to make better decisions. Techniques such as the balanced scorecard, dashboards, and benchmarks are needed to ensure that an organization aligns the work completed with its strategic goals and that each initiative has metrics to show that targets are being met.

A balanced scorecard is a series of measures on different dimensions for achieving a holistic view of the organization. A scorecard typically defines strategic objectives for finances, customers, internal processes, and learning and growth. Other perspectives can be defined, as appropriate, for the organization. Each objective is linked to one or more initiatives that each have defined targets for performance and measures of those targets. The balanced scorecard shifts attention from management by objectives to management by results. A balanced scorecard presents an overview of all critical organizational activities, can improve decision making, and can align operations to business strategy.

To develop individual metrics, the SMART method—that is, creating specific, measurable, actionable, relevant, and timely measures—is recommended. It is important that these measures are summarized and translated to fit the audience. Strategic and customer-oriented metrics are metrics that report at a level of meaning to the user. Creating customer-oriented measures requires that customer needs and expectations are defined to match the way the customer thinks about the process area. The needs and expectations are then translated into metrics that are meaningful to the customer. Strategic and customer-oriented metrics improve the perceived quality of the service being measured and provide a basis for impact analysis of costs, billing, and changes. In addition, customer understanding of all aspects of their IT support is enhanced. Conversely, strategic and customer-oriented metrics increase the accountability of the service provider, require new ways of interpreting operational information, and frequently meet with resistance from individuals who are reluctant to change.

A dashboard is a visual, usually real-time, online series of performance reports that depict the health of organizational components, usually with drill-down capabilities. Dashboards can present many different perspectives from functional to strategic to geographical ones. Design of dashboards is an art that requires deep understanding of the goals, uses, context, and content of the final product, combined with an ability to visualize information in simple ways. Dashboards provide an instant snapshot of business conditions, can improve executive knowledge and understanding of the organization, and provide feedback to allow strategy-initiative links to be adjusted when needed. Dashboards can hinder organizational management if missing key information or if poorly designed. They are also expensive to develop.

External benchmarks compare performance, processes, or strategies with those of other organizations and help contextualize interpretation of measures collected and reported about ongoing operations. Benchmarks can be arranged to be one on one, group, or mediated. The outcome of benchmarking is development of improved performance standards that become the basis for defining performance targets.

Monitoring and improvement is the periodic assessment of processes for change. In periodic assessment, an ad hoc team is convened to conduct an overall assessment of all organizational processes, selecting a subset for further investigation. From their investigation, the team develops a report on the "health" of each process analyzed in detail, recommending improvement projects for those found wanting. Periodic monitoring and improvement gives companies an opportunity to become world-class by comparing them to the best performers and setting higher targets for performance.

In any process improvement engagement, the final report summarizes the tasks and recommendations in the most objective manner in order to provide a compelling case for change as well as a road map for the changes. The final report differs from a case for change, as it may or may not include the financial analysis, jobs and roles affected by proposed changes, or project plan for the changes.

A service is a nonreturnable good designed to satisfy some customer need. Services have characteristics that are defined in order to determine how the service is defined. The service characteristics include aspects of I-P-O extent of customer contact, capital intensity, tangibility, and level of employee discretion. The characteristics of the service determine the methods of service delivery. The ability to define, analyze, improve, and measure processes are the first steps in being able to define services.

This book applies a practical approach toward developing process management disciplines. First, waste removal is applied to the overall process to ensure that only needed steps are kept. Then, each remaining step is further analyzed to ensure its most efficient functioning. Finally, consideration of outsourcing, coproduction, and automation determine the most cost-effective method of product conduct. Once the process is redesigned, it is error-proofed to further improve quality functioning, and metrics for process management are defined. Finally, a final report describing the case for needed changes and their financial justification are completed. Upon acceptance of the suggested changes, one or more new projects to implement the changes are initiated. As we mature in our understanding of servitizing organizations, this work may also evolve. More processes will be automated and outsourced as companies realize that development of their distinctive competencies requires only the activities that are central to their business. The service industry has become a permanent economic reality. Process management is integral for allowing companies to best exploit service improvement. Process management is critical to performing required activities over time with repeatable quality. Managed processes will ultimately aide companies in staying competitive.

Final Report for the SCI Call Center: Technology Analysis

December 1, 2010

BY: David Birch
Cindy Allison
Enrique Estevez
Anil Henry
Sheri Jones
Brad Powell

Executive Summary

An analysis of technology use in the call center was done from August through October 2010. While many recommendations are detailed in the report, the main recommendations relate to two major areas:

1. *Call center technology*. The Davox and Siemens equipment should all be moved to a secure location. Documentation on the Davox should be secured. Training of dialer administrators (DAs) should be conducted to improve call center operations. Create software to guarantee customer service representative (CSR) logon to campaigns and to prevent DA overwrite of campaigns' collections. These suggestions should lead to fewer outages and improved call center operations (e.g., a lower hang-up rate) and should reduce calls to the vendor for support. SCI should reconfigure the data center to use a single network of fiber optic cable and should automate and fix many call center quality problems. A project to evaluate Voice over Internet Protocol (VoIP) to supplement or replace current long-distance providers is recommended. These changes will increase the amount and quality of collections.

2. *Call center management*. Standardize a balanced scorecard for all client organizations and several types of reports for call center managers, including a daily "report card" of the prior day's activity. Standard reports will decrease report development time and simplify and routinize operational shutdown. Process definitions should be used as the basis for training and management.

Without these changes, SCI will continue to experience outages, incorrectly completed transactions, lost campaign collections, and other errors that will collectively cause SCI to forego collecting over $1 million per year.

Introduction

SCI is a call center organization performing both collections and sales activities. The project details technology issues and problems in the call center and develops recommendations to improve call center operations. The project was sponsored by Bob Wentworth.

SCI experienced a negative trend in its collections activity, dropping from about $55 million per month to just over $24 million per month (see Figure A.1). When compared to other organizations and industry best practice, SCI's CSRs collect less per employee (see Figure A.2) and contribute less to net income per employee than local competition, industry average, or industry best practice. However, average revenue per employee is higher than the local company comparison and industry average.

These conditions motivated this study, which is to evaluate the technology in the call center to determine the underlying cause(s) of lower

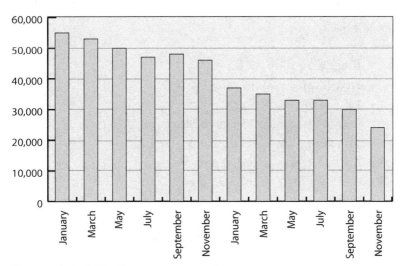

Figure. A.1. SCI collections per month.

	Income per employee	Revenue	Net income
SCI	26.6	42.5	4.25
A	31.0	40.0	4.65
Average	44.0	44.0	4.40
Best practice	50.0	50.0	5.00

Figure A.2. SCI financial comparison (in millions).

collections. In addition, the team created process maps to better understand the working life of CSRs and identified a number of significant
issues that also contribute to lower collections. The technical, process,
and management issues found during the course of the project and the
recommendations for their remediation are the subject of the remainder
of this report.

Project Methodology

Interviews, observation, document review, and technology reviews were
all conducted for this project. This section describes these activities and
the individuals involved in the process.

The SCI staff who were involved in one or more of the activities
include the following:

- Bruce Wentworth, COO
- Steve McHenry, Call Center Manager
- Pat Andrews, CIO
- Dennis McCardle, Operations Manager
- Juan Perez, Day-Shift Dialer Administrator
- Arlette Johnson, Client Services Manager
- Ann Paige, Accounting Manager
- Joey Harrington, Marion George, Sarah Capp, John Donovan,
  and Brian McDonald: First-Party Supervisors
- Raul Aguilar, Kristal Somers, Errol Pritzer, Chelsea Buchanon,
  Amber Wilson, and Austin Hoffman: First-Party CSRs
- Gregory Austin, Mandy Millikan, Andy Rogers, and Guillermo
  Gutierrez: Third-Party CSRs

The project team thanks all of the individuals for their time and
expertise in assisting us in performing the tasks involved in this project.
Any errors or omissions are those of the project team and not of any of
the previously mentioned individuals.

Interviews were held with the first five staff on the previously mentioned list. Each provided details of their area of responsibility and perceptions on the collections and sales processes. In addition all of the call
center supervisors, Steve McHenry and Bruce Wentworth participated in

reviews and validations of the current and proposed process maps. Many of the previously mentioned individuals were engaged to identify flaws in the processes and technology as well as how to fix them. The sequence of project events was the following:

- interviews of managers
- observation of collections and sales activities
- development of draft collections and sales processes with identified discrepancies
- walk-through of draft process maps
- revisions based on walk-through comments
- analysis of various aspects of collections activities, which included the following analyses:
  - brainstorming, Pareto, check list, and other techniques to identify problems
  - quality function deployment analysis to improve quality of collections
  - root-cause analysis for training issues
  - value-added analysis with cycle time analysis of collections processes
  - financial payback analysis of the value-added recommendations
  - analytic hierarchic analysis of dialer administration and account management
  - analysis of opportunities for coproduction engaging clients and customers
  - technical analysis of automation
- development of recommendations and proposed process map
- review and validation of the recommendations and proposed process map
- development of metrics and a balanced scorecard for call center activities

The following section discusses the current processes for each area, identifying issues and recommendations. Then, the recommendations are summarized in the following section. The next section describes the proposed process changes and provides a financial analysis justifying the changes and metrics to prove that the changes were successful. The appendices follow.

SCI Organization

The first activity was to develop an SCI organization chart (see Figure A.3). The diagram provided the project team a clear understanding of organizational responsibilities to ensure focus on the call center. Although some findings relate to other organizations, the call center remained the focus.

A baseline benchmark was created using as the average and best practice numbers, information from an industry association's call center website. As Figure A.4 shows, cost allocation information shows SCI spends significantly less than the industry average in most categories except real

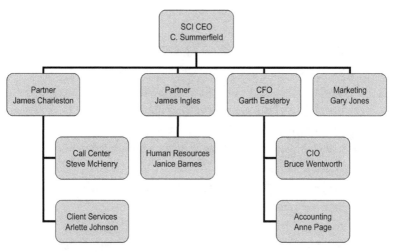

Figure A.3. SCI organization chart.

Metric	SCI	Average	Best practice
Salary and benefits as % of operating expense	52.67%	57.29%	54.61%
Recruiting, screening, and training	.6	4.62	3.22

Figure A.4. Cost allocations (percentage expenses).

estate. The low spending on computer software and telecom equipment may indicate that SCI's technology is inadequate for its use. This is further evaluated in the technology section of the report.

Other performance metrics were also evaluated (see Figure A.5). In virtually all categories, SCI measures indicate that performance is a significant problem with higher wait times, higher wrap times, and high numbers of abandoned calls, calls in queue, and errors per 1,000 calls.

Turnover in the call center, at 180%, is also significantly higher than the average of about 22%. Hiring cost is also significantly higher at $8,800, while the average is about $6,400 and best practice is about $4,000.

In other industry comparisons, best practice is to have all CSRs able to respond to customer e-mails with industry average of 75% of call centers

Metric	SCI %	Average %	Best practice %
Wait time (# seconds it takes for 80% calls to be answered)	1P – 30 seconds 3P – 75 seconds	36.7 seconds	18.3 seconds
Average speed of answer (seconds)	1P – 38.8 3P – 54	34.6	21.2
Average talk time (minutes) SCI time last quarter	1P – 2.2 3P – 2.2	6.1 minutes average	3.3 minutes average
Average wrap time (minutes)	1P – 7.5 3P – 8.3	6.6	2.8
Average percentage of calls abandoned	1P – 8.7 3P – 10	5.5	3.7
Average time in queue (seconds)	1P – 55 3P – 69	45.3	28.1
Average time before abandoning (seconds)	1P – 390 3P – 200	66.2	31.2
Cost per call	Unknown	$9.90	$7.12
Inbound calls per 8-hour shift	Unknown	69.0	73.9
Percentage attendance	90	86.8	94.7
Data entry error rate per 1,000 contacts sales/recordings	Collections 39 Sales 42	20.9	5.6

Figure A.5. Performance metrics.

having Internet and e-mail request and payment processing. At SCI, no CSRs have e-mail and the Internet is not used as a competitive resource.

By all of these measures, improvements in call center operations should be possible.

Analysis

The call center consists of first-party, third-party, and sales operations (see Figure A.6). A Davox predictive dialer for which start-up and shutdown processes are required on a daily basis supports these. Calls are made, evaluated, and forwarded by the Davox for processing after a formatting screen displays of the proper script and customer information. At the end of the day, the Davox is shut down and files are backed up for reporting and billing.

Each step of the diagram is reviewed in detail to discuss the findings and recommendations. The details of each process are in diagrams located in appendix A1. The project team was asked to omit sales from the project after the initial interviews. Therefore, the remainder of the discussion focuses on nonsales aspects of the call center. The detailed current process map for sales is stored with project documentation. Pricing for all recommendations is analyzed in the financial analysis section.

Dialer Administration

The DA performs start-up processing at the beginning of the work day. First, the Davox and Siemens equipment is started up. Then, Lyricall is

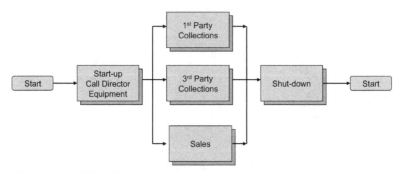

Figure A.6. SCI collection process summary.

initiated for campaign processing. While the start-up is taking place, the DA uses file transfer protocol through a PC to download client campaign files from the SCI website. Campaign files are transferred to the Davox when all downloads are complete. Campaigns to be processed are named, loaded into Lyricall, and prioritized for processing. As many as 10–15 campaigns might be running at any given time. As campaigns complete their cycles of calls, other campaigns are loaded and run throughout the day.

Once the initial load of campaigns is complete, the supervisors are notified verbally that processing can begin. CSRs may then logon to campaigns and begin work.

Some issues with dialer administration are the following:

- Training is on the job, usually with a prior DA who is leaving the company. DAs only can learn what the prior DA knows. As a result, DA knowledge has deteriorated and should be remedied by sending both DAs and at least one backup to Davox and Siemens vendor training.
- In the process of bringing a campaign into Lyricall for processing, the DA names the campaigns. There is no process or defined format for the names, thus they are difficult to track and prone to errors. At least once per month, the DA overwrites an already collected campaign with another of the same name for the same client. The problems usually are not recognized until billing time when there is a gap in the information. Then, Dennis McCardle, IT operations manager, must try to recreate the campaigns from the AS/400 files. The average recovery time from such a problem is about 10 man-hours and there is no guarantee that all collections are recovered. Further, there is no longer an audit trail for the collections. This overwriting of Lyricall campaigns should be prevented by creation of software to automatically add a three digit number to the campaign as entered, thus guaranteeing uniqueness and no overwrite. In addition to this software, a process for naming campaigns should be created jointly with customer service and marketing for uniformity throughout SCI.

- Campaign information fluctuates, depending on contract requirements, which are not standardized. Plus, contract terms are passed verbally between the units, which is an error-prone process subject to forgetting. As a result, there is no way to ensure that all contractual obligations are actually met. In addition, every nonstandard contract requires 2–10 hours of customer programming for website functioning and dealing with downloaded information. To improve quality of contract processing, the following recommendations are made:
  - o Standardize contract terms and require executive approval for variances.
  - o Develop a quality review of contracts that will determine the information to be shared.
  - o Develop a web page to convey contract information and implement it on the intranet.
  - o Marketing should e-mail contract information to customer service, the call center manager, and IT to trigger the contract quality review process.
- When Davox problems occur, there is no on-site knowledge. Thus the call center shuts down while the Davox is restarted. Problems of a longer duration require Davox support for recovery. Davox support is for 2-day response and the average time to repair is approximately 3 days. Thus the call center could be out 3 days because there is no on-site knowledge of the equipment. To prevent this situation, the operations manager should be sent to Davox internals training and a set of Davox documentation should be purchased for IT use.

Collections

Agents performing first-party collections act as agents of the client organization, announcing themselves as employees of that organization. Agents performing third-party collections are agents of SCI in the transaction. Both collections groups seek to collect past-due debts, updating databases at both SCI and the customer site (as required) with monies collected. All payment processing is essentially the same for both first- and third-party processing. The difference is that first party follows Lyricall scripts for the entire process while third party does not. The third-party CSRs must manually call up the screens they need to process payments or manage promise-to-pay (PTP) transactions.

Once logged on to the Davox to start a session, the CSR logs on to Lyricall and activates a campaign. However, CSRs can take calls without having logged on to a campaign. First, right-party contact is verified. Then, payment requirements and options are discussed. This results in the following: refuse to pay, dispute, already paid, PTP, direct check, or credit card. If any of the first three result options, then a termination code is entered in the result field and information about the result is entered into the notes field. If a PTP, the date, amount, and payment type is entered into appropriate fields, then PTP is entered in the result field, and the transaction is ended. If a direct check, then a validation screen is called up, the ABA routing number is entered and sent for validation by AS/400 software. If a credit card, then a credit card payment screen is raised and the card number is entered for validation through the AS/400, using web-based software. Errors in these two options often result in the PC freezing and a restart to the transaction. If the ABA or credit card is valid, then the remaining information is entered and the payment part of the transaction is complete. Within the Davox software, all of these transaction processing takes place. In addition, a screen for AS/400 transaction recording is raised and the same information is reentered. Finally, for some clients, a screen is raised to support direct A/R application entry and the transaction is again entered and saved.

At the end of a workday, CSRs all log off of their machines and the Davox is put through end-of-day processes to generate reports and close down database and client processing.

One major issue is time lost to raise screens. Wrong-party processing is particularly time-consuming and wastes CSR payment collection time. A value-added analysis of each process was conducted and shows that raising individual screens is a very time-consuming process that should be reduced. Wrong-party processing is used as the example of this waste.

Figure A.7, the value-added analysis for wrong-party processing, shows that CSRs spend almost 1 minute of time per transaction waiting for screens to display. Part of the problem relates to the network configuration (see the technical analysis section). By eliminating this wasted

Role	Process step	Time	VA	NVA	NVAU
Customer	Wrong-party response	:10		X	
CSR	Get wrong-party response	:01		X	
CSR	Enter wrong # term code	:05		X	
Lyricall	Get term code	:01		X	
Lyricall	Save term code	:00		X	
Lyricall	Display save	:05			X
CSR	Get confirmation	:01		X	
CSR	Enter "message left"	:10		X	
Lyricall	Get request for message	:01		X	
Lyricall	Display notes	:05			X
CSR	Get notes display	:01		X	
CSR	Enter message to call back	:20		X	
Lyricall	Get message	:01		X	
Lyricall	Save message	:00		X	
Lyricall	Confirm save	:00		X	
CSR	Get confirmation	:05			X
CSR	Terminate call	:02		X	
Customer	Terminate call	:00		X	
CSR	Enter customer update information	:20			X
Campaign collections DB	Get term code	:01		X	
Campaign collections DB	Save term code	:00		X	
Campaign collections DB	Display save	:05			X
CSR	Get save display	:01		X	
CSR	Enter call record code	:02		X	
Davox	Get call code	:01		X	
Davox	Save call code	:00		X	
Davox	Display save	:05			X
CSR	Get save display	:01		X	
CSR	End call	:02		X	
Davox	Return to request call	:10			X
	TOTAL TIME	1:56	:00	1:01	:55

Figure A.7. Value-added analysis for wrong-party processing.

time, collections should increase by about $6,800 per day assuming each CSR averages 100 wrong-party calls per day.

In addition to wrong-party screen processing, assuming all transaction types are approximately evenly distributed across all calls, then the average wait for screen displays is 68 seconds per transaction. At that rate, daily revenue of $3,474 is foregone. If screen processing could be reduced across all calls, the call center should increase revenue without any change in process. This change requires reconfiguration of the network, which is discussed in the technical analysis section.

Agent success information is shown in Figure A.8. This diagram shows that by moving agents to the periods of time that are most productive, the success rates on collections can also be improved. For instance, the highest success rates are at the lowest utilization hours for all inbound and first-party outbound processing. Therefore, hours of work for CSRs should be changed to have most CSRs working evening hours, when the percentage of success is highest, and fewer CSRs working early morning hours, when the percentage of success is lowest.

This move might have two impacts on SCI's business. First, they can complete contracts faster. Then, by completing contracts faster, they can sell more contracts. Both activities should increase collections substantially.

Other issues with CSR collections processes are the following:

- CSRs can begin taking payment calls without logging in to a campaign. The result is that the CSR is not paid for those collections and SCI must recover the transactions from the AS/400 records at the end of the month as they are not entered into the Davox files unless the Lyricall logon is completed. To remedy these issues, software should be created such that when a CSR logs on to the PC, they are automatically directed on to a campaign logon screen.
- There is no single process followed by all CSRs. The documented process maps should be made available through an intranet capability for all CSRs to access as needed. The process maps should also be used as the basis for all training with written testing of all CSRs on a regular basis to ensure their understanding and knowledge of the process.

Agent group	Most busy hour	Least busy hour	Total calls/ day	Avg, calls/ hour	Highest success rate	Lowest success rate	Highest util. hour	Highest util./agent	Lowest util. hour	Lowest util./agent
Inbound first party	6:00 p.m.	9:00 p.m.	2,522	210	9:00 p.m. at 82%	8:00 a.m. at 53%	11:00 a.m.	84%	9:00 p.m.	40%
Inbound third party	3:00 p.m.	9:00 p.m.	2,260	151	9:00 p.m. at 74%	8:00 a.m. at 53%	11:00 a.m.	76%	9:00 p.m.	40%
Outbound first party	4:00 p.m.	9:00 p.m.	10,970	731	9:00 p.m. at 90%	9:00 a.m. at 40%	11:00 a.m.	86%	9:00 p.m.	40%
Outbound third party	8:00 p.m.	9:00 p.m.	1,792	128	7:00 p.m. at 92%	9:00 a.m. at 40%	5:00 p.m.	86%	9:00 p.m.	40%

Figure A.8. Agent success rates.

- The first-party collection CSRs deviate from their script verbiage, which is stilted or not exactly appropriate to the situation. There is no process or other means for either first-party collection CSRs or sales CSRs to report and suggest changes needed to scripts that do not work. The recommendation is to develop a process for CSRs to suggest script changes to the client organizations.

- Approximately 40 errors per 1,000 customer contacts cause a significant number of billing issues. By using process maps for training and testing knowledge of processes, the error rate should be reduced. But the rates might be reduced faster and more permanently if a bonus structure were developed for individuals with so many days of perfect collections and for groups with some number of days with perfect collections.

- To reduce the incidence of frozen PCs as a result of software failures in the credit card and bank number validation processes, full testing of those processes (i.e., not just software but also all network connections) should be conducted to determine and remedy the source of problems. If feasible, the software to do these validations should be moved to the Davox and Internet access should be moved to the Davox as well.

- There is significant variation in termination code entries with about 55 errors per 1,000 calls. The outcome of these errors are customers who are angry that they are called when they should not be, calls that should be made again that are not, or outcomes that are reported incorrectly and could lead to incorrect collections amounts. To remedy these errors, a list of term codes should be created and attached to every cubicle as a reminder. In addition, software to provide a pull-down menu for selection of the term code should be created and added to the Lyricall screen to prevent entry of a wrong code. Software should be considered that tracks type of transaction from the entries made and force a correct result, entering the term code automatically if that proves feasible.

- To remedy the problem of time lost from collections for wrong-party transactions, those transactions should be fully automated and executed within the Siemens call director equipment.

- Different screens are required for each transaction type, yet several of the transactions use the same set of fields with different termination codes. Therefore, to eliminate moving from one screen to several, the processing for PTP, disputes, rejects, and already paid transactions should be consolidated on a single screen.

- As payments are made, as many as three screens are required—Davox, Lyricall, AS/400, and client A/R, each taking 5+ seconds to load and each requiring duplicated data entry. Software should be developed to automatically update all required payment files using a single Lyricall screen.

- Training for CSRs is an issue. Training is cut short, not set up when needed, has insufficient training cases for practice calling, and has an ill-prepared instructor. The analysis of training is documented in appendix A2. Human resources (HR) should notify the trainer, DA, and operations manager when training is planned. Then, the trainer should test that all capabilities are available 2 days prior to training. In addition, there should be at least 30 call records available for each person being trained, to provide five of each type for practice. The trainer should be sent to train-the-trainer courses to better prepare her for her position.

- Training for call center supervisors does not exist. The trainer has no experience of supervisor duties and is not respected by the supervisors as being able to teach them anything. Upon completion of train-the-trainer courses, the trainer should be given on-the-job duties as a supervisor in between training assignments. Within 6 months, she should be able to develop supervisor processes, validate them, and use them as the basis for developing supervisory training. In addition to the coursework, all new supervisors should be overseen by the call center manager for at least 1 hour per day their first week of work, and should be mentored by another supervisor for at least 3 months.

- Training should integrate the process maps, and tests of CSR process knowledge should be given. In addition, measures for training satisfaction should be taken and managed.
- Reports for managing the call center are lacking. All reports available in the Davox should be documented and training provided to the call center manager and supervisors to provide them better workday reports on which to base their actions. In addition, the daily report card (see appendix A4) created as part of this project should continue to be used and should be augmented every 3 months or so to guarantee its continuing usefulness.
- Policies in the call center should all be reviewed. Firing for every offense is used as a motivator for CSRs but has the opposite effect. Rather than excel, CSRs believe they will all be fired eventually and that it is only a matter of time. Therefore, while they are diligent, they may not be presenting SCI in the best light. Policies for tardiness, days off, and so on should be reviewed to determine punishments other than firing.
- The position of call center manager has been a revolving door for the past 36 months. Stability in the call center manager position is needed to deal with the many insidious issues, such as training, reporting, and CSR inconsistency, that have developed. Further, the manager should be encouraged to learn everyone personally so that if transgressions do occur, the extenuating circumstances might be considered in an equitable manner.
- Cost per call in the call center is unknown. The ability to manage is determined by the costs of all activities. When the cost of each activity is unknown, the ability of the manager to manage is diminished. Therefore, SCI should develop metrics that lead to development of a cost per type of call. Then, the process for each call type should be reevaluated to determine if parts of the processes can be further optimized to reduce the cost.
- When problems with transactions occur, the CSR goes to someone who has e-mail to send a trouble ticket to the Operations manager, who is responsible for help desk functioning. The CSR may or may not receive an acknowledgement of the

request and may or may not receive a confirmation of request completion. There is no accountability for trouble ticket processing and no process. This is an important problem as the ability of a CSR to get help on technical problems gives them greater confidence in the technology and IT staff. Help desk software should be obtained through a formal acquisition process that matches the requirements for potential target software. Once software is obtained, a process should be developed for help desk processing and trouble ticket reporting, including escalation to the CIO if no resolution is found within a reasonable time (e.g., 2 hours). Accountability for help desk responsiveness and quality should be created and the Help desk should be managed with regular oversight.

- Campaign information is shared verbally from Customer Service to the call center and from the call center manager to the DA and supervisors. This communication should be formalized and routinized by joint development of Customer Service with the call center and IT, since all three need notification of new campaigns. Then, the communication should be placed in a public area of an intranet for sharing with all interested parties. Fewer mistakes will result from having a process for all information users.

- There is no Internet payment processing and no capability to manage customer e-mail. Few CSRs have e-mail and none have Internet access. To reduce the CSR load but still increase collections requires some type of web presence. The recommendation is to develop and deploy payment processing for customers through the Internet and provide CSRs with e-mail to address customer problems with standard text. Many of the common questions on cut-off of service (e.g., hard and soft cut-offs) should be explained in frequently asked questions (FAQs) on the SCI website. By providing Internet accessibility for payment and question services, collections should increase.

- Problems with collections files are not known until the end of the month when they are compared for billing purposes. To improve the quality of collections, daily reconciliation of all transactions should be done with errors traced back to CSRs for retraining.

- Using the AS/400 for dual-write capability for transactions causes significant slow-down in transaction time. This capability should be moved to the Davox if feasible to optimize speed of processing.

Technology Analysis

Connections within the computer configuration are suspected of contributing to the multisecond delays in call center transaction processing. The 10/100 line across the center of the page identifies the Ethernet connection that connects all of the CSRs to the computer network (see Figure A.9). The Davox (top center of the diagram) is connected to the call center through first Unison Smart Center management equipment that connects to a 100 MB subnet to the other computer equipment, and to the call center through a network bridge. The Siemens, on the left, connects directly to the Ethernet for incoming calls only. The PCs on the right are for Compose-it, the software used to create scripts, the web server composed of two PCs, and a PC used as the download server (that physically sits in dialer administration). Davox, Siemens, and CSR PC equipment are on the call center floor. The rest of the equipment is in a locked, secure computer room with environmental control equipment.

Configuration

By tracing the number of interactions between the PC, Davox, and AS/400 for a single outgoing transaction (see Figure A.10), the bottleneck locations become clear: the Unisom, network bridge, and 10Base-T network. This configuration appears as if it is not a star-type topology when in fact, with all traffic being managed through the Davox, it is the center of the "star" and needs to be configured in a way that does not impede access to it. While specific recommendations cannot be made from this analysis in terms of network reconfiguration, the recommendation is that tracing of transaction times through each waypoint (Unisom and the bridge) and monitoring of traffic on the network should be performed to continue to assess the configuration. It appears that by

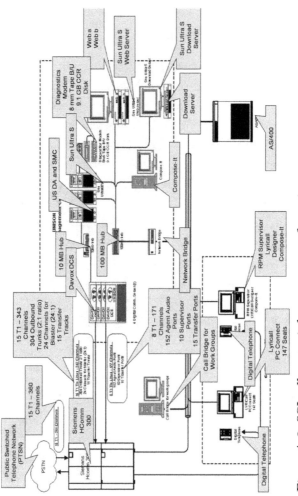

Figure A.9. SCI call center infrastructure configuration.

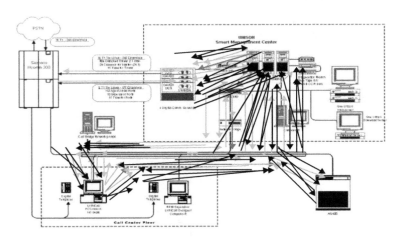

Figure A.10. Outgoing call tracing.

removing the bridge from the middle of the links between Davox and Ethernet, and by moving from 10Base-T to fiber optic backbone, traffic speed should increase substantially. If this does not solve the problems, then it may be beneficial to keep the bridge but split the Ethernet into subnets by groups that perform their work differently, for example, 50 first-party + 50 third-party CSRs on a single subnet to ensure that the traffic patterns do not cause problems and to improve the traffic statistics by having subnets. In any case, the network configuration places the burden of its traffic on the Unisom and network bridge equipment that may not be able to handle it.

Call Management Technology

Information about some of the network equipment and its functioning is presented in Figure A.11, which shows that the Davox trunk group is over 100% utilization, another factor that would contributes to slow response.

Except for the Davox trunk group that is over 100% utilization, the other circuits might be cut back. The Davox future group, if it can be moved into mainstream use, should be immediately deployed to reduce Davox line utilization. VoIP should be evaluated to replace some or all

Group	Function	Weekly average # calls	Utilization
Local Call Office	Internal administrative phone resource for corporate use. 7 in/outbound lines.	426	.05%
WorldCom OUT	Interstate primary call center in/outbound lines service through the Davox. 5 T1 lines = 120 lines.	94,733	39.7%
Davox	Core call center functions. 2 Davox DCS platforms, each supporting 6 T1 circuits connected to the switch, total capacity 12 T1 circuits. Lines from Davox to Siemens are 288.	102,639	114%
GTE	Call center in/outbound lines support CSRs and outbound manual CSR calls, Davox predictive dialer, and inbound non-call director (ACD) calls, consists of 2 T1 circuits or 46 lines.	1,491 in 5,306 out	31.5% in 21.2% out
Quest	Five T1 circuits (120 in/outbound lines) to support intrastate Davox predictive dialing. High percentage of inbound traffic for 32 1-800 numbers.	5,729 in 9,931 out	30% in 3% out
Davox Future	12 lines (½T1 switch) listed as future use but with traffic. Needs analysis.	8,149	25% 14% busy

Figure A.11. Phone connection utilization.

of the long-distance services into a single VoIP service that would be cheaper with no loss of speed. The WorldCom links especially, which carry a large number of interstate calls, could be replaced by VoIP. VoIP adoption should significantly reduce SCI's long-distance charges.

The seven lines for "other than call center use" seem not to be warranted as they have less than 1% utilization. These, too, might be completely replaced with a VoIP service at significantly lower cost to the company.

Davox-Sun Configuration

Figure A.12 shows additional agent statistics that were computed to show that the Davox was at 96.3% utilization (see Figure A.10) with its three Sun Ultra 60s, which combined can manage 40,000 transactions per day. With outbound activity at 38,500 transactions per day, this configuration is close to saturated. This, too, can be a source of slow response time. By adding an additional Sun Ultra 60, the utilization would still be about 75%. Therefore, the company should evaluate adding two Sun Ultra 60s, moving to larger capacity equipment, or outsourcing some of the computing resource needs as utilization hits some predetermined threshold.

In addition to supporting information on technical issues with the call center, Figure A.13 also shows that agents are unlikely to increase utilization statistics without changing the transaction mix or, as we recommend, fully automating some of the transactions. When or if this change takes place, there will be even more pressure on the dialer and line

Activity	Statistic
Agent talk + wrap time	40 seconds
Agent utilization	80%
Agent connect %	30%
Agent connects per hour	72
Transaction rate per seat per day	240
Number of seats	152
Outbound transactions per day	38,513

Figure A.12. Agent activity summary.

configurations. Therefore, the link problems are more pressing than the network configuration and should be fixed before or at the same time as the network reconfiguration changes.

CSR PC Technology

The PCs in the call center appear to have response delays that relate to slow or insufficient memory. The PCs evaluated spent about 10 seconds in page swapping for each screen load. The recommendations is to evaluate each PC for updating the chipset, memory, or both as needed to improve responsiveness.

Summary of Recommendations

All recommendations are summarized in this section. The categories of recommendations relate to the area of the problem: quality of collections, call center training, call center support, and technology recommendations.

Quality of Collections

These recommendations were developed to meet the overall goal of "increased customer satisfaction." Customer satisfaction should be met by proving that contracts were met and providing accurate collection and billing information. Meeting the following recommendations will require cooperation between marketing, customer services, and the call center. The recommended changes included the following:

1. Standardize contracts.
2. Develop a quality review of contracts.
3. Standardize campaigns and campaign information.
4. Develop a quality review for campaigns.
5. Develop a form to convey campaign information (and make it available on an intranet).
6. E-mail contract and campaign information to customer service, IT, and the call center as they are completed.
7. Develop software to provide single-screen payment processing.

Agent group	Max. calls	Max. hours	Max, talk	Max. wrap	# agents	Agent util. %
Inbound first party	320	17.3	3.0	.43	26	83.9%
Inbound third party	258	16.0	3.7	.58	27	76.2%
Outbound first party	1,972	37.2	.8	.2	62	73.1%
Outbound third party	2,722	28.9	.6	.1	38	86.0%
TOTAL	5,507	21.0	1.7	.3	168	81.1%

Figure A.13. Agent group activity.

8. Consolidate promise-to-pay, refuse-to-pay, dispute, and already paid processes on a single Lyricall screen.

9. Automate wrong-party transaction processing within the Davox.

10. Develop a single screen for payment processing.

11. Develop dual-write capability to provide backup for Davox collection information. This recommendation also includes ceasing dual-write capability on the AS/400.

12. Create custom software to error-proof collection process and termination code entry.

13. Create custom software to error-proof CSR campaign logon.

14. Create custom software to error-proof DA campaign handling by adding a three-digit number to every campaign entered.

15. Fully test credit-card and direct-check payment validation software to prevent frozen PC problems.

16. Move credit-card and direct-check payment validation processes to the Davox if feasible.

17. Develop a capability for Internet customer payments and client FAQ processing.

18. Provide CSRs with e-mail and standardized text for responses to questions.

19. Develop a capability to reconcile collections on a daily basis.

20. Develop a process for CSRs to suggest script changes to clients.

21. Develop procedures to improve quality controls on billing information.

22. The hours of work for CSRs should be changed to have most CSRs working evening hours, when the percentage of success is highest, and fewer CSRs working early morning hours, when the percentage of success is lowest.

23. Continue to use the daily report card created for this project.

24. Standardize and create new management reports for the call center. To the extent allowed by contracts, discontinue customer reports for each customer unless paid for by the client.

25. Establish a reward structure for zero errors in collections for both individuals and groups.

26. Develop a means of measuring cost per call by type.

27. Stabilize call center management and begin to move beyond collections as the only measure to evaluating call center management
quality of several types:

a. Evaluate the purchase of surveillance equipment to equip all
supervisors to monitor CSR calls.

b. Develop a communications program for regular communications
to CSRs about policy and practice changes. Communications
should be in the form of town meetings, bulletin board notices,
and newsletters. When an intranet is established, it should also be
used to pop up new changes or important information to ensure
clear communications.

c. The call center manager and HR should reevaluate the use of part-
time, young collectors and of using firing as motivation. Both of
these practices appear to contribute to poor collections quality.

The matrix in Figure A.14 shows recommended organization or role
responsibility for the previously mentioned changes. In addition, supporting participants to each change activity and those who should be
informed about devisions and changes are also identified.

Call Center Training

The recommendations in this section all relate to call center training. The
training for CSRs is often cut short, inadequately prepped, and insufficient for full training of new staff. As a result, error rates are significantly
higher than industry average. The recommendations are the following:

- Send the trainer to train-the-trainer courses.
- The trainer should perform as a supervisor for at least 3
months to develop the skills required to develop supervisory
training.
- The process maps should also be used as the basis for all training with written testing of all CSRs on a regular basis to ensure
their understanding and knowledge of the process, transaction
codes, and so on.
- Develop and deploy standardized supervisor training for all
supervisors. The call center manager should personally monitor

Legend:

⊙ Primary   ◯ Support   △ Inform

Tasks/ Organization	CIO	Operations	Call Center	Customer Service	Marketing	Accounting	Finance	Executive	HR
Standardize contacts					⊙			⊙	
Develop contract QC procedure					⊙			◯	
Standardize campaigns and campaign information		◯	◯	◯	⊙			◯	
Develop campaign QC procedure				◯	⊙			△	
Develop campaign form			⊙	⊙	⊙			△	
Develop intranet	⊙	⊙	◯			◯		◯	◯
Develop procedure for e-mail contract and campaign information		◯	◯	⊙	◯			△	
Set up e-mail for all employees	⊙	◯	△	△	△	△	△	△	△
Develop Davox dual-write capability	⊙	◯	△					△	
Create software to error-proof collections	⊙	◯	◯					△	
Create software to error-proof CSR logon	⊙	◯	◯					△	
Create software to error-proof campaign handling	⊙	◯	◯					△	
Develop daily reconcilliation capability	△		⊙	△		⊙	◯	◯	
Develop QC for billing information	△		△			⊙	◯	△	
Standardize new management reports	⊙	◯	⊙	◯	◯	△		◯	

Figure A.14. Responsibility matrix.

new supervisors for at least the first week. Mentors should be assigned for at least the first 3 months.

- Document and train the call center manager and supervisors in the use of Davox reports for intraday management.
- Training should be coordinated through HR with e-mail notices sent to the training, DA, and operations manager at least 3 days prior to training.
- The trainer should test adequacy and readiness of training technology setup at least 2 days in advance of training.
- The operations manager should create at least 30 test customers, 5 of each type, for each student undergoing CSR training.
- Initiate a process to report student satisfaction and follow-up on all training.
- Regular testing on termination codes, collections processes, and other call center operational aspects should be conducted.
- End the process of cutting training short when new people are hired for a specific campaign.

Call Center Support

This section summarizes the changes recommended to provide better continuity and availability of computing resources in the call center:

- Help desk software should be obtained through a formal process and deployed.
- Help desk processes and metrics should be developed to track requests, escalate after some period of time, and monitor success rates.
- The help desk should be managed properly with oversight and review of metrics on a monthly basis.
- The DAs and operations manager should be sent to Davox and Siemens vendor training.
- A set of Davox documentation should be obtained and retained in the operations manager's office. He should be responsible for on-site support for Davox operations and should troubleshoot most problems without relying on Davox.

Technology

This section summarizes the changes relating to computing equipment that supports call center activities. No other SCI computing activities were evaluated:

- Add two Sun Ultra 60 processors.
- Add two T1 trunks to the Davox configuration.
- Change from a 10/100 LAN to a fiber optic backbone that eliminates one router.
- Evaluate upgrading all equipment both in the data center and in the call center.
- Evaluate the use of VoIP for long-distance calling.
- Evaluate the potential for outsourcing some or all of the computing to support call center operations.

Financial Analysis

The previously listed recommendations should not be undertaken if they do not lead to added collections in the call center. However, it is believed that they will not only add to the collection rate but also improve the quality of collections by adding the recommended computing and software changes. The financial analysis presented in Figure A.15 shows that the net present value (NPV) on the investment to conduct all recommended activities should more than make up the company's losses within the first year. Assumptions for this analysis are in Figure A.16. For every dollar invested, the return will be approximately $30, arguing for all of the recommended changes.

The greatest contribution comes from automation of wrong-party calls. By saving 20,000 minutes per day and assuming the normal collection rate of approximately $118, the added $61 million in revenue is the most important change. The next closest change in terms of financial impact is to consolidate all payment screens into a single screen and process. This change will add $1 million in revenue the first year. Replacing 20% of the PCs in the call center can also reduce the time to process by about 1 minute per transaction, thus adding $1 million in revenue per year. The fourth really significant change is for data center infrastructure

	Year 0	Year 1
Expense reduction		**$180,000**
Revenue generation		
Infrastructure + reconfiguration (.5 minute/transaction saved)		$923,052
Automate wrong-party calls (2 minute/transaction saved)		$9,836,736
Single payment screen (1 minute/transaction saved)		$1,844,388
Term code drop-down		$5,000
Test and fix payment errors		$10,144
Automate campaign logon		$0
Lyricall screen consolidation		
Help desk software		$10,000
E-mail throughout the call center		$5,000
Internet payment processing		$60,000
DA and ops manager training and Davox manuals		$0
Intranet design, contracts documentation, deployment		$5,000
Speed transactions from replacing 20% of PCs		$1,844,388
Proposed process investment		
Infrastructure + reconfiguration	($150,000)	
DA campaign intercept and append 3-digit number	($6,000)	
Automate wrong-party calls	($10,000)	
Single payment screen	($15,000)	
Term code drop-down	($15,000)	
Test and fix payment errors	($20,000)	
Automate campaign logon	($6,000)	
Lyricall screen consolidation	($6,000)	
Help desk software	($15,000)	
E-mail throughout the call center	($30,000)	
Internet payment processing	($15,000)	
DA and ops manager training and Davox manuals	($8,000)	
Intranet design, contracts documentation, deployment	($20,000)	
Replace 20% of PCs	($72,000)	
TOTAL	($388,000)	$13,186,718
Return on investment		$29.64
Net present value at 10%		$11,518,846

Figure A.15. Financial analysis: all changes.

Assumption	Statistic
240 transactions/seat/day	240
140 seats average	140
Total transactions/day	33,600
Collection/day	$92,308
Average collection/transactions	$2.75
Collection/minute	$118.34
Total successful transactions/day at 40% success	13,440

Figure A.16. Financial assumptions.

and network upgrades, which should translate to almost $1 million per year. These estimates are based on the value-added analysis of call center transactions. The increased revenue estimates are based on removing unproductive time from each transaction type.

The other changes have different expectations. The automated campaign logon has no direct return but directly impacts the cost avoidance by eliminating the need to recreate transactions. E-mail is expected to have a positive impact on client relations but not to necessarily generate added revenue. Having the Davox training and manuals is expected to have a minimal effect but should pay off in other ways by smoothing out call center operations, reducing hang-ups and wait time. Posting contracts, process maps, and other call center–related material on the intranet should increase information accountability and indirectly should have a positive impact on collection quality. Nominal returns were estimated for these changes.

Proposed Process

The proposed process includes all recommended changes (see the appensix). The changes are not substantively different in terms of the process. Rather, they differ in that the software, screen, and computing support all are improved.

Davox start-up and shutdown are unchanged with the exception of software to automatically add a three-digit number to campaigns when added. This process will be invisible to the DA and CSRs, but it will prevent accidental overlay of campaigns with collections.

When a CSR logs on to their PC, they will have an automatic pop-up to log on to a campaign. In this way, the campaign cannot be circumvented.

Processing for wrong-party transactions will be fully automated within the Davox and removed from the CSR process.

All transactions operate as they currently do with the addition of required termination code selection from a pull-down menu of preset options. This will prevent, to the extent possible, entry of wrong term codes. Several screens will be consolidated so fewer screen displays are required. A single screen replaces the 2–3 screens for payment processing file updates.

Shutdown processing is unchanged.

Benchmarks and Measures

The baseline benchmark taken at the beginning of the project should be used as a basis against which to determine if the changes recommended have fulfilled the goal of increasing collections. An individual should be named responsible for monitoring and reporting baseline measures.

The major metrics focus on collections and may miss personnel issues or other problems that might arise in the call center. These metrics are presented in Figure A.17. In addition, other measures are provided in appendix A4. However, it is recommended that these measures *not* be implemented immediately to minimize the amount of change and scrutiny in the call center. Rather, these might be considered for implementation after 6 months of stable operations as an impetus to further improvements.

In addition, other measures were created using a failure mode and effect analysis to first prevent problems but then to recognize their existence if they were to occur. These measures are provided in appendix A5. However, it is recommended *not* to implement these measures immediately to minimize the amount of change and scrutiny in the call center. Rather, these might be considered for implementation after 6 months of stable operations, as an impetus to further improvements.

Perspective	Objective	Initiative	Target	Measure
Financial	Adopt balanced scorecard	Create dashboard of metrics	March 31, 2011	Completion date and real-time thereafter; 98% uptime
	Reduce expense per call	Daily report	January 5, 2011	Completion by 8:30 am daily
Client	Improve relations with top three clients	Create dashboard of metrics	April 30, 2011	Completion date and real-time thereafter; 98% uptime 9 am est to 9 pm pst
	Diversify sales	Increase volume of placements from existing clients	25% increase from at least 25% of clients	6.5% increase in volume from at least 6.5% of clients per quarter
		Obtain more large clients	1–2 clients	Contract starts by June 1 and December 1 (i.e., 1 per 6 months)
Internal Process	Motivate and inspire employees to become more committed	Self-training courses in, e.g., phone skills, negotiation, leadership	10 completions per month per course	Improved collections by 15% within 6 months; sustain the new level of collection; climate survey EO4Q
	Create a culture that supports innovation and ownership of issues	Suggestion box Bonus for $ saved if signed	Immediate	# Suggestions %, # Suggestions acted on $ Bonus paid Climate survey 4Q
'		Monthly Newsletter	End of current quarter	Climate survey 4Q

Figure A.17. SCI scorecard definition.

Perspective	Objective	Initiative	Target	Measure
Internal Process	Create a culture that supports innovation and ownership of issues	Daily collection tips	Collection: Now Dissemination: end of month	Improved collections Climate survey 4Q
	Improve IT resources	Design and implement reports	End of current quarter	
		Upgrade ACD technology	Within 6 months	
		Error-proof dialer, software	End of current month	Zero overlaid campaigns
		Error-proof call software	End of current quarter	Zero call errors
		Error-proof payment software	End of current quarter	Zero payment errors; zero PC freezes
		Build and deploy software to force CSR campaign logon	End of current quarter	100% CSR campaign logon
Innovation and learning	Improve morale and reduce turnover	Develop group bonus policy and practice	End of current month	Increase collections by 15% within 6 months; sustain the new level of collection
		Revise termination offenses	End of current month	Reduce problems, terminations; increase compliance, collections.
		Investigate work-at-home	End of current quarter	Decision on work-at-home

Figure A.17. SCI scorecard definition (continued).

Perspective	Objective	Initiative	Target	Measure
Innovation and learning	Upgrade supervisor/manager skills	Provide essential training to supervisors and managers	1 new course per quarter starting EO2Q: 10 completions per month per course.	Improve collections by 15% within 6 months; sustain the new level of collections; climate survey EOQ4.

Figure A.17. SCI scorecard definition (continued).

Summary

The analysis of SCI's call center technology and processes identified a number of areas for improvement. Based on the financial analyses, the recommended efforts that require software or hardware expenditures would pay for themselves within the first year. By implementing these changes, SCI can return to its prior level of success and would be well situated to accommodate future growth.

Project Approval

SCI Corporation:

_____   _____
Bruce Wentworth, COO   Date
Project Team:

_____   _____
David Burch, Project Manager   Date

Appendix A1

Current process maps are in this appendix. The following diagrams are included: Dialer admin—start of day (Figure A.18a), third-party collections (Figure A.18b1), wrong-party processing (Figure A.18b2), direct check processing (Figure A.18b3), credit card processing (Figure A.18b4), promise-to-pay and nonpayment processing (Figure A.18b5), first-party collections (Figure A.18c), and end-of-day processing (Figure A.18d).

Appendix A2

This section contains the analysis of training and quality collections. First, a root-cause analysis (RCA) of training issues is presented. A responsibility matrix is presented to document responsibility for quality changes, with participation by other parties and oversight by others. The analyses for these techniques are incorporated in the report. Details of each analysis are documented in the project website on the SCI intranet.

SCI RCA

Shaded areas identify root causes and the responsible part from among SCI management. Italicized areas identify root causes for attention by SCI management.

Q.   Why is check processing (CP) problematic?
A.   Because agents do it differently.
  Q.   Why do agents do CP differently?
  A.   *Supervisor issues*, turnover, and lack of training
    Q.   Why is supervision an issue?
    A.   Not enough agent observation and feedback, little direction, and no training
    Q.   Why is there insufficient agent observation?
    A.   Equipment lacking, supervisor training, and no time
      Q.   Why is *equipment lacking?*
      A.   *Not enough equipment to go around*; software doesn't cover all environments; and observation only allows audio surveillance, not visual, that is, what is done on screens.
        Q.   Why is there *not enough equipment* to go around?
        A.   *The headsets and software are expensive; SCI pays for 5 seats but has 3 quality assurance (QA) people and 8 supervisors, so there are 11 people who need the 5 seats of software. Everyone has his own headset.*
        Refer to Steve McHenry and Bob Wentworth.

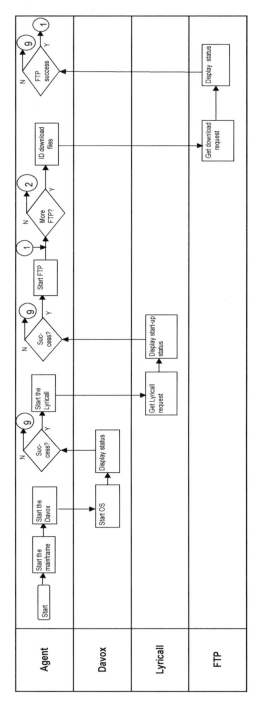

Figure A.18a. Dialer admin—start of day.

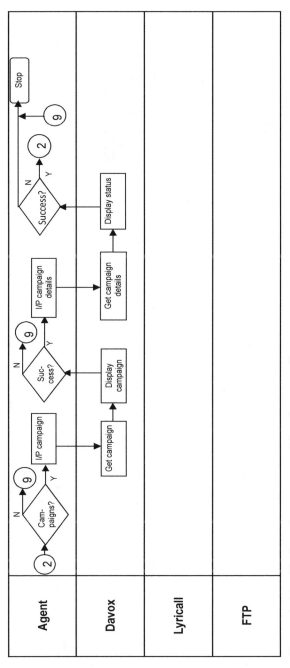

Figure A.18a. Dialer admin—start of day (continued).

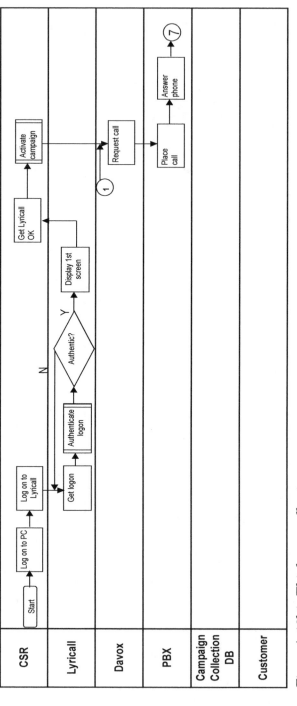

Figure A.18b1. Third-party collections.

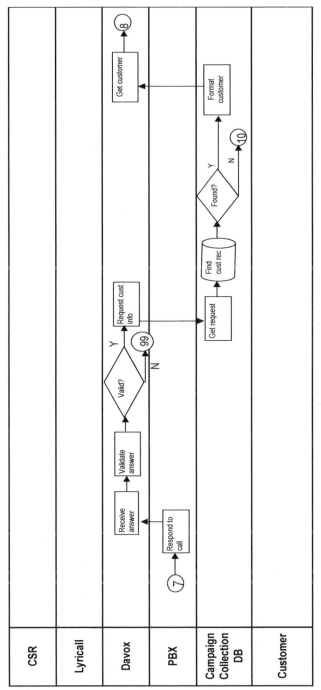

Figure A.18b1. Third-party collections (continued).

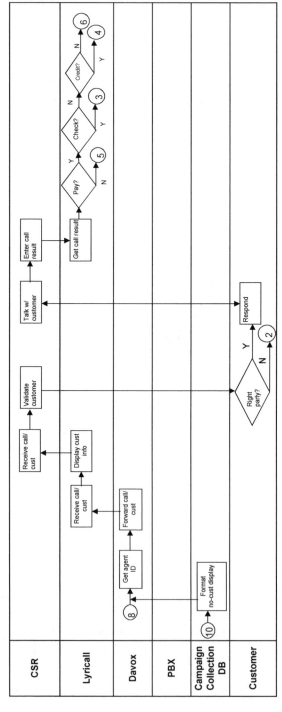

Figure A.18b1. Third-party collections (continued).

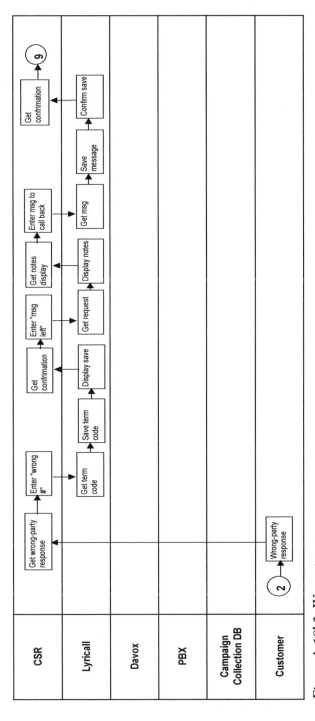

Figure A.18b2. Wrong party.

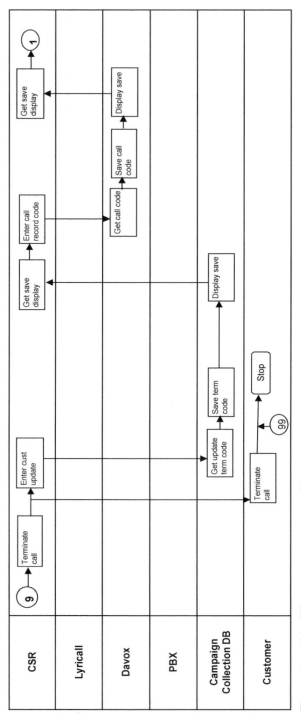

Figure A.18b2. Wrong party (continued).

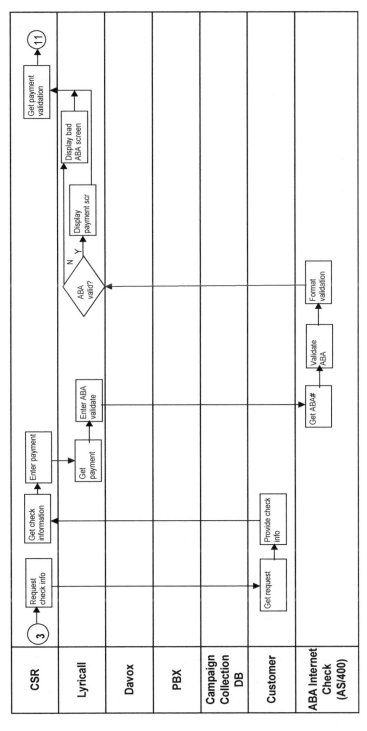

Figure A.18b3. Direct check.

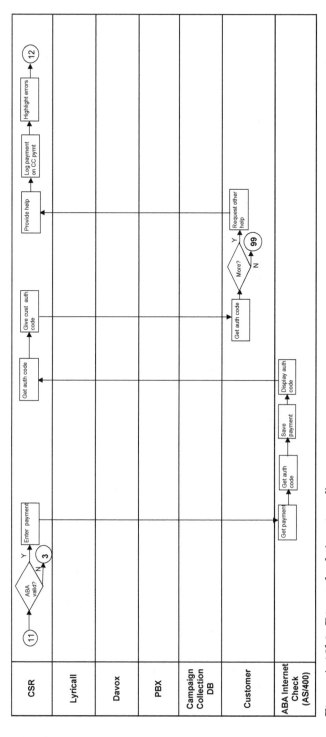

Figure A.18b3. Direct check (continued).

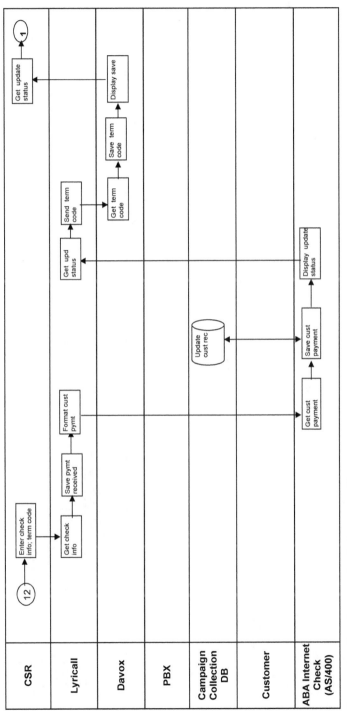

Figure A.18b3. Direct check (continued).

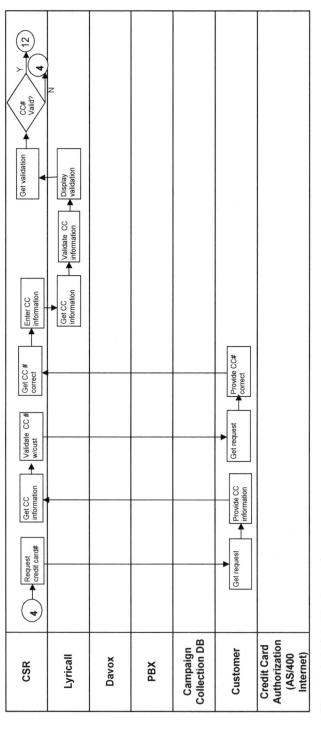

Figure A.18b4. Credit card.

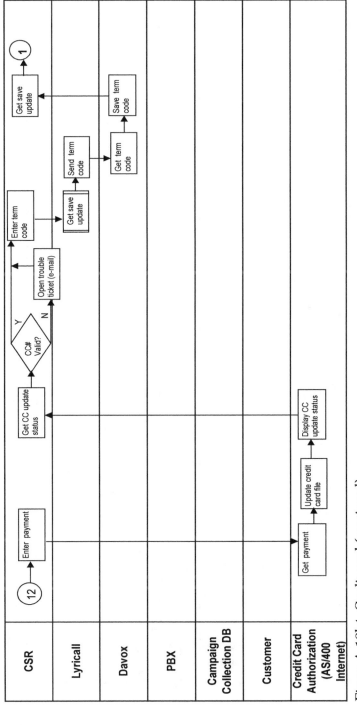

Figure A.18b4. Credit card (continued).

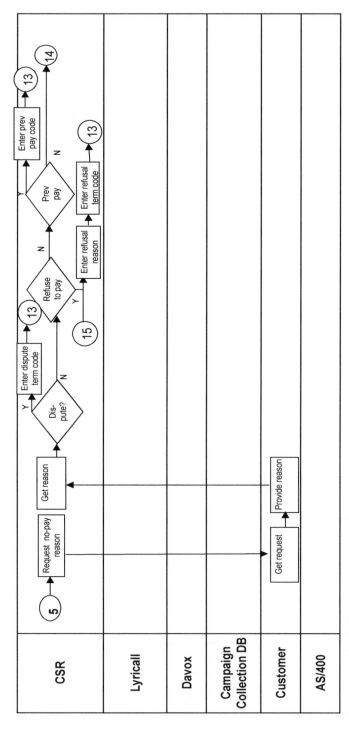

Figure A.18b5. Promise to pay and nonpayment.

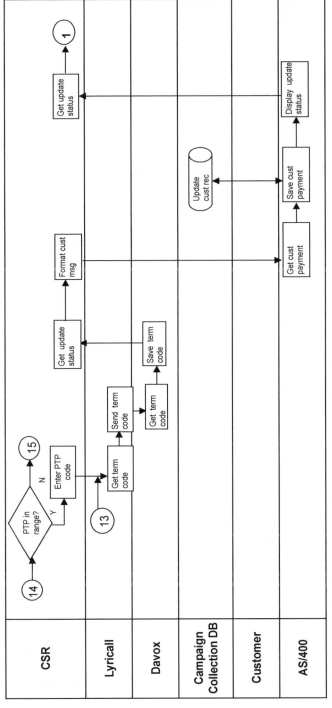

Figure A.18b5. Promise to pay and nonpayment (continued).

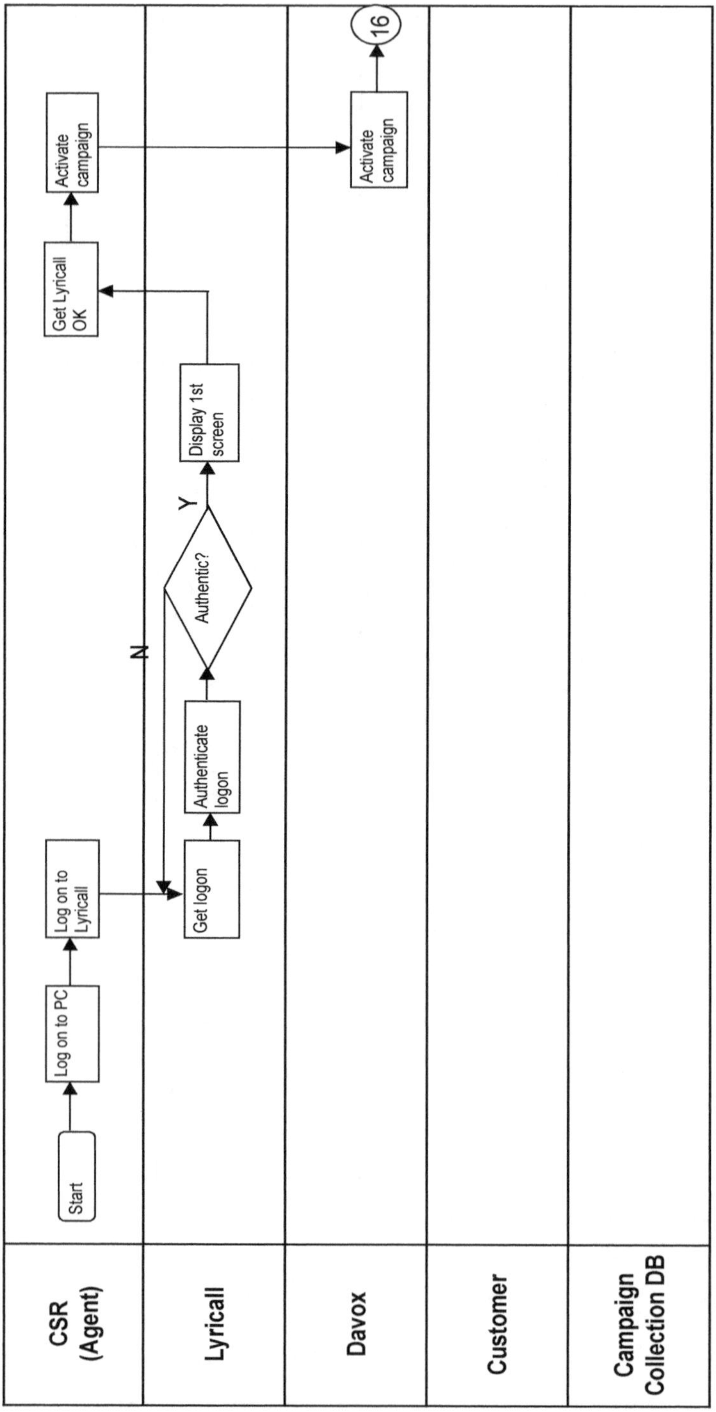

Figure A.18c. First-party collections.

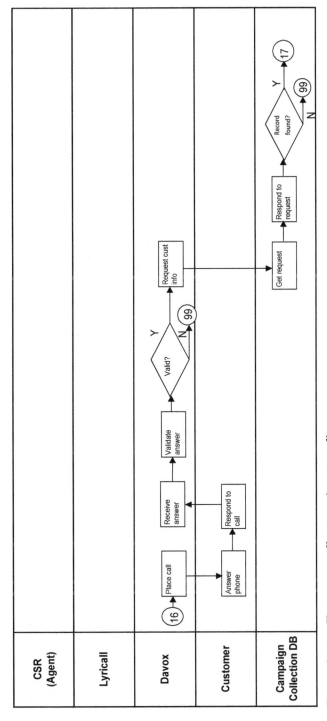

Figure A.18c. First-party collections (continued).

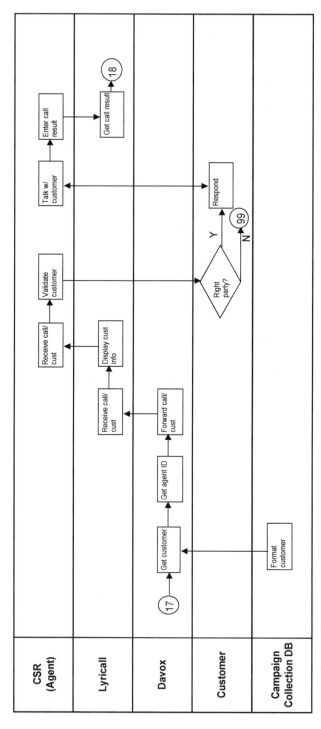

Figure A.18c. First-party collections (continued).

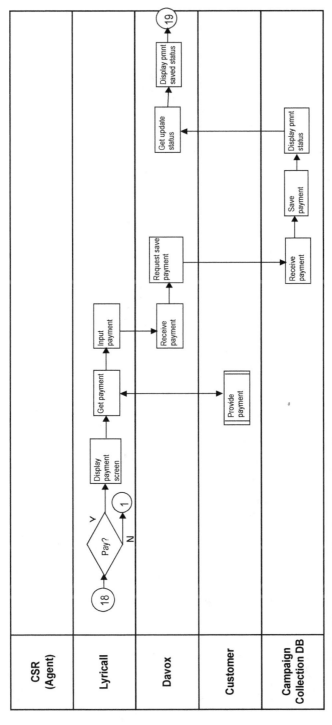

Figure A.18c. First-party collections (continued).

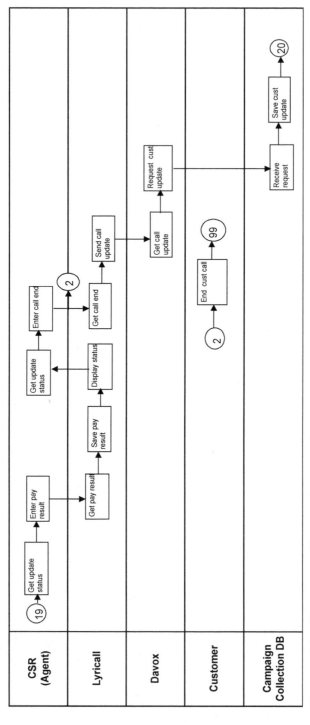

Figure A.18c. First-party collections (continued).

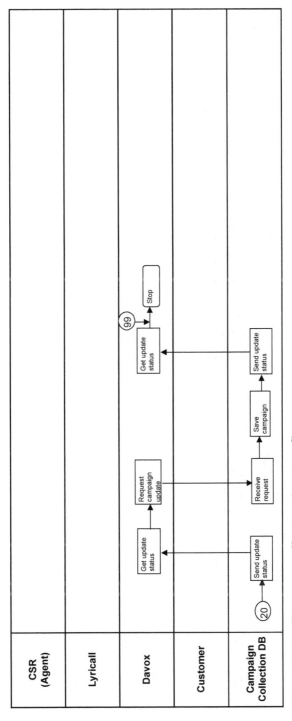

Figure A.18c. First-party collections (continued).

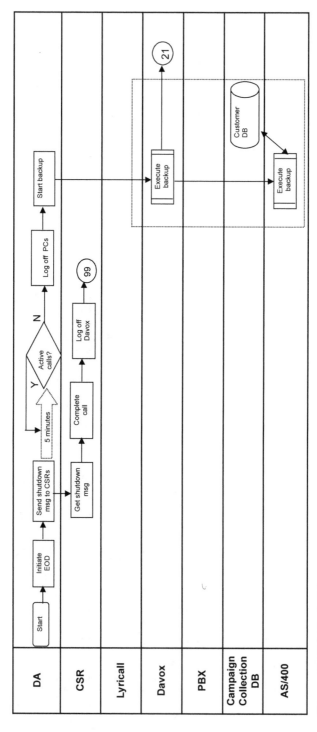

Figure A.18d. End of day.

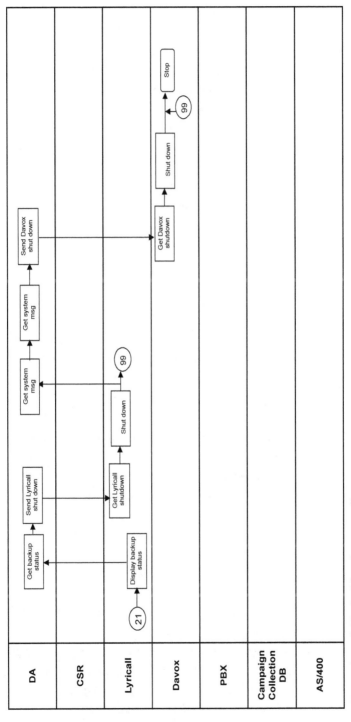

Figure A.18d. End of day (continued).

A. Not enough equipment to go around; *software doesn't cover all environments*; and observation only allows audio surveillance not visual, that is, what is done on screens.

Q. Why does *software not cover all environments?*

A. There is no software to monitor all of the environments the CSRs interact with: Davox, Lyricall, AS/400, scripts, and sometimes PCs.

Q. Why is there no software to monitor all environments?

A. There is no evaluation software to monitor all environments; there is software that allows monitoring of screens.

Q. Why has no one evaluated software that allows monitoring of all screen activity?

A. They have. Software to allow looking at screens as well as audio is over $10,000, and SCI does not want to spend the money.

Q. Why does SCI not want to spend money for audio and video monitoring?

A. *They feel the return would not justify the expense. Refer to Steve McHenry and Bob Wentworth.*

A. Not enough equipment to go around; software doesn't cover all environments; and *observation only allows audio surveillance not visual, that is, what is done on screens.*

Q. Why does *observation software only support audio?*

A. Software to allow looking at screens as well as audio is over $10,000, and SCI does not want to spend it.

Q. Why does SCI not want to spend money for audio and video?

A. *They feel the return would not justify the expense. Refer to Steve McHenry and Bob Wentworth.*

A. Equipment lacking, supervisor training, and no time

Q. Why is *supervisor training* an issue?

A. *Not enough supervisor training,* no one to train, the supervisors usually learn from each other, not enough time, and no follow up on on-the-job training (OJT).

Q. Why is *there not enough supervisor training?*

A. *Time pressure on the job; CSRs slack off if not monitored*
Refer to Steve McHenry.
Q. Why is there *too much time pressure* on the job?
A. First Party clients have contractual commitments about % collection by # agents in Y time. Since collections have the highest priority, SCI loses money on agents, time, or both if needed to comply with client contracts.
Q. Why do clients have these assurances?
A. *According to marketing, "That's the way contracts have always been done."*
Refer to marketing, Steve McHenry, and Bob Wentworth.
A. Time pressure on the job; CSRs slack off if not monitored
Q. Why do *CSRs slack off* if not monitored?
A. *According to supervisors, monitoring motivates people to work. According to the Process Improvement Team, in over 30 hours of observation with and without supervisors around, CSRs did not slack off.*
Refer to Steve McHenry.
A. Not enough supervisor training, *no one to train*, the supervisors usually learn from each other, not enough time, and no follow up OJT.
Q. Why is *there no one to train supervisors*?
A. The trainer has never been a supervisor and does not know enough about the job to develop and deliver training; supervisors do not trust the trainer.
Q. Why is the trainer not trained?
A. *She does not know supervisor jobs.*
Refer to Steve McHenry.
Q. *Why do supervisors not trust the trainer?*
A. *Supervisors perceive the trainer as a gossip and "spy for management."*
Refer to Steve McHenry.
A. Not enough supervisor training, no one to train, *the supervisors usually learn from each other*, not enough time, and no follow up on OJT.

Q.   Why is *a supervisor learning from other supervisors a problem?*

A.   Some supervisors refuse to help people they don't like or don't think should be supervisors, and no one tells them to stop this behavior.

Q.   Why are supervisors allowed to choose whom they will help?

A.   *It seems to have fallen through the cracks relating to high manager turnover in the call center.*
Refer to Steve McHenry.

A.   Not enough supervisor training, no one to train, the supervisors usually learn from each other, *not enough time,* and no follow up on OJT.

Q.   Why is there *not enough time to train supervisors?*

A.   First Party clients have contractual commitments about % collection by # agents in Y time. Since collections has a higher priority, SCI loses money on agents, time, or both if needed to comply with client contracts.

Q.   Why do clients have these assurances?

A.   *According to marketing, "That's the way contracts have always been done."*
Refer to marketing and Bob Wentworth.

A.   Not enough supervisor training, no one to train, the supervisors usually learn from each other, not enough time, and *no follow up on OJT.*

Q.   Why is there *no follow-up on supervisor OJT?*

A.   Management turnover in the call center and poor follow-up.

Q.   Why is management turnover so high?

A.   *One call center manager falsified his resume and was fired; one call center manager stole equipment and was fired; Steve McHenry is the third call center manager in 6 months.*
Refer this issue to Steve McHenry and Bob Wentworth.

Q.   Why is management follow-up so poor?

A.   *It seems to have fallen through the cracks relating to high manager turnover in the call center.*

Refer this issue to Steve McHenry.

A.   Equipment lacking, supervisor training, and no time.

Q.   Why is *supervisor not having enough time* an issue?

A.   First Party clients have contractual commitments about %
collection by # agents in Y time. Since collection activity
is the highest priority, SCI loses money on agents, time,
or both if needed to comply with client contracts.

Q.   Why do clients have these assurances?

A.   *According to marketing, "That's the way contracts have
always been done."*
Refer this issue to marketing and Bob Wentworth.

A.   Supervisor issues, *turnover*, and lack of training.

Q.   Why is *turnover* an issue?

A.   Turnover is currently running at about 180% per year, and
the churn causes supervisors to spend time helping people
get started rather than longer term people to improve or follow the standards.

Q.   Why is there *180% turnover per year?*

A.   *HR policy is to hire 90% part-time employees with average age
18. This demographic has a high turnover rate. SCI's turnover
is double that of other call centers in the same metro area.*
Refer to Steve McHenry and HR.

A.   HR policy is to hire 90% part-time employees with average
age 18. This demographic has a high turnover rate. SCI's
turnover is double that of other call centers in the same
metro area

Q.   Why is SCI's *turnover so high?*

A.   *Firing for petty offences is used to keep people motivated.*
Also, SCI is not perceived as having good salaries, and
many managers has led to many policy changes in the call
center. Turnover doubled in the last year.

Q.   Why is *firing used as a motivator?*

A.   *It is management policy.*
Refer to Steve McHenry and HR.

A.   Firing for petty offences is used to keep people motivated.
Also, *SCI is not perceived as having good salaries,* and

many managers has led to many policy changes in the call center. Turnover doubled in the last year.

Q. Why is *SCI not perceived as having good salaries?*

A. Poor internal communications and recent changes to the commission structure.

Q. Why are internal communications poor?

A. *SCI base salaries are the highest in the metro area. The commission structure is comparable to the competition. Changes were made without any discussion or public announcement. CSRs found out about the changes via memo.*

Refer to Steve McHenry and Bob Wentworth.

Q. Why did the *commission structure* change?

A. *Analysis of financial strength of the company led Bob to recommend changing the commission structure. The changes lead to similar payouts but require higher base collections to begin receiving bonuses.*

Refer to Steve McHenry and Bob Wentworth.

A. Firing for petty offences is used to keep people motivated. Also, SCI is not perceived as having good salaries, and *many managers has led to many policy changes in the call center.* Turnover doubled in the last year.

Q. Why have there been *so many call center managers?*

A. *One call center manager falsified his resume and was fired; one call center manager stole equipment and was fired; Steve McHenry is the third call center manager in 6 months.*

Refer to Steve McHenry and Bob Wentworth.

A. Firing for petty offences is used to keep people motivated. Also, SCI is not perceived as having good salaries, and many managers has led to many policy changes in the call center. *Turnover doubled in the last year.*

Q. Why *has turnover doubled?*

A. Firing for petty offences is used to keep people motivated. Also, SCI is not perceived as having good salaries, and many managers has led to many policy changes in the call center. Turnover doubled in the last year.

Q.   Why is *firing used as a motivator?*

A.   *It is management policy.*

Refer to HR and Steve McHenry.

A.   Supervisor issues, turnover, and *lack of training.*

Q.   Why is lack of training an issue?

A.   CSR training sessions are inconsistent from one group to another; training sessions have technology problems and sometimes are cut short. Not everyone gets the same training (OJT and in class).

Q.   Why are *CSR training sessions inconsistent?*

A.   One individual who has never had teaching training does training, time and job pressure on the trainer, and technology problems during training.

Q.   Why is the *trainer untrained?*

A.   *Previous to having a trainer, OJT was the only method of training. SCI promoted a CSR who wanted to do training to the position when they realized that people could not walk in off the street and start the job, since OJT was too inconsistent. The trainer took the job materials and successfully created training modules, but the call center manager had not given the trainer any other training.*

Refer to Steve McHenry.

A.   Training sessions are inconsistent from one group to another; *training sessions have technology problems and sometimes are cut short.* Not everyone gets the same training (OJT and in class).

Q.   Why are there *technology problems during training?*

A.   Special test customer files need to be loaded on the Davox, related AS/400 customer records need to be "reset," and test logons and passwords need to be activated. These setups require coordination between the trainer and DA for the Davox and the operations manager in IT. They are usually given 2 days notice via e-mail sent from the trainer for setups. Occasionally, one or more of the setups are not timely. The trainer does not test the setup until it is needed. If one or both of the required people are away from their desks when a problem is noticed, then the class is cut short.

Q. *Why are the DA and the operations manager not notified automatically when training is scheduled?*

A. *This would require HR involvement.*

Refer to Steve McHenry and HR.

Q. *Why does the trainer not test the setup before the training?*

A. *No known reason.*

Refer to Steve McHenry and trainer.

A. Training sessions are inconsistent from one group to another; training sessions have technology problems and sometimes are cut short. *Not everyone gets the same training (OJT and in class).*

Q. Why are *training sessions inconsistent?*

A. Training is usually 1 full day in the classroom and 1 full day of OJT listening to a CSR for half of the day and talking with the CSR, and listening and offering suggestions for improvements. When a new account opens or turnover has been particularly high, there is pressure to get new CSRs "on the phones" and collecting or selling. Thus the classroom training becomes ½ day (or less if there are technical problems), and the OJT is ½ day. Agents trained in ½ time are not as familiar with termination and error codes or with payment processing, resulting in inconsistent performance.

Q. Who authorizes the 1-day training?

A. *This is not clear. It appears that HR and a previous call center manager (not McHenry) initiated this practice. Then, as call center managers turned over, whenever the conditions recurred, the trainer continued the practice on her own.*

Refer to Steve McHenry.

Root Cause Issue Summary

Once RCA is complete, a summary of issues is created and presented to the people charged with remedying the situation. In some cases, that may be the RCA group, but for SCI, that means giving issues back to the various managers as identified previously. The root causes are summarized here for each person or department.

Steve McHenry

- Supervisor training:
  - CSRs are thought to require constant supervision, resulting in no supervisor training.
  - The trainer is not trained and does not know supervisor jobs so she is not qualified to train them.
  - Supervisor OJT is selective with some supervisors refusing to help others.
  - Supervisors perceive the trainer as a "gossip" and "spy for management"
  - There has been no follow-up on (lack of) supervisor training.
- The trainer:
  - The trainer has never been formally trained on how to create or deliver training.
  - The trainer does not test training setup before sessions begin.
  - A practice initiated under prior management reduces training by half when new client pressures were high. The trainer has continued this practice automatically whenever there is a new client.

Steve McHenry and Bob Wentworth

- There is insufficient software for monitoring. SCI pays for 5 seats but has 11 people who need monitoring software.
- Audio/video monitoring costs $10,000.
- Failures in communicating to CSRs about commission restructuring are causing perceptions of SCI having poor salaries.
- The need for higher base collections to receive bonuses is causing perceptions of SCI having poor salaries.
- Management turnover in the call center is partially responsible for poor supervisor training

Steve McHenry and HR

- High turnover may relate partly to use of firing as a motivator.
- Automatic notice to the DA and operations manager when training is scheduled may cut down on technical problems with training.
- High turnover partly may relate to policy on hiring part-time, young people.

Steve McHenry, Marketing, and Bob Wentworth

- Supervisors not trained because of collections pressures relating to contracts.

Steve McHenry

- Testing for training setups should be conducted the day prior to training to allow for any missing setup or technology fixes to be completed.

Other analyses were conducted and are available upon request or through the SCI intranet at D:\share2010ccevalindex.htm.

Appendix A3

This appendix documents the impacts of recommended changes on the call center processes. The processes affected include collections (Figure A.19a), payment and nonpayment (Figure A.19b), and end-of-day processing (Figure A.19c). There are no changes to the start-of-day process.

Appendix A4

This appendix contains two documents:

- Daily performance report (Figure A.20) for monitoring of critical collections statistics

- Key performance indicators to measure key areas of the call center operation (Figure A.21)

The recommended daily performance report shows caregories for call center management by type of collections. This report should be available at least daily for the prior day's activity.

The recommended measures in Figure A.21 are designed to identify situations requiring attention during the calling day. To provide this capability, the metrics should be designed to be available on demand by all supervisory and managerial staff. In addition, for each metric, a threshold of acceptable performance should be defined such that automated alerts are generated to appropriate managers when a threshold is reached.

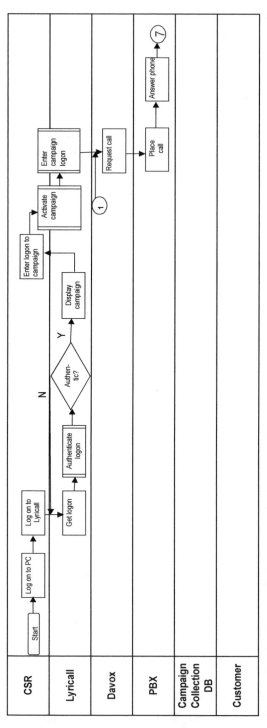

Figure A.19a. Proposed changes to third-party collections.

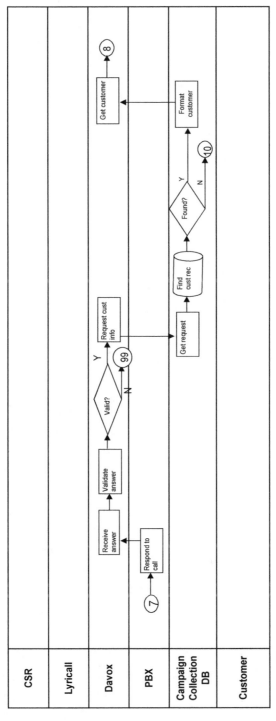

Figure A.19a. Proposed changes to third-party collections (continued).

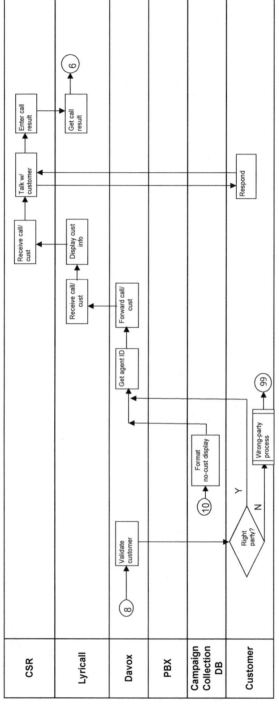

Figure A.19a. Proposed changes to third-party collections (continued).

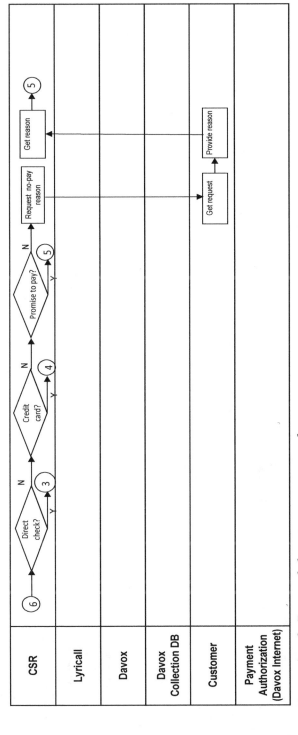

Figure A.19b. Proposed changes to payment and nonpayment.

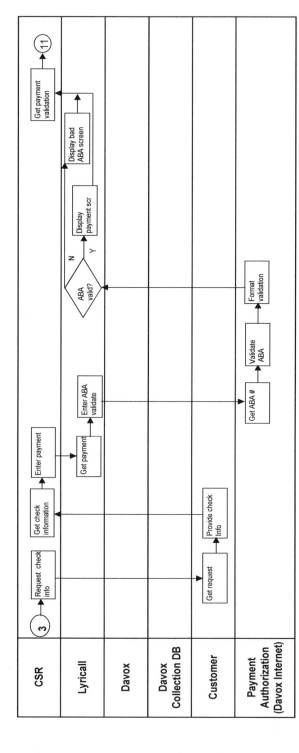

Figure A.19b. Proposed changes to payment and nonpayment (continued).

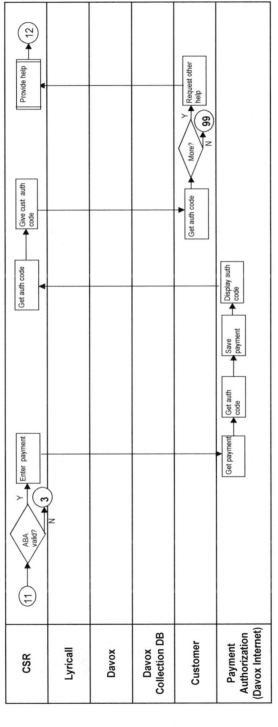

Figure A.19b. Proposed changes to payment and nonpayment (continued).

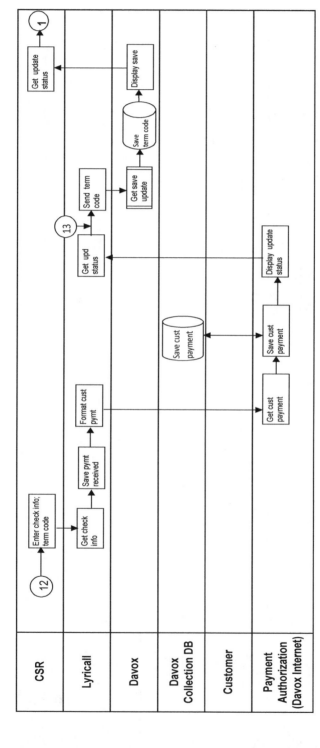

Figure A.19b. Proposed changes to payment and nonpayment (continued).

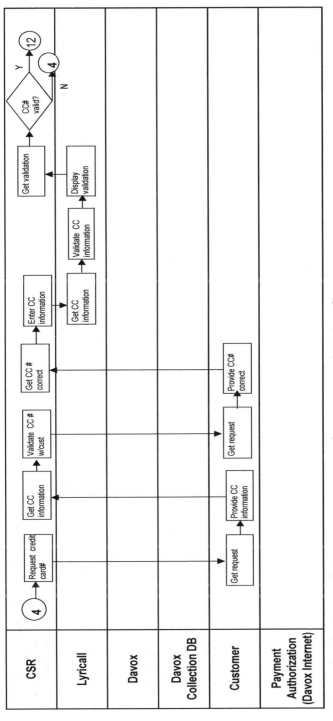

Figure A.19b. Proposed changes to payment and nonpayment (continued).

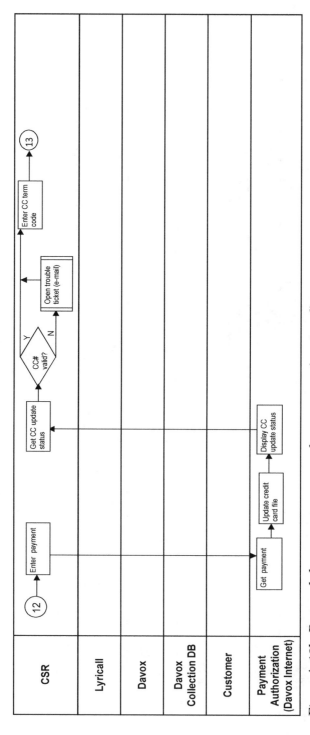

Figure A.19b. Proposed changes to payment and nonpayment (continued).

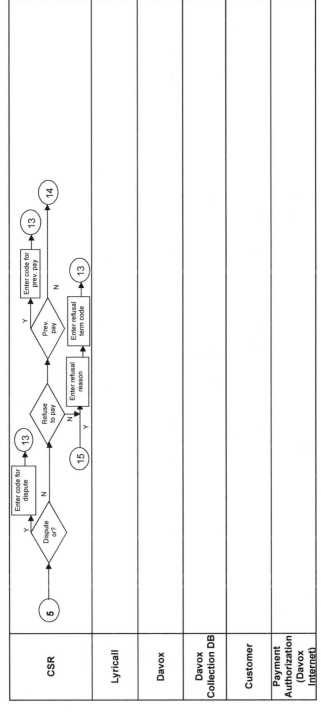

Figure A.19b. Proposed changes to payment and nonpayment (continued).

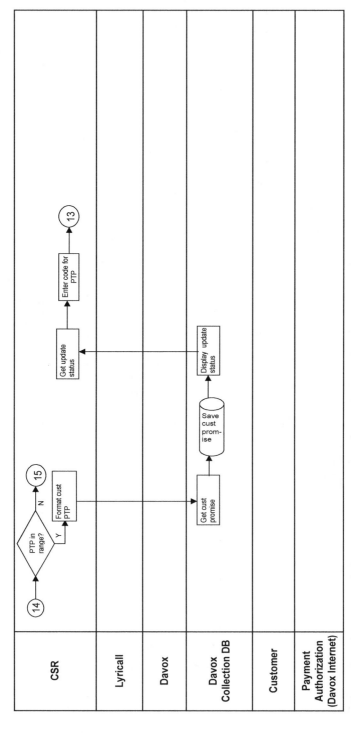

Figure A.19b. Proposed changes to payment and nonpayment (continued).

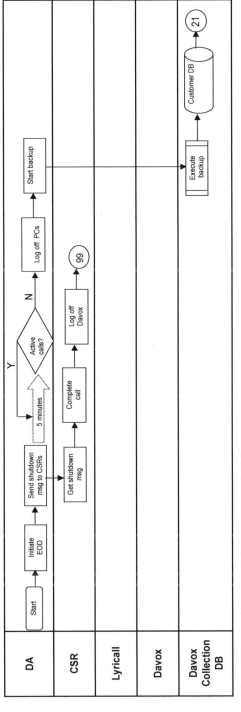

Figure A.19c. Proposed changes to end of day.

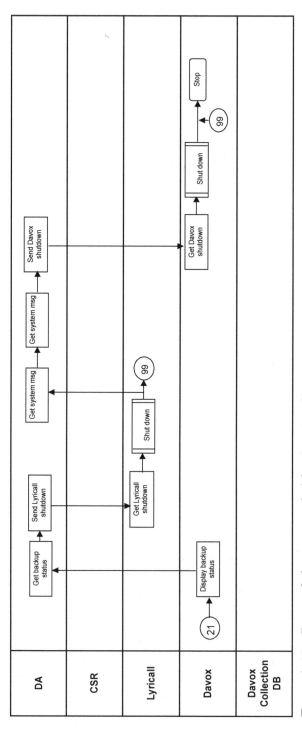

Figure A.19c. Proposed changes to end of day (continued).

Daily SCI performance report for	Third party		First party			
Last run on 5/09/xx 05:01:56 PM	First tier	Second and third tier	Apex	Pinnacle	TX Telecomm	Top 25
Campaigns	Actual	Actual	Actual	Actual	Actual	Actual
Download #s	100,252	96,062	5,272	1,914	2,811	10,192
# dial Attempts	17000	429	4,017	1,928	2,103	2,384
$ downloaded placement (DP)	$540,240.20	$25,048,161.92	$638,273.49	$111,232.04	$169,901.91	$808,593.56
$ collected	$425,024.25	$0.00	$29,463.35	$10,359.72	$4,569.39	$2,393.71
% $ collected/DP amount	78.67%	0.00%	4.62%	9.31%	2.69%	0.30%
Agents						
Total FTEs logged on	11.25	1.45	7.66	2.60	2.88	4.80

Figure A.20. Proposed daily performance report.

	First tier	Second and third tier	Apex	Pinnacle	TX Telecomm	Top 25
Agents						
Average login duration/FTE	6.35	1.66	1.86	1.48	2.56	2.13
Total talk time	1,546.25	9.12	54.91	20.26	17.66	27.45
% TT/hour	75.43%	78.49%	89.66%	97.50%	76.62%	71.54%
% TT/hour/FTE	55.42%	47.28%	48.32%	65.69%	29.92%	33.56%
Inbound efficiency						
Total inbound hours	20.5	8.09	34.64	19.38	4.12	0
Total agents logged on	11	4	12	10	2	0
Total FTEs logged (inbound)	1.25	1.01	4.33	2.42	0.52	0.00
Average login duration/FTE (inbound)	3.02	2.02	2.89	1.94	2.06	0.00
Total talk time (inbound)	220.45	8.09	34.64	19.38	4.12	0

Figure A.20. Proposed daily performance report (continued).

Inbound efficiency	First tier	Second and third teir	Apex	Pinnacle	TX Telecomm	Top 25
% calls answered within 30 seconds	35.00%	0	0	0	0	0
Seconds to answer 90% of calls	80%	0	0	0	0	0
# abandon	1,540	0	0	0	0	0
% abandon	9.06%	0	0	0	0	0
% idle time (in-bound only)	38%	20%	16%	22%	53%	0%
Total # calls	14,050	0	0	0	0	0
Total # direct check payments taken	3,322.00	0	120	42	26	17
$ direct checks	$63,753.64	$0.00	$15,025.48	$4,723.35	$2,766.10	$2,393.71
Total # credit card payments taken	2,522	0	144	57	23	0
$ credit cards	$85,004.85	$0.00	$14,437.87	$5,636.37	$1,803.29	$0.00

Figure A.20. Proposed daily performance report (continued).

	First tier	Second and third tier	Apex	Pinnacle	TX Telecomm	Top 25
Inbound efficiency						
Total # collections	5,844	0	264	99	49	17
$ collected	$148,758.49	0	29463.35	10359.72	4569.39	2393.71
% # collections/# calls	41.59%	0.00%	0.00%	0.00%	0.00%	0.00%
Outbound efficiency						
Total outbound hours	20.5	3.53	26.6	1.4	23.05	38.37
Total agents logged in	11	3	21	4	9	18
Total FTEs logged (outbound)	6.25	0.44	3.33	0.18	2.88	4.80
Average login duration/FTE (outbound)	3.02	1.18	1.27	0.35	2.56	2.13
Total talk time (outbound)	128.125	1.03	20.27	0.88	17.66	27.45

Figure A.20. Proposed daily performance report (continued).

Outbound efficiency	First tier	Second and third tier	Apex	Pinnacle	TX Telecomm	Top 25
Total # calls	128,000	88	2190	95	1272	4002
Total # right-party contact (RPC)	12,045	0	155	20	286	390
% RPC/total calls	9.41%	0.00%	7.08%	21.05%	22.48%	9.75%
% idle time (outbound only)	48%	50%	9%	14%	13%	21%
Total # direct check payments taken	3577	0	0	0	0	0
$ direct checks	$148,758.49	$0.00	$0.00	$0.00	$0.00	$0.00
Total # credit card payments taken	4244	0	0	0	0	0
$ credit cards	$127,507.28	$0.00	$0.00	$0.00	$0.00	$0.00
Total # collections	7,821	0	0	0	0	0
$ collected	$276,265.76	$0.00	$0.00	$0.00	$0.00	$0.00
$ downloaded placement for RPC calls	$0.00	$0.00	$16,211.09	$1,020.44	$16,989.23	$29,817.58

Figure A.20. Proposed daily performance report (continued).

	First tier	Second and third tier	Apex	Pinnacle	TX Telecomm	Top 25
Outbound efficiency						
$ collected/hour	$0.00	$0.00	$0.00	$0.00	$0.00	$0.00
$ collected/call	$31.10	$0.00	$0.00	$0.00	$0.00	$0.00
% # collections/# calls	48.80%	0.00%	0.00%	0.00%	0.00%	0.00%
% $ collected/$DP for outbound RPC calls	0.00%	0.00%	0.00%	0.00%	0.00%	0.00%
% $ collected/$DP	78.67%	0.00%	0.00%	0.00%	0.00%	0.00%
Payments posted						
Total # collections posted	13,665	904	0	0	0	0
$ posted	$425,024.25	$77,686.48	$0.00	$0.00	$0.00	$0.00

Figure A.20. Proposed daily performance report (continued).

KPI #	Related to	Factor	Measure	Explanation
1	Call	Average calls abandoned	Number	The average number of callers that hang-up before reaching a CSR.
2	Call	Abandon time	Seconds	The average time (seconds) a caller waits before hanging up without talking to a CSR.
3	CSR	Average talk time	Minutes/Seconds	Total number of seconds the caller was connected to a CSR.
4	CSR	Average after-call work time	Minutes	The average amount of time after a call is completed during which CSR completes paperwork and termination tasks.
5	CSR	Average handle time	Minutes	The sum of talk time and after call work time.
6	CSR	Occupancy rate	Percentage	(Talk time + Hold time)/(Talk time + Hold time + Idle time) × 100.
7	CSR	Calls per hour	Number	The average number of calls that an agent handles per hour computed as total calls handled during a working shift divided by total time logged into the system.
8	CSR	Percentage of calls transferred	Percentage	The percentage of total calls transferred from the original CSR to someone else.
9	CSR	Wrap-up time	Seconds	The time after a call is completed during which CSR completes paperwork and termination tasks.
10	DA	Total calls offered	Number	All calls incoming and outgoing including blocked, abandoned, and handled.
11	DA	Average number of rings	Number	The average number of rings the customer hears before the call is answered by a CSR, voice recording, and so on.

Figure A.21. SCI key performance indicators.

KPI #	Related to	Factor	Measure	Explanation
12	DA	Percentage agent utilization	Percentage	Calculated by (Talk time + Hold time)/(Manned time) × 100.
13	DA	Percentage and number calls blocked (calls blocked)	Percentage and number	The percentage and number of callers who received a busy signal.
14	DA	Percentage agent turnover (turnover)	Percentage	The number of agents who left in less than 12 months as a percentage of the total number of FTE CSRs working during that period.
15	DA	Queue time	Seconds	The average number of seconds that a caller spends waiting for a CSR to answer the telephone after being placed in the CSRs queue by the ACD.
16	DA/Call	Percentage of calls in queue	Percentage	The number of calls placed in the queue divided by the total of all calls.
17	DA/Call	Percentage abandonment (abandon)	Percentage	The number of abandoned calls that get connected to the call center but are disconnected by the caller before reaching a CSR or information announcement.
18	DA/Call	Average speed of answer	Seconds	Total time in queue divided by the total number of calls answered.
19	DA/Call	Average time in queue	Seconds	The average length of time (in seconds) a caller waits before connection to a CSR.
20	Management	Average sale value per collection	Currency	Total collections divided by total calls during a period.
21	Management	Cost per call	Currency	Average cost per call; the sum of all costs for running the call center for the period divided by the number of all incoming and all successful outgoing calls in the call center for the same period.

Figure A.21. SCI key performance indicators (continued).

KPI #	Related to	Factor	Measure	Explanation
22	Management	Cost per contact	Currency	An internal metric that is the sum of all costs for running the call center for the period divided by the number of incoming and outgoing calls for the same period. This includes all calls for all reasons, whether handled by human or computer.
23	Management	Efficiency index	Index <=1.0	A combination of 10 performance metrics that are related to productivity. Examples would be average talk time, average after-call work time, calls per CSR per shift, and the like.
24	Management	Effectiveness index	Index <=1.0	A combination of 10 performance metrics that are related to quality. This index includes percentage caller satisfaction, calls handled on the first call, and percentage no-error transactions.
25	Management	Call center performance index (CPI)	Index <=1.0	A balanced scorecard that combines the effectiveness index and the efficiency index into one combined index of performance. SCI's performance index is calculated by statistically weighing metrics for turnover, cost per call, average abandon rate, percentage first-time final calls, percentage adherence to schedule, percentage caller satisfaction, and percentage complete and accurate collection. (Other measures are available at http://www.benchmarkportal.com.)
26	Management	Calls handled per 8-hour shift (calls per shift)	Number	Calls handled per 8-hour shift.
27	Management	Average calls/shift/CSR	Number	Average number of calls per CSR per 8-hour shift.

Figure A.21. SCI key performance indicators (continued).

KPI #	Related to	Factor	Measure	Explanation
28	Management	Average percentage attendance	Percentage	The total number of CSRs that show up for work divided by total CSRs expected for each period of time × 100.
29	Management	Percentage adherence to schedule (adherence)	Percentage	A measure of whether agents are "in their seats" as scheduled. This is calculated as occupancy factor divided by total CSR scheduled time × 100.
30	Management	Occupancy factor	Percentage	The percentage of time that a CSR is in his or her seat and ready to handle calls.
31	Overall	Percentage of first-time final calls (first/final)	Percentage	Percentage calls handled on the first call (i.e, that require no added or return calls).

Figure A.21. SCI key performance indicators (continued).

Additional Reference Materials

Al-Mashari, M., Zahir, I., & Zairi, M. (2001). Holistic business process reengineering: An international empirical survey. Retrieved from http://csdl .computer.org/comp/proceedings/hicss/2001/0981/08/09818022.pdf

Amer, C. K. (n.d.). Quality cost analysis: Benefits and risks. Retrieved from http://www.kaner.com/qualcost.htm

Andersen, B. (1999). *Business process improvement toolbox.* Milwaukee, WI: ASQ Quality Press.

Arveson, P. (1999). What is balanced scorecard? Retrieved from http://www .balancedscorecard.org/basics/bsc1.html

Arvidsson, A. (2008). The ethical economy of customer coproduction. *Journal of Macromarketing, 28*(4), 326–330.

ASA Quality and Productivity Conference Committee. (1999). Introduction to Six Sigma. Retrieved from http://www.amstat-online.org/sections/qp/qpr/ QPRC1999/six_sigma_intro.pdf

Balancedscorecard.org. (n.d.). Cause and effect diagrams. Retrieved from http:// www.balancedscorecard.org/files/c-ediag.pdf

Beecroft, G. D. Cost of quality, quality planning and the bottom line. Retrieved from http://www.g-dennis-beecroft.ca

Benyon, R., & Johnson, R. (2006). *Service agreements: A management guide.* Zaltbommel, Netherlands: Van Haren Publishing.

Bertels, T. (2007). A lean-Six Sigma duo of the office: A case study. Retrieved from http://europe.isixsigma.com/library/content/c040714b.asp

Bitner, M., & Brown, S. W. (2008). The service imperative. *Business Horizons, 51*(10), 39–46.

Boland, L., & Coleman, E. (2008). New development: What lies beyond service delivery? Leadership behaviours for place shaping in local government. *Public Money & Management, 28*(5), 313.

Bordley, R. F., & Kirkwood, C. W. (2004). Multiattribute preference analysis with performance targets. *Operations Research, 52*(6), 823–816.

BPEL references. (n.d.). In *Wikipedia, the free encyclopedia.* Retrieved from http://en.wikipedia.org/wiki/BPEL#The_BPEL_language

Brassard, M., Field, C., Oddo, F., Page, B., Ritter, D., & Smith, L. (2000). *The problem solving memory jogger.* Salem, NH: GOAL/QPC.

Brown, P., & Szefler, M. (2003). BPEL for programmers and architects. Retrieved from http://www.bptrends.com/publicationfiles/BPEL4ProgArchies.pdf

Buthmann, A. (2007, May 2). Cost of quality: Not only failure costs. Retrieved from http://europe.isixsigma.com/library/content/c070502a.asp

Campanella, J. (Ed.). (1999). *Principles of quality costs: Principles, implementation, and use* (3rd ed.). ASQ Milwaukee, WI: Quality Press.

Citibank. (2007). Pay your utility bills on Citibank online. Retrieved from http://www.online.citibank.co.in/portal/newgen/seo/cbol/bill-pay.htm

Cobbold, I. C., & Lawrie, G. J. G. (2002). The development of the balanced scorecard as a strategic management tool. *Proceedings of the Third International Conference on Performance Measurement and Management*, Boston, MA. Retrieved from http://www.2gc.co.uk/pdf/2GC-W0412.pdf

Cohen, L. (1995). *Quality function deployment: How to make QFD work for you.* Reading, MA: Addison-Wesley.

Concordia University. (n.d.). Coast Guard process improvement guide. Retrieved from http://web2.concordia.ca/Quality/tools/6cksheet.pdf

Costich-Sicker, R., Sheehy, P., Navarro, D., Silvers, R., Keyes, V., Dziark, J., & Dixon, D. (2002). *The black belt memory jogger.* Salem, NH: Goal/QPC.

Crowley, L. D. (2008). Introduction to cost of quality. Retrieved from http://www.sasqag.org/pastmeetings1998.htm

Davison, D. (2009, January 16). How to make offshore outsourcing deals withstand crisis situations. *CIO Magazine.* Retrieved from http://www.cio.com/article/print/476715

Donovan, R. M. (n.d.). The order to delivery cycle: Quick response is essential. Retrieved from http://www.rmdonovan.com/cycle_time-reduction

Dorgan, S. J., & Dowdy, J. J. (2004). When IT lifts productivity. *McKinsey Quarterly.* Retrieved from http://www.adamsmithesq.com/blog/pdf/McKinsey.When.IT.Lifts.Productivity.pdf

Dossenbach, T. (n.d.). Manufacturing cycle time reduction: A must in capital project analysis. Retrieved from http://www.iswonline.com/wwp/dossenbach/doss1000.shtml

European Charter for Small Enterprises. (2007, February 20). EU countries set to reduce administrative burdens. Retrieved from http://www.bundesregierung.de/nn_6538/Content/EN/Artikel/2007/02/2007-02-20-eu-wettbewerbsrat__en.html

European Charter for Small Enterprises. (2003). *Implementation report 2003.* Retrieved from http://ec.europa.eu/enterprise/enterprise_policy/charter/004_charter_docs/report-germany-2003-en.pdf

Europa Press Releases. (2008). Cutting red tape at maximum speed: Citizens and enterprises save billions. Retrieved from http://europa.eu/rapid/pressReleasesAction.do?reference=IP/08/115&format=HTML&aged=0&language=EN&guiLanguage=en

Federal Express. (2009). http://www.fedex.com

Frailey, D. J. (n.d.). Meeting tight software schedules through cycle time reduction. Retrieved from http://www.pnsqc.org/proceedings/pnsqc00.pdf

Business Week. (2006, January 30). The future of outsourcing: How it's transforming whole industries and changing the way we work. *Business Week.* Retrieved from http://www.businessweek.com/magazine/content/06_05/b3969401.htm

Genba-kanri.com. (2009). Genba-kanri: An overview. Retrieved from http://www.genba-kanri.com/gkweb/Briefweb.htm

George, M. (n.d.). Reducing delays in service processes with rapid setup. Retrieved from http://finance.isixsigma.com/library/content/c040714a.asp

Goyal, N. (2007). Applying lean manufacturing to Six Sigma: A case study. Retrieved from http://www.isixsigma.com/library/content/c020225a.asp

Hass, R., & Meixner, O. (2009). *An illustrated guide to the analytic hierarchy process.* Retrieved from http://www.boku.ac.at/mi/ahp/ahptutorial.pdf

Hiroshi, W., Suzuki, J., & Katsuya, O. (2008). Early aspects for nonfunctional properties in service oriented business processes. *Proceedings of IEEE Congress on Services*, Honolulu, HI.

Hiroshi, W., Suzuki, J., & Katsuya, O. (2009). A feature modeling support for nonfunctional constraints in service oriented architecture. *Proceedings of the 4th IEEE International Conference on Services Computing*, Salt Lake City, UT.

HRWorld Editors. (2008). 100 small business tips and tricks for effectively outsourcing to India. Retrieved from http://www.hrworld.com/features/100-tips-outsourcing-india-021508

HRWorld Editors. (n.d.). Outsourcing checklist: What to ask before deciding to outsource. Retrieved from http://www.hrworld.com/whitepaper/pdf/outsourcing-checklist_8-07.pdf

Ishikawa, K. (1991). *Guide to quality control.* Tokyo: Asian Productivity Organization.

isixsigma.com. (n.d.). Dictionary of Six Sigma terms. Retrieved from http://www.isixsigma.com/dictionary/5Z-1904.htm

ITGI.org. (2006). COBIT and IT governance case study: Harley-Davidson. Retrieved from http://www.itgi.org/Template_ITGI.cfm?Section=Case_Stu

dies1&CONTENTID=27036&TEMPLATE=/ContentManagement/Co
tentDisplay.cfm

Kaplan, R. S. (1994). Devising a balanced scorecard matched to business strategy. *Planning Review, 22*(5), 15–24.

Kaplan, R. S., & Norton, D. P. (1992). The balanced scorecard: Measures that drive performance. *Harvard Business Review, 70*(1), 71–79.

Kaplan, R. S., & Norton, D. P. (1993). Putting the balanced scorecard to work. *Harvard Business Review, 71*(5), 134–147.

Katz, J. (2006, February 14). Continuous improvement: Taking a big-picture approach to lean. *Industry Week*. Retrieved from http://www.industryweek.com/PrintArticle.aspx?ArticleID=11432

Kendrick, C. (2007, February 14). Statistics on outsourcing, outsourcing news. Retrieved from http://www.outsourcing-weblog.com/50226711/statistics_on_outsourcing.php

Kimbler, D. L. (1991). *Etcetera, Inc.: A case study in quality improvement*. Clemson, SC: Clemson University.

Klass, G. (2001). *How to construct bad charts and graphs*. Normal, IL: Illinois State University. Retrieved from http://lilt.ilstu.edu/gmklass/pos138/datadisplay/badchart.htm

Kurtzman, J. (1997, February 17). Is your company off course? Now you can find out why. *Fortune, 135*, 128–130. Retrieved from http://www.maaw.info/ArticleSummaries/ArtSumKurtzman97.htm

Lacity, M. C., & Willcocks, L. P. (1998). An empirical investigation of information technology sourcing practices: Lessons from experience. *MIS Quarterly, 22*(3), 363–408.

Lacity, M. C., Willcocks, L. P., & Rottman, J. W. (2008). Global outsourcing of back office services: Lessons, trends, and enduring challenges. *Strategic Outsourcing: An International Journal, 1*(1), 13–34.

Lawrie, G. J. G., Cobbold, I., & Marshall, J. (2004). Corporate performance management system in a devolved U.K. governmental organisation: A case study. *International Journal of Productivity and Performance Management, 53*(4), 353–370. Retrieved from http://www.2gc.co.uk/pdf/2GC-P1003.pdf

Lawrie, G. J. G., Kalff, D., & Andersen, H. V. (2005, September). *Balanced scorecard and results-based management: Convergent performance management systems*. Presented at 3rd Annual Conference on Performance Measurement and Management Control, The European Institute for Advanced Studies in Management (EIASM), Nice, France. Retrieved from http://www.2gc.co.uk/pdf/2GC-C060130.pdf

Lewis, P. J. (1999). *The project manager's desk reference* (2nd ed.). Loveland, CO: Prosci. Retrieved from http://www.prosci.com/project-planning.htm

Mautner, T. (Ed.). (2005). *The Penguin dictionary of philosophy* (2nd ed.). New York, NY: Penguin Books.

Morisawa, T. (2002). *Building performance measurement systems with the balanced scorecard approach.* Nomura Research Institute, Paper No. 45. Retrieved from http://www.nri.co.jp/english/opinion/papers/2002/pdf/np200245.pdf

Morrow, R., & Wells, A. (n.d.) Beef farm sustainability checksheet. Retrieved from http://attra.ncat.org/attra-pub/PDF/beefchec.pdf

Mottier, S., & White, F. (2003). *Co-production as a form of service delivery.* Workshop on New Approaches to Decentralized Service Delivery, Santiago, Chile. Retrieved from http://www.ids.ac.uk/logolink/resources/downloads/Chile%20Workshop/Mottiarbgpaper.pdf

National Institute for Health. (2007). Workflow/business process management (BPM) service pattern. Retrieved from http://enterprisearchitecture.nih.gov/ArchLib/AT/TA/WorkflowServicePattern.htm

Ordanini, A., & Pasini, P. (2008). Service co-production and value co-creation: The case for a service-oriented architecture (SOA). *European Management Journal, 26*(5), 289–297.

Osgood, N. (2004). Problem diagnosis and introduction to project dynamics. Retrieved from http://ocw.mit.edu/NR/rdonlyres/Civil-and-Environmental-Engineering/1-040Spring-2004/55BC6C7D-6489-4717-BA26-4B06AFDFE047/0/l16diagnsprjctrl.pdf

Pexton, C. (2004). Ideas for achieving higher reliability in healthcare. Retrieved from http://healthcare.isixsigma.com/library/content/c040901a.asp

Prabha, C., & Connaway, L. S. (2007). What is enough? Satisficing information needs. *Journal of Documentation, 62*(1), 74–87.

Pradesh, A. (2006). Now, pay electric bill at the bank. Retrieved from http://www.thehindu.com/2006/09/14/stories/2006091410460300.htm

Ravichandran, J. (2007). Using weighted-DPMO to calculate an overall sigma level. Retrieved from http://www.isixsigma.com/library/content/c060320a.asp

Russell, B. (n.d.). Continuous improvement: Changing processes by streamlining. Retrieved from http://www.circuitree.com/CDA/ArticleInformation/features/BNP__Features__Item/0,2133,21565,00.html

Saaty, T. (2005). *Theory and applications of the analytic network process: Decision making with benefits, opportunities, costs, and risks.* Newark, CA: RMS Publications.

SaferPak. (2003). Cause and effect diagram. Retrieved from http://www.saferpak.com/cause_effect.htm

Statit. (n.d.). Introduction to statistical control processes. Retrieved from http://www.statit.com/statitcustomqc/StatitCustomQC_Overview.pdf

U. S. Department of Commerce, National Institute of Science & Technology. (2006). *Engineering statistics handbook.* Washington, DC: National Institute for Science and Technology. Retrieved from http://www.itl.nist.gov/div898/handbook/eda/section3/scatterp.htm

U. S. Department of Defense. (1993). *Integration definition for function modeling (IDEF0)*. Washington, DC: U. S. Department of Defense.

U. S. Government Accounting Office. (1999). *Information security risk assessment: Practices of leading organizations*. Washington, DC: U.S. Government Accounting Office. Retrieved from http://www.gao.gov/special.pubs/ai00033.pdf

U. S. Securities and Exchange Commission. (1998). A plain English handbook: How to create clear SEC disclosure documents. Retrieved from http://www.sec.gov/pdf/handbook.pdf

University of Wisconsin. (2000). *Cycle time reduction: Figuring the savings*. Madison, WI: University of Wisconsin. Retrieved from http://www.engr.wisc.edu/ie/newsletter/2000_winter/cycletime.html

Van Bon, J., Pieper, M., & van der Veen, A. (2005). *Foundations of IT service management*. Amersfoort, Netherlands: Van Haren Publishing.

Vargo, S. L., Maglio, P. P., & Akaka, M. A. (2008). On value and value co-creation: A service systems and service logic perspective. *European Management Journal, 26*(3), 145–152.

White, S. (2006). *Introduction to BPMN*. Armonk, NY: IBM Corporation. Retrieved from http://www.bpmn.org/Documents/Introduction%20to%20BPMN.pdf

Willcocks, L., Hindle, J., Feeny, D., & Lacity, M. (2004). IT and business process outsourcing: The knowledge potential. *Information Systems Management, 21*(3), 7–15.

Womack, J. P., & Jones, D. T. (1998). *Lean thinking*. New York, NY: Free Press.

Zbikowski, E. (2007, February 7). How does your call center stack up? *Call Center Magazine*. Retrieved from http://www.callcentermagazine.com/showArticle.jhtml?articleID=197004092

Internet References

Balanced Scorecard

http://en.wikipedia.org/wiki/Balanced_Scorecard
http://www.ihi.org/resources/continuousimprovement/index.asp
http://www.valuebasedmanagement.net/methods_balancedscorecard.html
http://www.sc.doe.gov/bes/archives/plans/GPRA_PL103-62_03AUG93.pdf
http://images.google.com/imgres?imgurl=http://www.balancedscorecard.org/images/BSC.jpg&imgrefurl=http://www.balancedscorecard.org/basics/bsc1.html&h=406&w=513&sz=128&tbnid=cmCXZbO4aZg8JM:&tbnh=104&tbnw=131&prev=/images%3Fq%3Dbalanced%2Bscorecard&start=2&sa=X&oi=images&ct=image&cd=2

Benchmarking

http://www.benchmarkportal.com/newsite/index.html
http://www.benchmarkcc.com
http://www.benchmark-research.co.uk/attachments/PRCS%20DATAPOINT
%20UK%20Call%20Centre%20Environment%20Report%202004.pdf
http://www.benchmark-research.co.uk/attachments/Research.pdf

Business Process Execution Language

http://en.wikipedia.org/wiki/BPEL#The_BPEL_language

Cause-and-Effect Diagrams

http://www.skymark.com/resources/tools/cause.asp
http://www.deming.eng.clemson.edu/pub/tutorials/qctools/cedm.htm
http://www.isixsigma.com/library/content/t000827.asp
http://www.hci.com.au/hcisite3/toolkit/causeand.htm
http://erc.msh.org/quality/pstools/pscsefdg.cfm
http://www.tin.nhs.uk/index.asp?pgid=1132

Check Sheets

http://www.asq.org/learn-about-quality/data-collection-analysis-tools/overview/
check-sheet.html
http://mot.vuse.vanderbilt.edu/mt322/Check.HTM
http://www.tin.nhs.uk/index.asp?pgid=1359
http://nhcs.k12.nc.us
http://www.hinkingmaps.com
http://mapthemind.com
http://smartdraw.com
http://mindtools.com

Continuous Improvement

http://www.isixsigma.com/dictionary/Continuous_Improvement-149.htm
http://www.ihi.org/resources/continuousimprovement/index.asp
http://deming.eng.clemson.edu/pub/psci
http://www.mapnp.org/library/quality/cont_imp/cont_imp.htm
http://www.mapnp.org/library/quality/tqm/tqm.htm

http://www.vitalentusa.com/products/kdrs/kdrs_learn_about.php
http://systems2win.com/solutions/lean.htm
http://www.mapnp.org/library/org_perf/methods.htm
http://www.eagle.ca/~mikehick/continue.html
http://www.nwlink.com/~donclark/perform/process.html
http://www.southalabama.edu/mcob/jeffery/REF%20ID%20ATS-158%20.doc
http://www.mapnp.org/library/quality/cont_imp/cont_imp.htm
http://www.mapnp.org/library/org_perf/methods.htm

Coproduction

http://www.timebanks.org/co-self-assess.htm
http://wpcarey.asu.edu/csl/Customer-Co-Production.cfm
http://www.marketingpower.com/content-printer-friendly
   .php?&Item_ID=17613

Criteria Testing

http://www.jpbowen.com/pub/compsac2003.pdf
http://www.jpbowen.com/pub/compsac2001.pdf
http://ise.gmu.edu/~aynur/rsrch/eval.html
http://ts.nist.gov/Standards/scopes/cct.htm

Cycle Time Reduction

http://www.rmdonovan.com/cycle_time-reduction.htm
http://www.lean.org/WhatsLean/Principles.cfm
http://www.isixsigma.com

Dashboards

http://www.dashboardspy.com
https://www.qimacros.com/pdf/dashboard-user-guide.pdf
http://upload.wikimedia.org/wikipedia/commons/f/f7/US_Flag_color_blind
   .png
http://www.dmreview.com/article_sub.cfm?articleId=1011285
http://www.celequest.com/products/lava/PerformanceDashboards.aspx?cid
   =googleadwords&gclid=CJXI7fmL_YoCFRBPUAodtkP5_Q
http://www.idashboards.com/financial.shtml

http://www.forbes.com/video/?video_url=http://www.forbes.com/video/fvn/
business/tm_hyper103105&id=murphy_hyper&title=Video%3A+Executive+
Dashboard+Light

Financial Cost Models

http://www.itilpeople.com/Glossary/Glossary_c.htm
http://www.isixsigma.com/dictionary

Genba Kanri

http://www.genba-kanri.com/gkweb/Briefweb.htm
http://www.abdn.uk.net/Who%20facilitiates.htm
http://www.isixsigma.com/dictionary/5Z-1904.htm

Graphics

http://www.math.yorku.ca/SCS/Gallery/context.html
http://www.stattucino.com/berrie/graphs.html
http://www.math.yorku.ca/SCS/Gallery
http://www.stattucino.com/berrie/normal.html
http://stattrek.com/Lesson2/Poisson.aspx

Histogram

http://www.shodor.org/interactivate/activities/histogram
http://www.stat.sc.edu/~west/javahtml/Histogram.html
http://www.luminous-landscape.com/tutorials/understanding-series/
understanding-histograms
http://www.isixsigma.com/library/content/c010527c.asp
http://www.itl.nist.gov/div898/handbook/eda/section3/histogra.htm
http://www.ruf.rice.edu/~lane/stat_sim/histogram/index.html
http://www.stat.sc.edu/~west/javahtml/Histogram.html
http://www.itl.nist.gov/div898/ handbook/eda/section3/histogra.htm
http://www.sytsma.com/tqmtools/hist.html
http://www.luminous-landscape.com/tutorials/understanding-series/undestanding
-histograms.shtml
http://nlvm.usu.edu/en/nav/frames_asid_174_g_2_t_5.html?open=instructions

Pareto Diagrams

http://www.hpl.hp.com/research/idl/papers/ranking/ranking.html

Quality Function Deployment

http://www.qfdi.org
http://www.isixsigma.com/tt/qfd
http://www.npd-solutions.com/qfdsteps
http://www.icqfd.org

Quality Cost Analysis: Benefits and Risks

http://www.kaner.com/qualcost.htm

Scatterplots

http://ocw.mit.edu/NR/rdonlyres/Civil-and-Environmental-Engineering/
   1-040Spring-2004/55BC6C7D-6489-4717-BA26-4B06AFDFE047/
   0/l16diagnsprjctrl.pdf

Simple Language

http://www.muhlenberg.edu/muhlinfo/accessibility/point1.html
http://www.w3.org/TR/1999/WAI-WEBCONTENT-19990505/full-checklist.pdf
http://www.tokipona.org/intro.html
http://www.law.ucla.edu/volokh/legalese.htm
http://en.wikipedia.org/wiki/Wikipedia:Simple_English_Wikipedia
http://www.basic-english.org/institute.html

Spider Diagrams

http://web2.concordia.ca/Quality/tools/23radar.pdf
http://www.kuleuven.ac.be/stwav/arbstat2000/nl/presentaties/WZB%20
   radar%20charts.ppt

Standards Organizations

http://www.iso.org
http://www.iec.org
http://www.etsi.org
http://www.ansi.org
http://www.ieee.org
http://www.w3c.org

Statistical Process Control

http://www.statit.com/statitcustomqc/StatitCustomQC_Overview.pdf
http://www.itl.nist.gov/div898/handbook/pmc/section1/pmc12.htm
http://www.1stnclass.com/spc_tutorial.htm
http://www.goldpractices.com/practices/spc/index.php
http://plantweb.emersonprocess.com/Customer/Pharmaceutical_index.asp
http://www.hanford.gov/safety/vpp/spc.htm
http://www.qualityamerica.com/Support/spccc-support.htm
http://www.isixsigma.com/offsite.asp?A=Fr&Url=http://www.skymark.com/
    resources/tools/control_charts.htm
http://www.isixsigma.com/st/control_charts
http://www.wikipedia.com
http://www.spcpress.com
http://www.spcforexcel.com
http://lorien.ncl.ac.uk/ming/spc/spc8.htm
http://www.statsoft.com/textbook/stquacon.html

Telecommuting

http://www.joannepratt.com

Trend Analysis

http://www.investopedia.com/terms/t/trendanalysis.asp
http://www.questionpro.com/trend

Value-Added Analysis

http://www.grand-blanc.k12.mi.us/qip/Value-Added%20Activity.htm
http://www.qfdi.org

http://www.shef.ac.uk/~ibberson/qfd.html
http://www.grand-blanc.k12.mi.us/qip/Value-Added%20Activity.htm
http://www.qfdi.org
http://www.shef.ac.uk/~ibberson/qfd.html

Yet Another Workflow Language

http://en.wikipedia.org/wiki/YAWL

Notes

Chapter 1

1. Dorgan and Dowdy (2004).
2. Behr, Kim, and Spafford (2007), p. 91.
3. Behr et al. (2007), p. 91; Baschob and Piott (2007).
4. Carr (2003), p. 449.
5. Dorgan and Dowdy (2004).

Chapter 2

1. A *rule of thumb*, or heuristic, is a principle with general applicability that cannot be assumed to apply to every situation.
2. Other terms by which an SOW may be known include contract, project plan, feasibility study, or some similar name.
3. SCI is based on a real organization, with dates and names changed to provide anonymity.

Chapter 3

1. Please note that flow of process is *not* flow of data. This is not a different kind of data flow diagram.
2. Some process mapping methods (or near-process methods) include Business Process Execution Language (BPEL), Enterprise Distributed Object Computing (EDOC), Uniform Modeling Language (UML), EDOC Business Processes, UML Activity Diagrams, Business Process Specification Schema (BPSS), Event-Process Chains, and Activity-Decision Flow Diagrams.
3. This is called overloading.
4. The open source version, developed by universities in the Netherlands and Canada is called YAWL (Yet Another Workflow Language).
5. White (2004).

Chapter 4

1. Both definitions are paraphrased from http://www.wordnik.com, a linguistics dictionary.

2. The condition only has a "yes" leg out and requires a "no" leg for completeness.

Chapter 5

1. Klass (2001).
2. Tufte (2010).
3. Brassard, Field, Oddo, Page, Ritter, and Smith (2000).
4. Criterion is singular, criteria is plural.
5. Crosby (1979).
6. HIPAA is the Health Information Portability and Accountability Act of 1996, and IT stand for "information technology."
7. Sarbanes-Oxley Act of 2002 (2002).
8. See NAICS codes at http://www.sec.gov/info/edgar/naicscodes.htm.

Chapter 6

1. See Ohno (1988, 2007), http://www.genba-kanri.com/gkweb/Briefweb .htm, and http://www.isixsigma.com/dictionary/5Z-1904.htm.
2. http://www.isixsigma.com.
3. See Ohno (1988).
4. Campanella (1999).
5. Campanella (1999).
6. Cohen (1995).
7. See, for example, Cohen (1995), which shows the Figure 6.8 symbols in the frontispiece of the book and recommends a different method (p. 155) than is suggested in Figure 6.10.

Chapter 7

1. iSixSigma LLC (2000–2006).
2. This is not very impressive quality. It means that for the 87,000 airline flights in the United States per day, 5,829 would crash or fail. No one would fly at that rate. Data on flights per day from Natca.org (2010)
3. 5Whys.org (2006).
4. Wordnik.com (2010).
5. German Government (2007).
6. Kronz and Zipse (2008).
7. Federal Express Corporation (2007).
8. Federal Express Corporation (2007).
9. Pexton (2004).

10. U.S. Securities and Exchange Commission (n.d.).

11. AHP and its related technique, analytical network process (ANP), which applies to more interrelated outcome analyses, were both developed by Thomas Saaty, starting in the 1970s while he was at the University of Pennsylvania's Wharton School of Business.

12. For more on this technique and its conduct, see Hass and Meixner (2005).

Chapter 8

1. Holcomb and Hitt (2007).

2. ITIL was originally developed by what is now the Office of General Counsel of the British government and defines best practices for aspects of support and delivery in primarily IT operations management. CMMI is the Capability Maturity Model developed by the Software Engineering Institute for controlled project management, primarily in IT application development or acquisition. COBIT is the Control Objectives for Information and Technology created by the IT Governance Institute and used by auditors around the globe as the basis for IT auditing. COBIT can be used as a guiding framework for both application and operations management but is unevenly both weaker and stronger than CMMI and ITIL in their own milieu.

3. See, for instance, Benyon and Johnson (2006).

4. Lacity, Willcocks, and Rottman (2008).

5. See Kern and Willcocks (2002).

6. See Kern, Lacity, and Lacity (2002).

7. See Arvidsson (2008).

8. See TimeBanks USA at http://www.timebanks.org/co-production.htm.

9. See TimeBanks USA at http://www.timebanks.org/co-production.htm.

10. See Arvidsson (2008).

11. See http://www.linkedin.com, http://www.facebook.com, http://secondlife.com/?v=1.1, http://digg.com, and http://twitter.com.

12. See http://www.us-cert.gov.

13. See http://www.joannepratt.com for many telework studies.

Chapter 9

1. U.S. Congress (2002).

2. Walker (2003).

3. Davis, Bagozzi, and Warshaw (1998) and the hundreds of articles that the Technology Adoption Model (TAM) spawned.

4. Adapted from Rogers (1983).

5. JISC Advance (2007).

6. U.S. Government Accounting Office (1999), p. 22.

7. This list is adapted from Statit Software, Inc. (2007).

Chapter 10

1. Kaplan and Norton (1992).
2. See Cobbold and Lawrie (2002) and Lawrie, Cobbold, and Marshall (2004).
3. iSixSigma LLC (2010).
4. Clayton (2003).
5. Clayton (2003), p. 3.
6. See Jensen (2006).
7. See Karni and Kaner (2007).
8. See Cook, Goh, and Chung (1999).
9. Office of General Commerce (2007), p. 45.
10. Another complication of virtualization and cloud computing is that finding errors is significantly more complex, as the exact location of an error, and therefore the ability to reproduce it, are lost as soon as the error occurs.

References

5Whys.org (2006, January). 5 Whys methodology. Retrieved on January 1, 2007, from http://www.5whys.org

Arvidsson, A. (2008). The ethical economy of customer coproduction. *Journal of Macromarketing, 28*(4), 326–330.

Baschob, J., & Piott, J. (2007). *The executive's guide to information technology* (2nd ed.). Hoboken, NJ: John Wiley & Sons.

Behr, K., Kim, K., & Spafford, G. (2007). *The visible ops handbook: Implementing ITIL in 4 practical and auditable steps.* Eugene, OR: IT Process Institute.

Benyon, R., & Johnson, R. (2006). *Service agreements: A management guide.* Zaltbommel, Netherlands: Van Haren Publishing.

Brassard, M., Field, C., Oddo, F., Page, B., Ritter., D., & Smith, L. (2000). *The problem solving memory jogger.* Salem, NH: GOAL/QPC.

Campanella, J. (Ed.). (1999). *Principles of quality costs: Principles, implementation, and use* (3rd ed.). Milwaukee, WI: ASQ Quality Press.

Carr, N. (2003). IT doesn't matter. *Harvard Business Review, 81*(5), 41–50.

Cherry, J., & Seshadri, S. (2000). Six Sigma: Using statistics to reduce process variability and costs in radiology. *Radiology Management, 22*(6), 42–45.

Clayton, J. (2003, August 1). Writing an executive summary (Prod. #: C0308E -PDF-ENG). Boston, MA: Harvard Business Review Newsletter Reprints. Retrieved from http://hbr.org/product/writing-an-executive-summary-that -means-business/an/C0308E-PDF-ENG?N=516169&Ntt=John+Clayton

Cobbold, I. C., & Lawrie, G. J. G. (2002). The development of the balanced scorecard as a strategic management tool. *Proceedings of the Third International Conference on Performance Measurement and Management,* Boston, MA. Retrieved from http://www.2gc.co.uk/pdf/2GC-W0412.pdf

Cohen, L. (1995). *Quality function deployment.* Reading, MA: Addison-Wesley.

Cook, D., Goh, C.-H., & Chung, C.-H. (1999). Service typologies: A state of the art survey. *Production and Operations Management, 8*(3), 318–338.

Crosby, P. (1979). *Quality is free.* New York, NY: McGraw-Hill.

Computer Emergency Readiness Team. (2010). Security notifications. U.S. Computer Emergency Readiness Team. Retrieved from http://www.us-cert.gov

Davis, F. D., Bagozzi, R. P., & Warshaw, P. R. (1998). User acceptance of computer technology: A comparison of two theoretical models. *Management Science, 35*(8), 982–1003.

Digg.com. (2010). [Social networking site.] http://digg.com

Dorgan, S. J., & Dowdy, J. J. (2004). When IT raises productivity. *The McKinsey Quarterly, 4*(8), 9–12.

Facebook.com. (2010). [Social networking site.] http://www.facebook.com

Federal Express Corporation. (2007). FedEx innovations. Federal Express Corporation. Retrieved from http://www.fedex.com/ca_english/about/pdf/ca_english_about_decades_innovation.pdf

Fitz-Enz, J. (1993). *Benchmarking staff performance: How staff departments can enhance their value to the customer.* San Francisco, CA: Pfeiffer & Company.

German Government. (2007, February 20). EU countries set to reduce administrative burdens. The Press and Information Office of the Federal Government, Germany. Retrieved from http://www.bundesregierung.de/nn_6538/Content/EN/Artikel/2007/02/2007-02-20-eu-wettbewerbsrat__en.html

Genba-kanri.com. (2010). Overview of genba-kanri principles. Retrieved from http://www.genba-kanri.com/gkweb/Briefweb.htm

Hass, R., & Meixner, O. (2005). *An illustrated guide to the analytic hierarchy process.* Vienna, Austria: Institute for Marketing and Innovation. Retrieved from http://www.boku.ac.at/mi/ahp/ahptutorial.pdf

Holcomb, T. R., & M. A. Hitt (2007). Toward a model of strategic outsourcing. *Journal of Operations Management, 25*(2), 464–481.

iSixSigma LLC. (2000–2006). Sigma level. iSixSigma LLC. Retrieved from http://www.isixsigma.com/index.php

iSixSigma LLC. (2010a). The 5 Zs. iSixSigma LLC. Retrieved from http://www.isixsigma.com/dictionary/5Z-1904.htm

iSixSigma LLC. (2010b). Six Sigma resources site. iSixSigma LLC. Retrieved from http://www.isixsigma.com

iSixSigma LLC. (2010c). Voice of the customer. iSixSigma LLC. Retrieved from http://www.isixsigma.com/dictionary/Voice_Of_the_Customer_(VOC)-391.htm

Jensen, A. (2006, October 9). Six Sigma courses focus on efficiency. *Northwest Arkansas Business Journal, 10*(15), 28.

JISC Advance. (2007). *Guidance on developing a business case for a change project.* London: JISC Advance. Retrieved from http://www.jiscinfonet.ac.uk

Kaplan, R. S., & Norton, D. P. (1992, January–February) The balanced scorecard: Measures that drive performance. *Harvard Business Review, 70*(1), 71–79.

Karni, R., & Kaner, M. (2007). Engineering design of a service system: An empirical study. *Information-Knowledge-Systems Management, 6*(3), 235–263.

Kern, T., & Willcocks, L. (2002). Exploring relationships in information technology outsourcing: The interaction approach. *European Journal of Information Systems, 11*(1), 3–19.

Kern, T., Lacity, M., & Willcocks, L. (2002). *Netsourcing: Renting business applications and services over a network.* New York, NY: Prentice Hall.

Klass, G. (2001). How to construct bad charts and graphs. Retrieved from http://lilt.ilstu.edu/gmklass/pos138/datadisplay/badchart.htm

Kronz, C., & Zipse, C. (2008, August 3). Too much bureaucracy? German Federal Statistical Office. Retrieved from http://www.destatis.de/jetspeed/portal/cms/Sites/destatis/Internet/EN/Navigation/Publications/STATmagazin/2009/Other2009__08,templateId=renderPrint.psml__nnn=true

Lacity, M. A., Willcocks, L., & Rottman, J. W. (2008). Global outsourcing of back office services: Lessons, trends, and enduring challenges. *Strategic Outsourcing: An International Journal, 1*(1), 13–34.

Lawrie, G. J. G., Cobbold, I., & Marshall, J. (2004). Corporate performance management system in a devolved UK governmental organisation: A case study. *International Journal of Productivity and Performance Management 53*(4), 353–370.

Linden Lab. (2010). [Social networking site.] http://secondlife.com/?v=1.1

LinkedIn.com. (2010). [Social networking site.] http://www.linkedin.com

NATCA.com. (2010) Air traffic control: By the numbers. Retrieved from http://www.natca.org/mediacenter/bythenumbers.msp#1

Ohno, T. (1988). *Toyota production system: Beyond large-scale production.* Florence, KY: Productivity Press.

Ohno, T. (2007). *Taiichi Ohno's workplace management.* Ed. J. Miller. Mukilteo, WA: Gemba Press.

Pexton, C. (2004). Ideas for achieving higher reliability in healthcare. Retrieved from http://healthcare.isixsigma.com/library/content/c040901a.asp

Pratt, J. (2010). Telecommuting references. Retrieved from http://www.joannepratt.com

Rogers, E. M. (1983). *Diffusion of innovations.* New York, NY: Free Press.

Statit Software, Inc. (2007). *Introduction to statistical process control techniques.* Corvallis, OR: Statit Software, Inc. Retrieved from http://www.statit.com/statitcustomqc/StatitCustomQC_Overview.pdf

TimeBanks USA. (2010). What is coproduction? Timebanks USA. Retrieved from http://www.timebanks.org/co-production.htm

Tufte, E. (2010) Minard's poster of Napoleon's march. Retrieved from http://www.edwardtufte.com/tufte/posters

Twitter.com. (2010). [Social networking site.] http://twitter.com

UK Office of General Commerce. (2007). *ITIL glossary of terms and definitions.* London: Author.

U.S. Congress. (2002). Sarbanes-Oxley Act of 2002. H.R. 3763, Pub. L. No. 107-204, 116 Stat. 745. Washington, DC: General Printing Office.

U.S. Department of Commerce. (1993). *Integration definition for functional modeling* (IDEF0). Washington, DC: National Institute of Science & Technology (NIST), U.S. Department of Commerce.

U.S. Department of Defense. (1993). *Integration definition for function modeling*. Washington, DC: Author.

U.S. Government Accounting Office. (1999). *Information security risk assessment: Practices of leading organizations*. Washington, DC: U.S. Government Accounting Office. Retrieved from http://www.gao.gov/special.pubs/ai00033.pdf

U.S. Securities and Exchange Commission. (n.d.). *A plain English handbook*. Washington, DC: U.S. Securities and Exchange Commission. Retreived from http://www.sec.gov/pdf/handbook.pdf

Walker, R. (2003, November 30) The guts of a new machine. *New York Times*. Retrieved from http://www.nytimes.com/2003/11/30/magazine/the-guts-of-a-new-machine.html

White, S. (2004). Introduction to BPMN. *BPTrends.com*. Retrieved from http://www.zurich.ibm.com/~koe/teaching/ETH2009/White-BPMN-Intro.pdf

Wordnik.com. (2010a). Optimize. Retrieved from http://www.wordnik.com/words/optimize

Wordnik.com. (2010b). Validation. Retrieved from http://www.wordnik.com/words/validation

Wordnik.com. (2010c). Verification. Retrieved from http://www.wordnik.com/words/verification

Index

Announcing the Business Expert Press Digital Library

Concise E-books Business Students Need for Classroom and Research

This book can also be purchased in an e-book collection by your library as

- a one-time purchase,
- that is owned forever,
- allows for simultaneous readers,
- has no restrictions on printing, and
- can be downloaded as PDFs from within the library community.

Our digital library collections are a great solution to beat the rising cost of textbooks. E-books can be loaded into their course management systems or onto student's e-book readers.

The **Business Expert Press** digital libraries are very affordable, with no obligation to buy in future years.

For more information, please visit **www.businessexpert.com/libraries**. To set up a trial in the United States, please contact **Sheri Allen** at *sheri.allen@globalepress.com*; for all other regions, contact **Nicole Lee** at *nicole.lee@igroupnet.com*.

CPSIA information can be obtained
at www.ICGtesting.com
Printed in the USA
LVHW081721280720
661749LV00008B/167